Soft Power and US Foreign Policy

The rise of widespread negative attitudes towards US foreign policy, especially following the war of aggression against Iraq and the subsequent military occupation – has brought new attention to the meaning and instruments of soft power. In this edited collection, an outstanding line up of contributors provides the most extensive discussion of soft power to date. Soft power is the use of attraction and persuasion rather than the use of coercion or force in foreign policy. It arises from the attractiveness of a country's culture, political ideals and policies, whereas hard power develops out of a country's military or economic might.

Soft power has become part of popular political discourse since it was coined by Harvard's Joseph Nye, and this volume features a brand new chapter by Nye outlining his views on soft, hard and smart power, and offers a critique of the Bush administration's inadequacies. He then goes on to examine the challenges for President Barack Obama. The other contributions to the volume respond to Nye's views from a range of theoretical, historical and policy perspectives giving new insights in to both soft power and the concept of power itself.

This is the most comprehensive and up-to-date analysis of this key concept in foreign affairs and is essential reading for scholars of US foreign policy, public diplomacy, international relations and foreign policy analysis.

Inderjeet Parmar is Professor of Government at the University of Manchester, UK. He is Vice Chair of the British International Studies Association, has published several books and is the co-editor of the *Routledge Studies in US Foreign Policy* series.

Michael Cox is Professor in the International Relations Department at LSE, UK. He is the author of numerous books and has edited several of the leading journals in international relations.

Routledge studies in US foreign policy

Inderjeet Parmar, *University of Manchester*
and John Dumbrell, *University of Durham*

This new series sets out to publish high quality works by leading and emerging scholars critically engaging with US Foreign Policy. The series welcomes a variety of approaches to the subject and draws on scholarship from international relations, security studies, international political economy, foreign policy analysis and contemporary international history.

Subjects covered include the role of administrations and institutions, the media, think tanks, ideologues and intellectuals, elites, transnational corporations, public opinion and pressure groups in shaping foreign policy, US relations with individual nations, with global regions and global institutions and America's evolving strategic and military policies.

The series aims to provide a range of books – from individual research monographs and edited collections to textbooks and supplemental reading for scholars, researchers, policy analysts and students.

United States Foreign Policy and National Identity in the 21st Century
Edited by Kenneth Christie

New Directions in US Foreign Policy
Edited by Inderjeet Parmar, Linda B. Miller and Mark Ledwidge

America's 'Special Relationships'
Foreign and domestic aspects of the politics of alliance
Edited by John Dumbrell and Axel R Schäfer

US Foreign Policy in Context
National ideology from the founders to the Bush Doctrine
Adam Quinn

The United States and NATO since 9/11
The transatlantic alliance renewed
Ellen Hallams

Soft Power and US Foreign Policy
Theoretical, historical and contemporary perspectives
Edited by Inderjeet Parmar and Michael Cox

Soft Power and US Foreign Policy

Theoretical, historical and contemporary perspectives

Edited by
Inderjeet Parmar
and Michael Cox

Routledge
Taylor & Francis Group

LONDON AND NEW YORK

First published 2010
by Routledge
2 Park Square, Milton Park, Abingdon, Oxon, OX14 4RN

Simultaneously published in the USA and Canada
by Routledge
270 Madison Avenue, New York, NY 10016

Routledge is an imprint of the Taylor & Francis Group

© 2010 Editorial selection and matter, Inderjeet Parmar and Michael Cox;
individual chapters the contributors

Typeset in Times New Roman by Glyph International
Printed and bound in Great Britain by TJ International Ltd., Padstow

British Library Cataloguing in Publication Data
A catalogue record for this book is available from the British Library

Library of Congress Cataloging in Publication Data
Soft power and US foreign policy : theoretical, historical and
contemporary perspectives / edited by Inderjeet Parmar and Michael Cox.
p. cm. – (Routledge studies in US foreign policy)
1. United States–Relations–Foreign countries. I. Parmar, Inderjeet. II. Cox,
Michael, 1947- III. Title: Soft power and United States foreign policy.
JZ1480.S64 2010
327.73–dc22   2009035653

ISBN 10: 0-415-49203-3 (hbk)
ISBN 10: 0-415-49204-1 (pbk)
ISBN 10: 0-203-85649-X (ebk)

ISBN 13: 978-0-415-49203-4 (hbk)
ISBN 13: 978-0-415-49204-1 (pbk)
ISBN 13: 978-0-203-85649-9 (ebk)

Contents

Contributors

Michael Cox is Co-Director of IDEAS and Professor of International Relations at the London School of Economics, UK.

Till Geiger is Lecturer in International History at the University of Manchester and has published widely on British and Irish foreign policy and transatlantic relations in the early Cold War. His publications include *Britain and the Economic Problem of the Cold War: The Political Economy and the Economic Impact of the British Defence Effort, 1945–1955* (Ashgate, 2004), (with Michael Kennedy, eds) *Ireland, Europe and the Marshall Plan* (Four Courts Press, 2004) and articles in *European Review of History* and *Irish Studies in International Affairs*. His current research is on Britain, Western Europe and American aid to Western Europe, 1948–60.

Christopher Hill, FBA, is Sir Patrick Sheehy Professor of International Relations, at the University of Cambridge. From 1974–2004 he taught in the Department of International Relations at the London School School of Economics and Political Science, where he was the Montague Burton Professor. His most recent books are *The Changing Politics of Foreign Policy* (Palgrave, 2003) and *The European Union in International Relations* (edited with Michael Smith, 2005).

John Krige is the Kranzberg Professor in the School of History, Technology and Society at Georgia Tech. He has published extensively on the intersection between scientific and technological collaboration and the foreign policy of nation states, both European and the US. He has participated in writing major histories of CERN (European Organization for Nuclear Research) and of ESA (European Space Agency). His most recent publications include an edited collection, *Global Power Knowledge: Science, Technology and International Affairs* (with K.H. Barth) published as Vol. 21 of OSIRIS (University of Chicago Press, 2005) and *American Hegemony and the Postwar Reconstruction of Science in Europe* (MIT Press, 2006). His current project deals with technological exchange between the USA and Western Europe in strategic domains, notably the nuclear and space.

Christopher Layne is Professor, and Robert M. Gates Chair in National Security at Texas A & M University's George H. W. Bush School of Government and

Public Service. His research interests are grand strategy, American foreign policy, and international relations theory. Professor Layne has written two books: *The Peace of Illusions: American Grand Strategy from 1940 to the Present* (Cornell University Press, 2006) and (with Bradley A. Thayer) *American Empire: A Debate* (Routledge, 2006). He has published five major articles in *International Security*. Additionally, he has contributed extensively to the debates about international relations theory and American foreign policy in several scholarly and policy journals. He also is a Contributing Editor to *The American Conservative*. Professor Layne is a member of the Council on Foreign Relations, and a consultant to the National Intelligence Council.

Edward Lock is a senior lecturer in International Relations in the Department of Politics, Philosophy and IR at the University of the West of England, Bristol. He writes on US grand strategy, strategic culture and constructivist theory. Currently, he is preparing a manuscript on the conceptual and practical limitations of the debate within the US foreign policy establishment regarding the nature, extent and future trajectory of American power.

Joseph S. Nye, Jr is University Distinguished Service Professor and former Dean of the Kennedy School of Government at Harvard University. He received his bachelor's degree *summa cum laude* from Princeton University in 1958, did postgraduate work at Oxford University on a Rhodes Scholarship, and earned a PhD in political science from Harvard. He joined the Harvard faculty in 1964. In 2008, a poll of 2700 international relations scholars listed him as one of the six most influential in the past 20 years and the most influential on American foreign policy.

From 1977–79, Nye was Deputy to the Undersecretary of State for Security Assistance, Science, and Technology and chaired the National Security Council Group on Nonproliferation of Nuclear Weapons. In 1993–94 he chaired the National Intelligence Council which prepares intelligence estimates for the president, and in 1994–95 served as Assistant Secretary of Defense for International Security Affairs. He won Distinguished Service medals from all three agencies.

Nye is the author of numerous books and more than 150 articles in professional and policy journals. His most recent books include *Soft Power* (New York: Public Affairs, 2004), *Understanding International Conflict* (7th ed), *The Powers to Lead* (New York: Oxford University Press, 2008) and *The Power Game: A Washington Novel* (New York: Public Affairs, 2004).

He is a fellow of the American Academy of Arts and Sciences, the British Academy, and the American Academy of Diplomacy. He is an honorary fellow of Exeter College, Oxford, and a Theodore Roosevelt Fellow of The American Academy of Political and Social Science. He is the recipient of Princeton University's Woodrow Wilson Award, and the Charles Merriam Award from the American Political Science Association.

Inderjeet Parmar is Professor of Government at the University of Manchester, UK. He was Head of Politics at Manchester (2006–9) and is currently Vice Chair of the British International Studies Association. Author and editor of several books and articles, he is writing a monograph entitled *Foundations of the American Century: Ford, Carnegie and Rockefeller Foundations and US Foreign Affairs* (Columbia University Press, forthcoming).

Leonardo Ramos is Assistant Professor in the Department of International Relations at the Pontifical Catholic University of Minas Gerais (PUC-Minas) and doctoral candidate in the Institute of International Relations at the Pontifical Catholic University of Rio de Janeiro (IRI/PUC-Rio). His current research focuses on the G8, and he has published articles on Gramsci, international political economy, globalization and civil society.

Giles Scott-Smith is a senior researcher with the Roosevelt Study Center and Associate Professor in International Relations at the Roosevelt Academy, both in Middelburg, the Netherlands. In January 2009 he was appointed the Ernst van der Beugel Chair in the Diplomatic History of Transatlantic Relations since WWII at Leiden University. He is co-editor of the *European Journal of American Studies* and on the management committee of the Transatlantic Studies Association. His research covers the role of non-state actors and public diplomacy in the maintenance of inter-state (particularly transatlantic) relations, and their contribution to the ideological 'battle of ideas' during the Cold War and beyond. His publications include *Networks of Empire: The U.S. State Department's Foreign Leader Program in the Netherlands, France, and Britain 1950–70* (Peter Lang, 2008), *The Politics of Apolitical Culture: The Congress for Cultural Freedom, the CIA, and Post-war American Hegemony* (Routledge, 2002) and numerous articles in journals such as *British Journal of Politics and International Relations*, *Cold War History*, *Revue Francaise d'Etudes Americaines*, *Journal of American Studies*, *Diplomacy and Statecraft*, and *Intelligence and National Security.*

Shogo Suzuki is Lecturer in Politics at the University of Manchester, UK. His research focuses on Sino-Japanese relations, Chinese foreign policy and Japanese foreign policy. He is the author of *Civilization and Empire: China and Japan's Encounter with European International Society* (Routledge, 2009), as well as articles that have appeared in *European Journal of International Relations*, *The Pacific Review*, *Third World Quarterly* and *International Relations.*

Angus Taverner specialises in international relations, political risk and strategic communications. He has been working with governments and organisations in the Europe, the USA and the Middle East since 2004, and has been involved with a number of projects involving: news analysis, interpreting international media perceptions, and commentary on strategic issues that influence political, diplomatic and economic relations in the region.

   Formerly an artillery officer in the British Army, Angus developed the UK Armed Forces' first formal doctrine for undertaking Media Operations and, while working for the UK Ministry of Defence, he conceived and established the UK's Defence Media Operations Centre. He planned the military-media support for initial operations in both Iraq and Afghanistan and evolved the UK policy for embedding war correspondents with UK forces.

   He holds a MA in Public Relations and Strategic Communications (2005) from the University of the Arts, London completing a dissertation on 'Terrorists' Use of Public Relations Techniques'. He continues to pursue research into the military approach to 'soft power' and the importance of understanding 'perception' as a key element of strategic and campaign planning. He has contributed to a number books including: *War and the Media: Reportage and Propaganda, 1900–2003* (I.B. Tauris, 2003) and *Communicating War: Memory, Media & Military* (Sage, 2007).

Philip M. Taylor is Professor of International Communications in the Institute of Communications Studies at the University of Leeds. His many publications include *War and the Media: Propaganda and Persuasion in the Gulf War* (2nd edition, 1997); *Munitions of the Mind: A History of Propaganda from the Ancient World to the Present Day* (3rd edition 2003); *Global Communications, International Affairs and the Media since 1945* (1997) and *British Propaganda in the 20th Century: Selling Democracy* (1999). His latest books are *Shooting the Messenger: The Political Impact of War Reporting* (co-authored with Paul Moorcraft, Potomac, 2008) and the *Routledge Handbook of Public Diplomacy* (co-edited with Nancy Snow, 2008).

Geraldo Zahran is a PhD Candidate at the Centre of International Studies, University of Cambridge. His work focuses on the influence of US liberal political tradition in international institutions.

Acknowledgements

As ever, the editing of a book is a team effort, with debts accumulated many times over. Not only must we thank the chapter authors, we also owe appreciation to all the speakers at the Symposium at Manchester in May 2008. Alas, it was not possible to include all contributions from the Symposium in this volume, though I am certain that those papers contributed in subtle ways to the same. A special thank you to Craig Murphy, a good friend and colleague, for helping to attract Joe Nye to the Symposium. Without Joe and, therefore, Craig, the Symposium would not have been possible. Once Joe came to Manchester, it was clear that the event would be a great success. The omens were good: Manchester United won the European Champions' League the night before the Symposium. It was very satisfying that Joe and several other speakers got to witness first-hand the joyous celebrations in Manchester city centre in the early hours of 22 May, 2008.

Without funding, of course, there is no way that we could have held a Symposium in the first place. A debt of gratitude is owed to the School of Social Sciences, the Politics Department, the Centre for International Politics, and the War and Peace Lecture Fund, all at the University of Manchester, for underwriting the event.

The event was the brainchild of the small group of colleagues at the heart of the Research Group on American Power (RGAP). They helped to develop the idea and translate it into a successful occasion. It took two years of planning and organization. Specifically, thanks to Mark Ledwidge, Piers Robinson, Leo McCann, Bill Cooke and Peter Knight. A panic shared is truly a panic halved!

Thanks also to Craig Fowlie and Nicola Parkin at Routledge: your encouragement and support has been wonderful!

This book is dedicated, however, to one who was not present at the Symposium and played no active part in its organization, my daughter, India Anoushka (now aged 4 years), who lights up my life. Her boundless energy and enthusiasm makes our home wonderful if, at times, a 'functioning anarchy', not unlike the country after which she is named.

Kuala Lumpur, August 2009

Introduction

Inderjeet Parmar and Michael Cox

This edited volume of original research papers draws its contributors and chapters principally from the Symposium on Soft Power and US Foreign Affairs organised by the Research Group on American Power (RGAP) at the University of Manchester, May 2008.

Soft power has become part of popular political discourse since it was coined by Harvard's Joseph Nye in his 1990 book, *Bound to Lead: The Changing Nature of American Power*, strengthened by his *Soft Power: The Means to Success in World Politics* (2004), and further elaborated in *The Powers To Lead* (2008). The rise of widespread anti-Americanism – or, at least, negative attitudes towards US foreign policy, especially following the war of aggression against Iraq and the subsequent military occupation of the country – has brought new attention to the meaning and instruments of soft power. The administration of President Barack Obama has overtly embraced soft power or, more accurately, its politically more acceptable version, *smart* power. It sounds a lot more attractive, especially to critics of military force, becoming a staple of Democratic Party opponents of the foreign policies of President George W. Bush; indeed, Nye was close to the more soft power-oriented election campaign of Senator Barack Obama and, after the 2008 elections, was touted as a possible US ambassador to Japan. Nye was also a member of the Project on National Security Reform (PNSR) – a high level congressionally mandated committee that examined, among other things, how better to integrate America's hard and soft power. Several members of the PNSR's leadership group were appointed to Obama's administration, including Dennis Blair (director, National Intelligence), Jim Jones (National Security Adviser) and James Steinberg (deputy secretary of state).

To Nye, soft power is the power of attraction, the influence of example – as opposed to the influence and power derived from military force, economic sanctions and even economic aid. 'Soft power is the ability to get what you want by attracting and persuading others to adopt your goals. It differs from hard power, the ability to use the carrots and sticks of economic and military might to make others follow your will. Both hard and soft power are important in the war on terrorism, but attraction is much cheaper than coercion, and an asset that needs to be nourished' (Nye, 2004).

Nothing very 'soft' about that!

Soft power is now a term used by scholars, policymakers, media analysts, etc. ...
A Google search reveals 93,200,000 sites that mention the term 'soft power'. Yet,
soft power is ambiguous and the term is used, even by Nye, in many different
ways. This has led to some interesting questions which this volume explores.
But first, it is vital to consider that before there can be any specific categories or
types of power, there is the very term 'power' itself that requires definition and
understanding. What is power? How does it work? How do we know it when
we 'see' it? What is the relationship between coercive power and authoritative
power? Between power that is 'legitimate' and that which is 'illegitimate'? These
questions are addressed in the course of this volume.

The first substantive chapter is the keynote lecture, 'The future of soft power in
US foreign policy', delivered by Joseph Nye at the Symposium, May 2008. It is
around this lecture and its themes that the volume hinges. In it, Nye explains
his notions of soft, hard and smart power and offers a critique of the Bush
administration's inadequacies. He then goes on to examine the challenges for
the new US president after November 2008.

The following section of the book consists of three chapters that carefully and
critically dissect the notion of soft power: Edward Lock's chapter on 'Soft power
as strategy', Zahran Ramos's neo-Gramscian critique, 'From hegemony to soft
power: implications of a conceptual change' (Chapter 3) and Christopher Layne's
'The unbearable lightness of soft power', present theoretical and methodological
critiques of Nye's concept of soft power. Zahran and Ramos explore Nye's soft
power concept, particularly its origins and development because he considers it
instructive as to its deeper meaning. They argues that Nye's 'soft power' concept
lies in Gramsci's understandings of power as 'consent'. This is highly interesting
and not widely understood, as Nye drops references to Gramsci in later renditions
of the term. Yet, if extracted from Gramscian hegemony theory, can soft power so
easily be applied outside its original framework without doing violence to it? And,
more broadly, is soft power in any way superior to hegemony in the Gramscian
sense? Zahran and Ramos scrutinise their chapter.

Since soft power is clearly a new term for an old concept, Chapters 5, 6 and 7
consider the concept in its historical application. Geiger's highly original chapter
(Chapter 5) examines the applicability of the concept, as suggested in Nye's
political novel, *The Power Game* (2004), to postwar American Marshall Aid
and other programmes designed to enhance US hegemony. Chapter 6 (Parmar)
considers the impacts of two soft power public diplomacy programmes – Henry
Kissinger's Harvard Seminar and the Salzburg Seminar in American Studies –
during the 1950s and 1960s which are suggestive of the importance of long-
term cultural engagement strategies of US hegemony-building; they are likely
to reappear in new form. John Krige argues in Chapter 7 that the USA used its
soft power in the 1950s and 1960s to try and enhance its own positions vis-a-vis
European defence cooperation.

Other important matters also arise at this point. What are the boundaries of
soft and hard power? Is soft power totally separate from hard (military and other
coercive) power? What is the relationship between hard, soft, and smart power?

How does the US military exercise soft power or consider it useful in the war on terror or in counter-insurgencies? Is soft power effective? In Gramsci's work, the consent of the governed is engineered by ruling class groups and their allies, particularly by state, church, school and party. Nevertheless, there is also the strong notion that the governed have to be persuaded to buy the line, to be given a 'stake' in the outcome. If that is the case in Nye's soft power concept, is *propaganda* an exercise in soft power? Are public and cultural diplomacy? Or is public diplomacy the result of the failure of soft power? Giles Scott-Smith examines this issue in regard to US public diplomacy in Chapter 8, Angus Taverner in relation to 'Strategic Communications' and information campaigns in the Middle East and Philip Taylor in connection with information strategies in the broader war on terror.

Clearly, soft power is exercised by a variety of states and other institutions and the following two chapters deal in turn with two such examples. Christopher Hill explores the politics of the European Union's soft power, an aspect of power that is, perhaps, the EU's hallmark (up to now, at least) in Chapter 11. Shogo Suzuki turns his attention to the rising power of China in Chapter 12, adding to the comparative character of this volume's examination of American soft power.

Finally, Joseph Nye responds to his admirers, critics and interlocutors in the last chapter of the volume. It is fitting that he should have the 'last word' on this subject, making this volume unique. Most of the chapters above were considered during the Symposium and subsequently rewritten to reflect the debates and discussions, with Nye's full participation.

1 The future of soft power in US foreign policy

Joseph S. Nye, Jr

The USA has lost a great deal of its soft power over the past eight years. While this is not true for all areas, public opinion polls show a serious decline in American attractiveness in Europe, Latin America, and most dramatically, across the entire Muslim world. When asked why they report this decline, respondents cite American policies more than American culture or values. In contrast to the arguments made by President George W. Bush, they hate us more for what we do than who we are. The resources that produce soft power for a country include its culture (where it is attractive to others); its values (where they are attractive and not undercut by inconsistent practices) and its policies (where they are seen as inclusive and legitimate in the eyes of others). Since it is easier for a country to change its policies than its culture, this implies the possibility that a future president could choose policies that could help to recover some of the soft power that the Bush administration squandered over the past eight years.

President Bush would certainly not agree with the view that he ignored American soft power. He could cite the Wilsonian rhetoric about the universal values of freedom and democracy that were central to his second inaugural address, or his recent speech urging Arab leaders to follow such principles. He might also cite his efforts to increase development assistance and combat AIDS in Africa (which may account for better poll results on that continent). However, the crucial flaw in this defense is the failure to understand that soft power is a relationship of attraction that depends on the eyes of the beholders. By failing to understand the need for the legitimacy of a broad coalition (such as his father assembled), his use of hard power in Iraq undercut American soft power. His failure to understand the cultural context of the Muslim world meant that his appeals for freedom and democracy failed to produce attraction. Furthermore, by cavalier civil liberty practices in the campaign against terrorism, the administration made its profession of universal values look hypocritical.

American foreign policy during the Bush administration has focused around what the president termed a 'global war on terrorism'. But there are serious problems with the idea of a war on terror, much less making that the theme for foreign policy. For example, Britain has recently told its officials not to use the words 'war on terrorism'. Americans have a rhetorical tradition of declaring war on abstract nouns like drugs and poverty, but the British have focused on concrete opponents. The basic British concern, however, lies in a different analysis of the problem. When interrogating arrested terrorists, British officials have found a common thread. Al-Qaeda and affiliated groups use a simple yet effective narrative to recruit young Muslims to cross the line into violence. While extreme religious beliefs, diverse local conditions or issues such as Palestine or Kashmir can create a sense of grievance, it is the language of war and a narrative of battle that gives recruits a cult-like sense of status and larger meaning that leads to action. The metaphor of war may have helped Bush to rally domestic opinion in the aftermath of 9/11, but he ignored the problem of multiple audiences. What appealed at home, failed abroad.

Al-Qaeda focuses a large portion of its efforts on communication, and it has learned to use modern media and the Internet very effectively. Potential recruits are told that Islam is under attack from the West, and that it is the personal responsibility of each Muslim to fight to protect the worldwide Muslim community. This extreme version of the duty of *jihad* (to struggle) is reinforced by videos and internet websites that show Muslims being killed in Chechnya, Iraq, Kashmir and Lebanon. This message uses the language of religion as justification, but its dynamic is like an ideology that seeks to harness the energy from a great variety of grievances. British officials have concluded that when we use the vocabulary of war and jihad, we simply reinforce al-Qaeda's narrative and help their recruiting efforts.

Former Secretary of Defense Donald Rumsfeld once asked what metric we should use to measure success in a 'war on terrorism'. He concluded that success depended on whether the number of terrorists we were killing or deterring was greater than the number the enemy was recruiting. By his metric, British and American intelligence estimates are not encouraging. The invasion of Iraq helped rather than hindered al-Qaeda recruitment.

Bush's legacy

Some pundits believe that no matter who wins the 2008 election, he or she will be bound to follow the broad lines of Bush's strategy. Vice-President Richard Cheney has argued, 'when we get all through 10 years from now, we'll look back on this period of time and see that liberating 50 million people in Afghanistan and Iraq really did represent a major, fundamental shift, obviously, in US policy in terms of how we dealt with the emerging terrorist threat – and that we'll have fundamentally changed circumstances in that part of the world.' President Bush himself has pointed out that Harry Truman suffered low ratings in the last year of his presidency because of the Korean War, but today is held in high regard and South Korea is a democracy protected by American troops. But this is an over-simplification of history. By this stage of his presidency, Truman had built major cooperative institutions such as the Marshall Plan and NATO.

The crisis of 9/11 produced an opportunity for George W. Bush to express a bold new vision of foreign policy, but one should judge a vision by whether it balances ideals with capabilities. Anyone can produce a wish list, but effective visions combine feasibility with the inspiration. Among past presidents, Franklin D. Roosevelt was good at this, but Woodrow Wilson was not. David Gergen, director of the Kennedy School's Center for Public Leadership has described the difference between the boldness of FDR and George W. Bush: 'FDR was also much more of a public educator than Bush, talking people carefully through the challenges and choices the nation faced, cultivating public opinion, building up a sturdy foundation of support before he acted. As he showed during the lead-up to World War II, he would never charge as far in front of his followers as Bush.' Bush's temperament is less patient. He saw himself as a transformational leader. As one journalist put it, 'he likes to shake things up. That was the key to going into Iraq.' But by failing to understand the cultural context, his transformation was for the worse, rather than better.

Contextual intelligence

The next president will need what I call 'contextual intelligence' in my new book, *The Powers to Lead*. In foreign policy, contextual intelligence is the intuitive diagnostic skill that helps you align tactics with objectives to create smart strategies in varying situations. Of recent presidents, Ronald Reagan and George H.W. Bush had impressive contextual intelligence, but the younger Bush did not. It starts with a clear understanding of the current context of American foreign policy, both at home and abroad.

Academics, pundits and advisors have often been mistaken about America's position in the world. For example, two decades ago, the conventional wisdom was that the USA was in decline, suffering from 'imperial overstretch'. It was during this debate that I coined the term soft power. After summarizing the hard military and economic resources of the USA, I realized that something was still missing. Particularly with the growth in the popularity of structural neo-realism, international relations theory suffered from a materialist bias that truncated our conceptions of power, and ignored the non-material factors that can influence behavior through attraction. That is what I tried to recover with the idea of soft power.

A decade later, with the end of the Cold War, the new conventional wisdom was that the world was a unipolar American hegemony. Some neo-conservative pundits drew the conclusion that the USA was so powerful that it could decide what it thought was right, and others would have no choice but to follow. Charles Krauthammer celebrated this view as 'the new unilateralism' and it heavily influenced the Bush administration even before the shock of the attacks on 9/11 produced a new 'Bush doctrine' of preventive war and coercive democratization. This new unilateralism was based on a profound misunderstanding of the nature of power in world politics. Power is the ability to affect others to get the outcomes one wants. Whether the possession of resources will produce such outcomes depends upon the context. In the past, it was assumed that military power dominated most issues, but in today's world, the contexts of power differ greatly on military, economic and transnational issues.

Contextual intelligence must start with an understanding of the strength and limits of American power. The USA is the only superpower, but preponderance is not empire or hegemony. America can influence but not control other parts of the world. Power always depends upon context, and the context of world politics today is like a three-dimensional chess game. The top board of military power is unipolar; but on the middle board of economic relations, the world is multipolar. On the bottom board of transnational relations (such as climate change, illegal drugs, pandemics and terrorism) power is chaotically distributed. We see a diffusion of power to non-state actors that Robert Keohane and I began to describe three decades ago. Military power is a small part of the solution in responding to these new threats. They require cooperation among governments and international institutions. Even on the top board (where America represents nearly half of world defense expenditures), the American military is supreme in the global commons of air, sea and space, but much more limited in its ability to control nationalistic populations in occupied areas.

Second, the next president must understand the importance of developing an integrated grand strategy that combines hard military power with soft attractive power. In the struggle against terrorism, we need to use hard power against the hard core terrorists, but we cannot hope to win unless we gain the hearts and minds of the moderates. If the misuse of hard power (such as in Abu Ghraib or Guantanamo) creates more new terrorist recruits than we kill or deter, we will lose. Right now we have no integrated strategy for combining hard and soft power. Many official instruments of soft power – public diplomacy, broadcasting, exchange programs, development assistance, disaster relief, military to military contacts – are scattered around the government and there is no overarching strategy or budget that even tries to integrate them with hard power into an overarching national security strategy. We spend about 500 times more on the military than we do on broadcasting and exchanges. Is this the right proportion? How would we know? How would we make trade-offs? What are the relevant time horizons? And how should the government relate to the non-official generators of soft power – everything from Hollywood to Harvard to the Bill and Melinda Gates Foundation – that emanate from civil society? A new administration will have to realize that it cannot control these actors who sometimes produce and sometimes consume soft power. It will have to think of public diplomacy as involving contacts and listening rather than just broadcasting values and policies that may be heard differently in other cultures. As Edward R. Murrow once put it, the most important part of public diplomacy is the last three feet of face-to-face interactions. Or to use a more modern metaphor, public diplomacy will have to be more like Web 2.0 where peer-to-peer interactions generate much of the content.

Soft and hard power

The Bush administration has drawn analogies between the war on terrorism and the Cold War. The president is correct that this will be a long struggle.

Most outbreaks of transnational terrorism in the past century took a generation to burn out. But another aspect of the analogy has been neglected. Despite numerous errors, the Cold War strategy involved a smart combination of hard coercive power and the soft attractive power of ideas. When the Berlin Wall finally collapsed, it was not destroyed by an artillery barrage, but by hammers and bulldozers wielded by those who had lost faith in communism.

There is very little likelihood that we can ever attract people like Osama bin Laden: we need hard power to deal with such cases. But there is enormous diversity of opinion in the Muslim world. Witness Iran whose ruling mullahs see American culture as the Great Satan, but where many in the younger generation want American videos to play in the privacy of their homes. Many Muslims disagree with American values as well as policies, but that does not make mean they agree with bin Laden. By Rumsfeld's calculus, we cannot win if the number of people the extremists are recruiting is larger than the number we are killing and deterring or convincing to choose moderation over extremism. The Bush administration is beginning to understand this general proposition, but it does not seem to know how to implement such a strategy. To achieve this – to thwart our enemies, but also to reduce their numbers through deterrence, suasion and attraction – we need better strategy.

In the information age, success is not merely the result of whose army wins, but also whose story wins. The current struggle against extremist jihadi terrorism is not a clash of civilizations, but a civil war within Islam. We cannot win unless the Muslim mainstream wins. While we need hard power to battle the extremists, we need the soft power of attraction to win the hearts and minds of the majority. Polls throughout the Muslim world show that we are not winning this battle, and that it is our policies not our values that offend. Presidential rhetoric about promoting democracy is less convincing than pictures of Abu Ghraib.

Despite these failures, there has not been enough political debate in the USA about the squandering of American soft power. Soft power is an analytical term, not a political slogan and perhaps that is why, not surprisingly, it has taken hold in academic analysis, and in other places such as Europe, China and India, but not in the American political debate. Especially in the current political climate, it makes a poor slogan – post-9/11, emotions left little room for anything described as 'soft.' We may need soft power as a nation, but it is a difficult political sell for politicians. Bill Clinton captured the mindset of the American people when he said that in a climate of fear, the electorate would choose 'strong and wrong' over 'timid and right.'

Of course soft power is not the solution to all problems. Even though North Korean dictator Kim Jong Il likes to watch Hollywood movies, that is unlikely to affect his nuclear weapons programme. And soft power got nowhere in attracting the Taliban government away from its support for al-Qaeda in the 1990s. It took hard military power to end that. But other goals such as the promotion of democracy and human rights are better achieved by soft power. Coercive democratization has its limits as the Bush administration has found in Iraq.

Smart power

I have used the term 'smart power' to describe strategies that successfully combine hard and soft power resources. The USA needs to rediscover how to be a 'smart power'. That was the conclusion of a bipartisan commission that I recently co-chaired with Richard Armitage, the former deputy secretary of state in the Bush administration. A group of Republican and Democratic members of Congress, former ambassadors, retired military officers and heads of non-profit organizations was convened by the Center for Strategic and International Studies in Washington. We concluded that America's image and influence had declined in recent years, and that the USA had to move from exporting fear to inspiring optimism and hope.

The Smart Power Commission is not alone in this conclusion. Recently Defense Secretary Robert Gates called for the US government to commit more money and effort to soft power tools including diplomacy, economic assistance and communications because the military alone cannot defend America's interests around the world. He pointed out that military spending totals nearly half a trillion dollars annually compared with a State Department budget of US$36 billion. In his words, 'I am here to make the case for strengthening our capacity to use soft power and for better integrating it with hard power.' He acknowledged that for the head of the Pentagon to plead for more resources for the State Department was as odd as a man biting a dog, but these are not normal times.

Smart power is the ability to combine the hard power of coercion or payment with the soft power of attraction into a successful strategy. By and large, the USA managed such a combination during the Cold War, but more recently US foreign policy has tended to over-rely on hard power because it is the most direct and visible source of American strength. The Pentagon is the best trained and best resourced arm of the government, but there are limits to what hard power can achieve on its own. Promoting democracy, human rights and development of civil society are not best handled with the barrel of a gun. It is true that the American military has an impressive operational capacity, but the practice of turning to the Pentagon because it can get things done leads to an image of an over-militarized foreign policy.

Diplomacy and foreign assistance are often under-funded and neglected, in part because of the difficulty of demonstrating their short term impact on critical challenges. In addition, wielding soft power is difficult because many of America's soft power resources lie outside of government in the private sector and civil society, in its bilateral alliances, multilateral institutions and transnational contacts. Moreover, American foreign policy institutions and personnel are fractured and compartmentalized and there is not an adequate inter-agency process for developing and funding a smart power strategy.

The effects of the 9/11 terrorist attacks have also thrown us off course. Since the shock of 9/11, the USA has been exporting fear and anger rather than our more traditional values of hope and optimism. Guantanamo has become a more powerful global icon than the Statue of Liberty. The CSIS Smart Power Commission acknowledged that terrorism is a real threat and likely to be with us for decades, but we pointed out that over-responding to the provocations of extremists does us more damage than the terrorists ever could. The commission argued that success in the struggle against terrorism means finding a new central premise for American foreign policy to replace the current theme of a 'war on terror'. A commitment to providing for the global good can provide that premise.

The USA should become a smart power by once again investing in the global public goods – providing things that people and governments in all quarters of the world want but cannot attain in the absence of leadership by the largest country. By complementing American military and economic might with greater investments in soft power, and focusing on global public goods, the USA can rebuild the framework that it needs to tackle tough global challenges.

Specifically, the Smart Power Commission recommended that American foreign policy should focus on five critical areas:

- We should restore our alliances, partnerships and multilateral institutions. Many have fallen in disarray in recent years of unilateral approaches and a renewed investment in institutions will be essential.
- Global development should be a high priority. Elevating the role of development in US foreign policy can help align our interests with that of people around the world. A major initiative on global public health would be a good place to start.
- We should invest in a public diplomacy that builds less on broadcasting and invests more in face to face contacts, education and exchanges that involve civil society. A new foundation for international understanding could focus on young people.
- Economic integration. Resisting protectionism and continuing engagement in the global economy is necessary for growth and prosperity not only at home but also for peoples abroad. Maintaining an open international economy, however, will require attention to inclusion of those that market changes leave behind both at home and abroad.
- Energy security and climate change are global goods where we have failed to take the lead but that will be increasingly important on the agenda of world politics in coming years. A new American foreign policy that helps shape a global consensus and develop innovative technologies will be crucial in meeting this important set of challenges.

Implementing such a smart power strategy will require a strategic reassessment of how the US government is organized, coordinated and budgeted. The next president should consider a number of creative solutions to maximize the administration's ability to organize for success, including the appointment of senior personnel who could reach across agencies to better align resources into a smart power strategy. This will require innovation, and that must be the agenda of the next president.

Leadership matters in foreign policy. States follow their national interests, but different leaders help to define national interests in different ways. For a powerful state such as the USA, the structure of world politics allows degrees of freedom in such definitions. It may be true, as structuralists argue, that the most powerful state is like the biggest kid on the block who will always engender a degree of jealousy and resentment, but it matters whether the big kid acts like a bully or a helpful friend. Both substance and style matter. If the most powerful actor is seen as producing global public goods, it is more likely to develop legitimacy and soft power.

Style also matters, even when public goods are the issue. For example, the Chair of the White House Council on Environmental Quality told the 2007 UN conference on climate change at Bali, 'The U.S. will lead, and we will continue to lead, but leadership requires others to fall into line and follow.' That statement became a sore point to other delegations. It illustrates the insensitivity to context and the eyes and ears of the beholders that has bedeviled the soft power efforts of the Bush administration.

Consultation and listening are essential in the generation of soft power. This is something that the USA is rediscovering after its infatuation with the 'unipolar moment and the new unilateralism'. The next administration, of whichever party, will have to learn better how to generate soft power, and relate it to hard power in smart strategies. This will require leaders with contextual intelligence. The bad news is that they will inherit a difficult international environment. The good news is that previous presidents have managed to employ hard, soft and smart power in equally difficult contexts. If it has happened before, perhaps it can happen again.

2   From hegemony to soft power

Implications of a conceptual change[1]

Geraldo Zahran and Leonardo Ramos

Introduction

The concept of soft power was introduced to the international relations literature by Joseph Nye in the early 1990s. In almost two decades, the concept has gained widespread acceptance and usage. In this chapter, we articulate the resemblance between Nye's concept of soft power and Antonio Gramsci's concept of hegemony. Nye himself provided our inspiration, as he has always acknowledged the similarities between soft power and the Gramscian concept of hegemony. Both concepts make reference to a set of general principles, ideas, values and institutions shared by, consented or regarded as legitimate by different groups, but that at the same time are resources of power, influence and control over one group by the other. Nevertheless, we argue that by not pushing the Gramscian analogy forward, Nye left open gaps in his conceptualization of soft power; Gramsci's work has implications that the concept of soft power cannot conceive.

To unfold this argument, we first present a historical analysis of how the concept was created and developed. The fact that Nye's work on soft power was always closely related to his work on US foreign policy clearly influenced the former. After that, we approach soft power in a more detailed way, carefully accessing its different definitions and meanings. Revisiting Nye's arguments about what is soft power and how it is constituted allows us to proceed with an internal critique of the concept, after which we can properly compare soft power with the Gramscian concept of hegemony. We do so by briefly exposing the thoughts of the Italian author on hegemony and its related concepts. From that point onwards we draw comparisons between hegemony and soft power, suggesting ways to better understand the concept and its dynamics, and finally offering a broader Gramscian reading of Nye's work.

A historiography of soft power

During the past two decades Nye has developed and advocated the use of the concept of soft power in a number of academic and non-academic publications. Broadly speaking, his efforts were a great success, as soft power became a widely known concept in international relations (IR) literature and elsewhere. In order to revisit this process we focus on three specific moments of the formulation of soft power: the three books published by Nye that in some degree dealt with this concept: *Bound to Lead*, published in 1990, *The Paradox of the American Power*, 2002 and *Soft Power*, 2004. It is worth noting that soft power was not the main topic of the first two books; they are primarily an analysis of US power and foreign policy. As we shall see, the origin of the concept being deeply related to analysis of US foreign policy produced a marked influence on soft power.

It all began during the 1980s, when declinist theories had strength and popularity in mainstream IR debates (Kennedy 1987). The central claim of declinist authors was that the US policies during the Cold War had reached a point of overstretch, the costs of which would start to undermine US power. In the end, this overstretch would be responsible for the weakening of the US position in the international system, combined with domestic upheavals against foreign policies and state expenditures abroad. Nye was one of the authors engaged in this debate, mainly criticizing declinist theories. And it was while doing so that he first articulated the concept of soft power (Nye Jr 1990).

In *Bound to Lead*, Nye argues that the declinist interpretation of the international order is distorted for two main reasons. The first criticism is aimed at the idea of a decline of US relative power, supported by an analysis of military and economic data from World War II onwards. Nye shows that the distribution of military and economic capabilities in post-war years was completely unbalanced due to the losses caused by the war. At this point, the USA had at its disposal an unmatched number of economic and military resources, simply because World War II was not fought on its own territory. Any analysis taking the distribution of resources in post-war years as its starting point would show a tendency towards decline, given that the USA had extremely high and distorted initial levels for comparison. Ignoring this initial distortion, the analysis of the same indexes would show much smaller variation between the 1970s and 1980s, refuting the idea of decline.

The second problem raised by Nye regarding declinist theories is their inability to deal with the changes the US power has been through in the international system. In Nye's view, declinists measure what he calls 'hard power': population, territory, natural resources, the size of the economy, armed forces, among others. However, they could not articulate a second characteristic of US actions during the Cold War, and one of the key measures of its relative power position in the international system: its soft power. Nye defines soft power as the ability to make others want what you want. In this sense, soft power is the opposite of hard power, the ability to make others do what you want. As traditionally understood in IR theories, hard power presupposes an active and direct engagement of the actors involved, expressed by incentives or threats, and is usually related to military force or economic resources. Soft power, which Nye also calls co-optive or indirect power, rests on the attraction a set of ideas exerts, or on the capacity to set political agendas that shape the preferences of others. Therefore, soft power is related to intangible resources like culture, ideologies and institutions (Nye Jr 1990: 31–5).

According to Nye, the development and exercise of soft power made the US position in the international system less difficult to maintain.[2] The set of liberal ideas promoted by the USA and shared by other Western states, such as democracy and free markets, made US policies abroad easier to implement. With other states sharing the same principles and values, the costs of maintaining the order through economic incentives or military threats were reduced. Moreover, Nye argues that the liberal ideas championed by the USA would be adequate to the reality of the international system in constant development, which had been characterized by processes of complex interdependence since the 1960s (Keohane and Nye Jr 1977). The incapacity of declinists to account for this change in the international system and in US power resources ended up condemning their predictions to failure. It is Nye's general conclusion that through its relative power position in the system, and through the characteristics of its soft power, the USA would be bound to lead.

In developing the idea of soft power, Nye makes reference to the analysis of economic orders in the nineteenth century and late twentieth century made by Robert Cox (1987). It is in following Cox's arguments that Nye considers the work of the Italian Marxist thinker Antonio Gramsci on the concept of hegemony (Nye Jr 1990: 32). Gramsci's influence on Nye is easy to see: hegemony, as soft power, works through consent on a set of general principles that secures the supremacy of a group and, at the same time, provides some degree of satisfaction to the other remaining groups. Gramscian authors would agree with Nye when he considers that a state would find less resistance in pursuing its goals if its own power is understood as legitimate by other states.

After defining soft power, Nye moves on to discuss and criticize theories that deal with hegemony and power transitions in the international system, such as the hegemonic stability theory, the world-system theory and the theory of long cycles (Nye Jr 1990: 40–8). However, even making use of the Gramscian concept of hegemony to develop his ideas on soft power, Nye does not take into account the contributions of neo-Gramscian authors, such as Cox or Stephen Gill, who distinguish themselves exactly by applying Gramsci's ideas to the study of IR. It was during the 1980s that the debate on the Gramscian concept of hegemony applied to IR gained strength, especially in the field of International Political Economy (Cox 1981, 1983; Van der Pijl 1984; Gill 1986; Gill and Law 1988, 1989). Neo-Gramscian analyses grew in number and relevance in the following decade, but were never incorporated by Nye in his subsequent works (Gill 1990, 1994; Rupert 1995; Robinson 1996).

Nye continued to work on the concept of soft power all through the 1990s in a great number of articles and publications. The concept was widely diffused and adopted by a large number of people, not just in academic circles. The international press and media, government representatives and decision makers started to use his terminology, even if not always with the same meaning as intended by its creator. In 2002, Nye revisits the theme of soft power in his book *The Paradox of American Power*. However, the international context had significantly changed in the 12 years between the publications of the two books. If in 1990 Nye was eager to criticize declinist authors, in 2002 he openly opposed a new group of thinkers influencing US foreign policy.

The end of the Cold War proved the declinists' theories wrong. The USA remained the single most-powerful state in the world, with unparalleled military might, with the strongest and most dynamic economy in the world and with a vibrant culture widely exported. Reflecting this new reality, two different approaches influenced debates on US foreign policy. One of them, isolationism, emerged at the end of the 1990s and was clearly present at the presidential elections of 2000. In face of the US preponderance in the international system and of the costs of its actions abroad, isolationists suggested that the country should restrain foreign policy. Isolationism however was always present in more or less degree in US foreign policy, and usually gains strength when the international system seems peaceful and stable, posing no immediate threats. This wave of isolationism was no more than a temporary influence and lost its significance after the events of 9/11.

Triumphalism was the second tendency influencing debates on US foreign policy even before 9/11, and much strengthened after the tragic events. Triumphalist pundits advocated that the US presence in the international system should not be restricted by existing institutions. They recognize the emergence of new threats from decentralized transnational networks that make good use of the information technologies to coordinate their actions, utilize terrorist tactics and present the worrying prospect of accessing weapons of mass destruction. The US unique position would make it the main target of the emerging threats, and international institutions would be obsolete to deal with them. As these institutions were designed to respect state authority and respond to security crises that emanate from other states, they would be of little value against an enemy that is not territorially located and does not follow international norms. Therefore, the USA should play an active role in responding to these new threats: it should act first, in a pre-emptive or even preventive manner if necessary. Alliances and legitimacy from the international community would be preferred, but not mandatory.

As an opponent to the triumphalist logic, Nye points out the mistakes that could lead US foreign policy to catastrophic results. According to him, the processes of globalization and the information revolution resulted in a transformation of the international system, which would be now composed of three different spheres: a military sphere, where the USA has unipolar control; an economic sphere, where there is a multipolarity shared by the USA, the European Union and Japan; and a third transnational sphere, where a diversity of state and non-state agents coexist and the debate over polarities is meaningless (Nye Jr 2002: 39). The characteristics of the emerging threats also have their origins in the processes of globalization and the information revolution: their main agents are non-state entities that exist and act in the transnational sphere. If hard power resources can be effective in the military and economic spheres, only soft power can work at the transnational level. Moreover, assertive and unilateral policies without the international community's legitimacy would only end up weakening US soft power. Transnational threats need to be countered through international cooperation, and in this respect consent and co-optation are essentials. Triumphalists' strategies would only undermine US soft power thus raising the costs of an effective foreign policy.[3]

Again, references to the work of Gramsci are present in Nye's conceptualization of soft power (Nye Jr 2002: 9). However, there is a slight difference in the way Nye deals with soft power. In *Bound to Lead*, Nye articulates soft power as a specific type of US power. He looks at US power resources and identifies some intangible resources that previous theories were not able to comprehend. In *The Paradox of the American Power*, Nye takes a different approach. The existence of soft power is taken for granted; what Nye argues for is a US foreign policy strategy that can make good use of it, instead of undermining its soft power resources with assertive and unilateral actions. This difference will be better explored in the next section, but it seems clear that its origins are related to the historical contexts in which Nye's works were being written.

In contrast with these two books, which were focused on US foreign policy and approached the concept of soft power as an aspect of it, Nye's 2004-book *Soft Power* is entirely devoted to the theoretical development of the concept and its implications. Nevertheless, as a conceptual elaboration, the book contains few innovations. Nye reworks the same ideas he has been advocating since 1990, with some updates and corrections. The author deals with issues such as the relations between hard and soft power, the origins and sources of soft power and states' misuses of their own soft power. The book is full of examples and references to contemporary cases of what is and what is not soft power, and what kinds of foreign policies are in harmony with it. It is worth noting that in his only proper theoretical book on soft power no reference is made to Gramsci's work on hegemony.

Scrutinizing soft power

After seeing the historical context in which the concept of soft power was developed, lets now look more deeply at its theoretical formulation. The concept of soft power that has been cited so far in this chapter is only the most common definition used by Nye; nevertheless, it is not the only one and its various definitions are not free of contradictions among them. Unfortunately, the definition of soft power given by Nye lacks rigour; its use is problematic and uncertain, making a strict definition of the concept hard to obtain.

As explained above, we are addressing the conceptualization of soft power given in Nye's three main books on the theme. In the first two works – and to some degree in the third too – the concept of soft power develops in a deep relation with thoughts on US power and foreign policy. But in all three books, Nye follows the same structure to present the concept. He articulates it in the exact same logical order, and apart from some updates, most of the ideas are expressed with strictly identical words. This makes it easier to reconstruct Nye's reasoning on soft power, and in the passages below the reader will find lots of cross-references to the three books.

The author begins with a brief discussion about the nature of power, admittedly one of the most disputed concepts in political science and IR. Nye opts for a succinct definition: 'power is the ability to influence the behaviour of others to get the outcomes one wants' (Nye Jr 1990: 25–9, 2002: 4–5, 2004: 1–5). This conciseness allows him to focus on other aspects of power in IR, as he moves on to articulate the distinction between hard and soft power. The concepts are twofold: 'The distinction between hard and soft power is one of degree, both in the nature of the behaviour and in the tangibility of the resource' (Nye Jr 1990: 267, 2002: 176, 2004: 7).[4] This distinction between power behaviours and power resources is the crucial element in Nye's concept of soft power.

According to Nye, power behaviours are ways of exercising power. Different types of behaviour form a spectrum ranging from command power to co-optive power. Command power is the ability to change what others do, while co-optive power is the ability to shape what others want. Therefore, command power is manifested through acts of coercion and persuasion, and co-optive power can be seen in the attraction exerted by a given agent and his capacity to define political agendas.

The second distinction between hard and soft power deals with the tangibility of power resources. However, the author does not apply any specific terminology at this point. Referring to tangibility, Nye uses the terms hard power resources and soft power resources. Hard power resources are well known: population, territory, natural resources, the size of the economy, armed forces, technological development, among others. These are tangible resources. In opposition, soft power resources are characteristically intangible resources: culture, ideology, values and institutions are the most common examples.

It is also worth noting that in all three books there is no discussion on the meaning of tangibility. The question of what would qualify a resource as tangible or intangible is not a simple one. Nye classifies economic resources as tangibles, but an argument could be made that most of the time they do not have a physical existence. A financial agreement lending money to a developing country could save its economy from a major crisis, but it is not easy to see the tangibility of this power resource – especially in credibility crisis, as economists well know. On the opposite side of the spectrum, Nye classifies institutions as intangible resources. It is comprehensible that he might be referring to institutional ideas and what they represent, but some institutions have physical existence, very important and present ones, running projects and programmes all over the world. The fact is that Nye leaves the reader with no criteria to address the tangibility of power resources.

In any case, the distinction between hard and soft power is given by taking together the nature of the agent's behaviour and the tangibility of the resources. However, a serious problem arises directly from this articulation. It has to do with the relation between power behaviours and power resources: '… soft power resources tend to be associated with co-optive power behaviour, whereas hard power resources are usually associated with command behaviour. But the relationship is imperfect' (Nye Jr 1990: 267, 2002: 176, 2004: 7). The logical consequence of the terminology used by Nye is that command power is related to hard power resources, and co-optive power to soft power resources. But these relations do not always hold true: it is possible for command power behaviour to utilize intangible soft power resources, in the same sense that co-optive power behaviour can make use of tangible hard power resources. Actually, it is even possible that command power creates soft power resources, or that co-optive power creates hard power resources.

It is not uncommon in the history of IR to see a state making use of an institution (a soft power resource) to coerce another state to adopt certain policies (a command power behaviour). In an identical way, there are cases in which a strong economy or high levels of technological development (hard power resources) are used to co-opt or attract other states to specific types of policies. After great conflicts, winning states can use their command power to build up institutions that will be seen as legitimate in the future, and will turn into soft power resources (Ikenberry 2001). Co-optive power behaviour can also be used to generate hard power resources in the form of military alliances or economic aid.

Nye is well aware of the difficulties in directly relating hard and soft power resources to command and co-optive power behaviours. Still, in dealing with the problem he argues that 'the general association is strong enough to allow the useful shorthand reference to hard and soft power' (Nye Jr 2002: 176). In short, Nye simply adopts the term hard power as a synonym for command power behaviour and hard power resources, and the term soft power as a synonym for co-optive power behaviour and soft power resources. In doing so the author simply dismisses the issue at hand and, at the same time, creates a deeper conceptual problem.

As seen above, resources are tangible or intangible capabilities, materials, goods, instruments at disposal. Behaviour is the action itself, the manner or way to act, the conduct of the agent. Clearly, the two concepts are related: a certain set of available resources favours some types of behaviours over others; in the same sense particular behaviours require specific resources. Nevertheless, an important part of this relation remains blurred. The coordination of one's actions and the resources at his disposal to achieve definite aims is the fundamental definition of the concept of strategy.[5] But Nye does not make this relation between behaviours, resources and strategy explicit. The problems with this unfinished articulation are recurrent in Nye's work, as demonstrated below.

The fact that Nye did not use a specific terminology to refer to the tangibility of power resources even worsens the case. As the author uses very similar terms when he discusses hard and soft power, it is difficult to be sure if the reference being made is to hard and soft power resources, to command and co-optive power, or to the broader concepts of hard and soft power. In some passages, while advocating the use of US soft power in the international system, the author seems to be calling for the use of co-optation behaviours, and not simply soft power resources. In his 1990 book, Nye appears to be more careful: the term co-optive power is used much more frequently than soft power. The first distinction offered to the reader is between command power and co-optive power; the term soft power only appears later and is related to resources of co-optive power. In his latter work, however, such diligence is not present. It appears that, despite its theoretical meaning, the term cooptation lacks the resonance, the appeal or even the romance of the term soft power.

Another question that is not properly explored in Nye's first books on soft power is the dependence of soft power resources on hard power resources: would soft power resources be effective only when hard power resources exist to sustain them? This question is not answered in the first two books, but in the last one the author affirms categorically: '... soft power does not depend on hard power' (Nye Jr 2004: 9). Instead of a theoretical argument, Nye presents examples to justify his statement. First, he presents the Vatican as an unquestionable example of soft power (after recounting Stalin's disdainful question about how many divisions the Pope controls).[6] Other examples are contemporary Norway, Canada and Poland that, according to Nye, have recently displayed a stronger influence on international politics than their hard power resources would predict, due to the use of soft power resources in their foreign policies. However, in all examples given by Nye the use of hard power resources is never absent. Peacekeeping operations can be legitimate, justified and pursued with altruistic intentions, raising a state's soft power. Nevertheless, the operations must be conducted with troops on the ground and substantial amounts of money, both hard power resources.

Even if one agrees with Nye's statement that soft power does not depend on hard power, another question can be posed: who are the agents that really hold soft power? Nye's definition of power – the ability to influence the behaviour of others to get the outcomes one wants – does not include any qualifications about agents. The definition of hard and soft power does not differentiate between agents either. One could relate the use of hard power with the state, assuming that the state holds the monopoly on the use of legitimate violence. Nevertheless, this relation is not unique: there are plenty of examples of non-state groups that use hard power resources for coercion. Terrorist groups, criminal organizations, political movements that recur to violence, as well as large corporations using their economic strength to implement particular interests are all examples of private non-state agents making use of hard power. The same questions are true regarding soft power. Institutions, large corporations, civil society entities and movements, and even individuals hold soft power. What surprises the reader is the lack of attention given to non-state agents by an author known as one of the fathers of interdependence theory. In fact, Nye is so focused on a change of US foreign policy with emphasis on its soft power that most of his attention is devoted to state actors.[7]

This emphasis on state actors has other implications as well. When Nye identifies three sources of soft power, it is difficult to assert the level of state control exerted on them. According to the author: 'The soft power of a country rests primarily on three resources: its culture (in places where it is attractive to others), its political values (when it lives up to them at home and abroad) and its foreign policies (when they are seen as legitimate and having moral authority)' (Nye Jr 2004: 11). It is clear that the state can influence these three elements: it can adopt policies that promote culture, act according to its own political values and implement a foreign policy in accordance with international society precepts. Yet, by Nye's definition of soft power, the relevance of these three elements rests only on the acceptance, attraction and legitimacy given by the subject, and not by the acting state. The fact that the state does not have full control on the creation of soft power is of little relevance according to Nye: '... the fact that civil society is the origin of much soft power does not disprove its existence' (Nye Jr 2004: 11). The problem here is that Nye's framework does not explain the linkage between civil society sources of soft power and different states. Large corporations, sports idols, pop culture symbols and a number of civil society groups create soft power of their own. At the same time, they can strengthen or weaken the soft power of different state and non-state agents whose images are related to these groups. It is usually regarded that the global proliferation of McDonald's restaurants, Coca-Cola, Starbucks coffee-shops and Hollywood movies promote a certain model of US society and values abroad. In some cases, this can be a useful resource of US soft power, but in other cases it can serve to undermine it too. Take for instance the Iranian reaction to the movie *300*, which tells the story of the Battle of Thermopylae from a very specific and caricaturized point of view. One cannot really say that the movie helped US–Iranian relations. The same comment could be applied to the controversy over the publication of cartoons containing images of Allah and the prophet Mohammed in European newspapers. Even though the Danish or the French governments do not control their press, their soft power resources as states were damaged by the publications. During the Cold War, the US took benefits of the diffusion of rock music over Soviet teenagers, even if groups like the Beatles or the Rolling Stones were in fact British. Rock music in general was related to US culture and way of life. But there is also soft power in non-state agents. The Greenpeace or the International Committee of the Red Cross are considered legitimate institutions by many without being related to any specific state; in fact they are considered legitimate because they are neutral and not related to any specific state. Influential individuals and some global causes also generate soft power on their own. Take for example Princess Diana's endorsement of the campaign to ban landmines. Again, it is a policy not related to any specific state, but that has soft power of its own.

The problem for Nye is that the state cannot fully control its soft power resources. It can influence them through a certain group of policies, but never fully manage them for two reasons: the state does not hold power over all soft power resources and the final relevance of these resources are given by acceptance, attraction and legitimacy of subject. Once again, the question between behaviours, resources and strategy comes into play, but is obfuscated by Nye's terminology. As the state cannot simply create soft power resources, it should adopt behaviours which exploit and reinforce the soft power resources it already has, and make sure its actions do not end up undermining them. Nevertheless, this balance between actions and resources is a question about strategy, not about soft power itself.

Presenting the Gramscian framework

To properly compare soft power with the Gramscian concept of hegemony, we must first present hegemony itself, and the framework of Gramscian thought that surrounds it.[8] As with any Marxist author, Gramsci's thoughts were influenced by the idea that the economic structures and the distribution of means of production strongly determine social relations. The question that puzzled Gramsci was how the capitalist structures of exploitation could be maintained in a democratic system with the consent of the unprivileged classes. In an authoritarian regime, economic structures that privilege elites would be easily maintained through coercion. But it would be expected that in a democracy the unprivileged classes would speak up and change the structures that suppressed them. That was not the reality seen by Gramsci at the beginning of the twentieth century, when many democratic states upheld capitalism without being contested. To address this question, Gramsci develops his concept of hegemony.

In short terms, hegemony is the capacity of a given group to unify a social body that is non-homogeneous and marked by contradictions. This process happens not only through material bases, but especially through ideational ones, developing a collective will towards an economic, social and political project that reproduces a given social order. In the process of establishing its hegemony, the group promoting it becomes the protagonist of a social order. It progressively incorporates some of the demands of other social groups, unifying them through ideational discourses and keeping them united. The establishment of hegemony involves all spheres of social live: economical, political and ideational. Hegemony, therefore, is not only economical or political but also cultural and moral; it is a conception of the world.

The hegemony of a social group works through what Gramsci calls the private apparatus of hegemony: an articulated network of cultural institutions that includes schools, churches, the press, the media and other institutions. They disseminate an idea of passive submission through a complex web of historically developed concepts. When this happens, this group reaches its moment of highest historical development (Sassoon 1980: 116). Even if in a passive form, hegemony creates submission between social groups; not submission to force, but submission to ideas. Gramsci speaks of hegemony as 'intellectual and moral guidance', affirming that this guidance should be exerted in the sphere of ideas and culture, manifesting a capacity to obtain consensus and create social basis for it – as there is no political guidance without consensus.

One of Gramsci's main influences comes from the works of Machiavelli, specifically from *The Prince* and his discussion of the creation of a new state (Cox 1994). While Machiavelli was concerned about creating a leadership and a social basis for a united Italy, Gramsci was looking for a new leadership that could be an alternative to fascism. But drawing from the Florentine author, Gramsci also makes a distinction between rule by force and rule by consent. This 'double perspective' corresponds 'to the dual nature of Machiavelli's Centaur – half-animal and half-human. They are the levels of force and of consent, authority and hegemony, violence and civilisation …' (Cox 1994: 33). Hence, there is for Gramsci a contrast between two ideal types: one is the exercise of power without the consent of the ruled; the other is an intellectual and moral leadership over the ruled.

According to Gramsci, coercion and consent are not opposites: in fact, force is a constitutive element of consent, to the extent that any rupture of consent brings forth instruments of coercion. These instruments are intrinsic to all spheres of social life and remain latent while there is enough consent to sustain the reproduction of social relations. Coercion is a latent element, inherent to consent: 'Coercion is thus ubiquitous; it is not reserved to any particular institution' (Przeworski 1985: 166–7).

The relation between coercion and consent is also present in Gramsci's conceptualization of the state. The author sees the concept of state in two different senses: the restricted state and the extended state. Gramsci also refers to the restricted state as the political society: the governmental apparatus of the state, administrative, legal and coercive (Gramsci 2001: 20–1). The concept of extended state is the sum of the political society and the civil society (Gramsci 1971: 261–3, 2002: 244, 254–5). Nevertheless, the division between civil society and political society is purely methodological, not organic (Gill 1990: 43).

Gramsci's concept of extended state diverges from the classical Marxist approach, which defines coercion as the basic feature of the state. In fact, Gramsci considered liberal democratic states as integral bodies, a merge of coercion and consent that secured its existence. The character of a state and its relation to civil society are not fixed, and vary throughout history. In this sense, Gramsci prescribes the necessity to examine the real nature of a given state and its civil society before making any decision regarding the political strategies against it. In places where hegemony is established, a strategy of 'war of movement', that is a direct assault on the state, would not be successful. What was needed was a 'war of positions', a struggle for hegemony in the civil society sphere to slowly create the social basis of new state.

At this point, the reader must already have noticed that the agents in Gramsci's thought are not states. While the individual is still the locus for transformation, Gramscian analysis is focused on classes and fractions of classes. A group establishing its hegemony is usually a social class related to the economic structures of the society. But as Gramsci avoids reductionism, he articulates society in its totality of political, ideational and economical spheres. In this sense, 'superstructures of ideology and political organization shape the development of both aspects of production and are shaped by them' (Cox 1994: 56). On the process towards hegemony the biding group evolves to the creation of a historic bloc: an alliance between classes and fractions of classes over a set of hegemonic ideas that give strategic guidance and coherence to its elements. The historic bloc is a dialectical concept as the interaction of its elements creates a larger unity (Gramsci 2002: 26). It must suppress the particular interests of some of its classes in favour of a universal ideology, and must also coordinate concrete interests of other unprivileged groups in a manner that at least some of them are fulfilled. And once the hegemony is established, the historic bloc keeps its social cohesion and unity through the diffusion of a common culture.

This process requires an intense dialogue within the bloc, which takes Gramsci to the role of the intellectuals. Intellectuals would play a fundamental role in the creation of a historic bloc according to Gramsci. In fact, they develop and sustain the mental images, the technologies and the institutions that hold the historic bloc together in a common identity: 'Intellectuals [...] are the "persuaders" of the dominant class, they are the "employees" of dominant class hegemony' (Gruppi 1978: 80). Intellectuals are not limited simply to technical questions of production, but they give the historic bloc its own conscience and role, both in the social and the political sphere; homogeneity and guidance.[9]

In general, the concept of historic bloc makes reference to those situations in which there is a strong level of political congruence between (1) the structural level, or the production forces, (2) the political level and (3) the military level. Regarding the political level, Gramsci identifies three different degrees of political conscience of the groups involved: first, the 'economic-corporative', reflecting the interests of a particular group, or group solidarity. Second, the 'class conscience', extended to an entire social class but still only at the level of economic interests. And third, the 'hegemonic', that creates harmony between the interests of the dominant class and of the subjugated class, and incorporates the latter under an ideational framework expressed in universal terms.

Therefore, the process towards hegemony is a movement from interests of a particular group or class to the creation of broader institutions and ideas. They will satisfy some of the interests of the unprivileged groups without undermining the leadership and interests of the hegemonic class. If the movement towards hegemony is complete, those ideas and institutions will not appear to reflect the interests of a particular group, but will be presented instead in a universal form (Gramsci 2002: 40–6). With this framework in mind, it is now possible for us to draw comparisons between the Gramscian concept of hegemony and Nye's concept of soft power.

From soft power to hegemony

In mainstream IR theory, hegemony is regarded as preponderance of one state over others, usually denoting a highly asymmetrical distribution of military and economic resources. As presented above, the concept of Gramscian hegemony has a completely different meaning. In this sense, hegemony is the process through which a group establishes a social order that combines power and leadership, coercion and consent, in a set of institutions that acknowledge some of the interests of unprivileged groups. Hegemony is created through material and ideational bases, conjugating the interests of different groups to sustain and regulate a given social order. Only by understanding hegemony in this manner can we then trace comparisons between hegemony and soft power. Nye acknowledges the influence of Gramsci in his work; nevertheless, the non-contemplation of hegemony in all its aspects, the use of the restricted concept of soft power and the missing dialogue with neo-Gramscian authors end up bringing relevant theoretical and practical implications to Nye's work.

The first implication of this conceptual change regards the relation between coercion and consent. According to Nye, the distinction between hard and soft power is a distinction of degree regarding the behaviour of the agent and the tangibility of the resources. Nevertheless, Nye argues that the existence of soft power does not require hard power: they are both related aspects of power, but are not dependant (Nye Jr 2004: 9). The concept of hegemony describes coercion and consent not as opposites but as complementary to each other (or command and co-optation in Nye's terms). Coercion is a mechanism intrinsic to consent: it lies down on a secondary level while the mechanisms of consent prevail in society, but it is still latent and emerges in moments of rupture of the consent. Disregarding hegemony, Nye creates the illusion of an aspect of power that could exist by its own only through consent, ignoring the social reality populated by intrinsic mechanisms of coercion.

A second critique comes from the way Nye approaches values, principles and ideas as a soft power resource. We have seen that hegemony is the capacity of a group to promote a social order not only through its material bases, but most importantly through a discourse reflected in the sphere of ideas and social institutions. It is clear, in this sense, that hegemony is the pursuit for consent where, logically, consent still does not exist. Those who try to establish hegemony struggle for consent with other pre-existent groups of distinct interests. Disregarding hegemony, Nye ignores the existence of a struggle over ideas and institutions in the international system. The concept of soft power hides the existing relations and disputes over ideas that work behind the processes of creation and sustainability of soft power itself.

A good example is Nye's characterization of US 'universal values' as a soft power resource. 'When a country's culture includes universal values and its policies promotes values and interests that others share, it increases the probability of obtaining its desired outcomes (...) The United States benefits from a universalistic culture ...' (Nye Jr 2004: 11). The problem here is the assumption that universal values exist. If one believes in the existence of universal values or a universalistic culture, it is obvious that they cannot articulate the struggle for the legitimization of these same principles and values. A more neutral analysis would recognize that any set of principles and values cannot be universal: ideas are always relative, they originate in a given society or culture, they are not absolute and usually mean different things for different people. Of course that values, principles and ideas can be universalized, acknowledged by others and legitimated (or imposed) by a series of processes, through consent or coercion. In this sense, US 'universal values' cannot be a soft power resource; the promotion of these same values or a 'universalistic culture' is an effective soft power or hegemonic strategy, but they are not resources on their own.

This criticism might seem abstract, but the international system is full of examples of groups struggling over legitimization of ideas. The celebrated discourse on human rights was not born as a universal principle: the prominence it enjoys came only after World War II, and even nowadays it is not a shared value in many parts of the world. Principles of humanitarian aid, the protection of refugees and internally displaced people still fight their way through the resistance of the sovereignty concept embedded in the international system. Environmental protection ideas are currently clashing with free-market principles, and free trade is not an idea shared by everyone and in everyone's benefit. One of the most notorious examples of the struggle over ideas is the World Social Forum (WSF). First held in 2001 as a counterpart to the World Economic Forum at Davos, the WSF is an open space for civil society organizations and movements to discuss alternative ways of globalization. The WSF has a new and inventive format: it is not an institution in the proper sense, it does not have a representative body, no one is allowed to speak on its behalf and it does not aim to produce statements of principles or policies that should be adopted by its members. It is simply an open space for discussion and articulation of civil society groups around the world. Many disregard the WSF as a meaningless event and ignore the existence of a global civil society, but it is clear that its ideas are being contested all over the world.

A third critical problem comparing hegemony and soft power regards the concept of state. It seems like Nye assumes the Weberian conception of the state. In this way, he identifies the state as the political society in Gramsci's terminology, the restricted concept of the state in its administrative, legal and coercive institutions. Nye's work does not articulate the state in its extended concept, that is, the conjunction of the political society and the civil society. In this way, Nye misinterprets the spheres of political and civil society, and therefore the relation between coercion and consent. The struggle for hegemony takes place in the civil society sphere, in which hegemony is manifested through consent. Coercion is an instrument of the political sphere, represented in the state apparatus. However, just as coercion is ubiquitous to consent, the distinction between civil society and political society is simply methodological, not organic. As Nye uses only the restricted concept of state and does not identify the peculiarities of each sphere, he cannot articulate coercion and consent in a coherent manner. It is for this reason that Nye comes to the point of stating that hard and soft power (or coercion and consent) are independent of one another.

As much as Nye emphasizes the need to give the due attention to soft power, he does not neglect the relevance of hard power. He labels this ability of combining hard and soft power as smart power (Nye Jr 2004: 43, 147; Armitage and Nye Jr 2007). During the Cold War, the USA and its allies would have used hard power to contain Soviet aggression, while soft power was used to undermine the beliefs and faith in the communist system: this was smart power. Nye clearly states that soft power is not the answer for all US problems and that hard power should be exercised when needed. But the concept of smart power is a limited articulation. As we know, intelligence cannot be attributed to non-sentient beings. We can even conceive that power is hard or soft, but never smart. Resources can be hard or soft, even behaviours can be harder or softer. But only strategies can be smart, as they are evaluated in accordance to the aims they plan to achieve. Therefore, smart power is a characteristic of a strategy and of the state that applies it, not of power itself.

This leads to a fourth and final point: the fact that Nye blurs a complex relation between behaviours, resources and strategy when he adopts the term hard power as a synonym for command power and hard power resources, and soft power as a synonym for co-optation power and soft power resources. This ends up by making Nye's texts easy to read, but confusing and unclear if one tries to examine the real meaning of his references to soft power. As for this and other criticism, a defence could be raised in the sense that his focus lies mainly on US foreign policy and in the need to give more emphasis to the country's soft power. Nye would be really interested in the practical applicability of the concept and permitted himself to ignore some theoretical questions and problems. Still, this defence is not very convincing in almost two decades of theoretical development on soft power, culminating with a book devoted to the theme. Even if Nye was only interested in the political implications of soft power, to ignore its theoretical foundations is counterproductive. Pushing forward the analogy between hegemony and soft power provides us with a better understanding of the instruments of coercion and consent, of the continuous struggle for the legitimization of ideas and values, and of the differences between the spheres of political and civil societies, therefore allowing analytical descriptions which are more adequate to inform and shape political actions.

An exercise of imagination

This last section provides a Gramscian interpretation of Nye's work on soft power and US foreign policy and will draw heavily on previous works by neo-Gramscian authors that apply the concept of hegemony to the international system. We must state from the beginning that this falls short from any conspiracy theory, and nothing in our minds suggests that Nye had anything less than the best intentions and academic rigour in pursuing his work on soft power. In fact, we are sympathetic with his recommendations on US foreign policy.

Neo-Gramscian authors consider the international system today as organized around a global capitalist order (Gill 1990). A globalist historic bloc promotes this order, and in its centre there is a transnational capitalist class, which encompasses owners and managers of transnational corporations that manage transnational capital (Robinson 1996). The globalist historic bloc also includes governors from developed and developing states, technicians and bureaucrats, international organizations and other transnational institutions. In addition, it includes organic intellectuals that provide legitimacy, ideology and technical solutions. At last, there is a small layer of middle class and cosmopolitan professionals that, even having no real power, form a weak cushion between the transnational elite and the unprivileged social groups.

Two points need further enlightenment. First, a historic bloc is an alliance between groups and parts of groups over a set of hegemonic ideas. In this sense, the historic bloc suppresses particular interests of some of its groups in favour of hegemonic ideas, and accommodates some of the interests of other unprivileged groups. As it is an alliance between groups of distinct interest, it is possible that tensions emerge within a historic bloc from time to time. Second, neo-Gramscian analysis does not focus on the US as a unitary agent, or on US hegemony, and the way forward is to deconstruct this image. When we talk about a globalist historic bloc we are not talking about the USA itself, but about a variety of groups of which many are US elite groups. If there is anything like the emergence of transnational elites, there is no doubt that US political, economical and intellectual elites are a central part of it.

How does Nye and soft power fit into this picture? The globalist historic bloc started its emergence in the 1970s. At that time, a series of economic crises culminated with the end of the Bretton Woods system. This was also a process of reformulation of the global capitalist order. The predictions of the decline of the nation-state or a general capitalist crisis deeply underestimated its capacity of reformulation (Gill 2003). In fact, the globalist historic bloc evolved into a new structure of transnational character (Robinson 2004). This process continued during the 1980s, evidenced in neoliberal economic policies, and was finally consolidated at the beginning of the 1990s. When Nye wrote *Bound to Lead* he was answering declinist theories about the collapse of US preponderance in the international system. Declinist authors failed to see the processes by which the global capitalist order was being reformulated, and therefore predicted US decline. In answering these authors, Nye coined the term soft power; what he was really doing was identifying the ideational aspects of the hegemonic project taking place. The universalization of liberal ideas and values, deeply embedded in the US society, is in fact one of the characteristics of the globalist historic bloc's hegemony.

During the mid-1990s, the globalist historic bloc started to suffer serious crisis that undermined its capacity to reproduce hegemony. Authors argued that the private interests of the financial capital, one of the groups within the globalist historic bloc, undermined the hegemonic project. This initiated a crisis in the global capitalist order expressed in a structural crisis of super accumulation and social polarization, and a crisis of legitimacy and authority. Its dual manifestation was evidenced in different social movements questioning economic globalization, most famously symbolized in the 1999 protests during the WTO Ministerial Conference in Seattle, and in various economic crisis during the decade, with the 1997 Southeast Asian crisis as it most notorious example.

Just as interests of financial capital groups undermined the hegemonic project during the 1990s, at the beginning of the 2000s another group placed private interests in first place. The political elite that took control of the US government in 2001 was a mix of old Cold War warriors, right-wing Christian groups and representatives of the energy and military industries. The assertive and unilateral foreign policy followed by these groups weakened the hegemonic project as a whole. When Nye wrote *The Paradox of American Power* he referred to policies that were undermining US soft power. It is enlightening to see how Nye described globalization processes and the informational revolution, or what neo-Gramscian authors would name the reformulation of the global capitalist order. The policies that undermined US soft power would be nothing less than interest of particular groups controlling the US government, in detriment to hegemony in a broader sense. It is worth noting that Nye wrote *The Paradox of American Power* before the events of 9/11, and the following war on terror and the Iraq invasion. As US foreign policy continued to undermine the hegemonic project, *Soft Power* can be seen a continuation of Nye's advocacy for a different set of police initiatives.

Taking all of this into account would lead us to name Nye as an organic intellectual. Through neo-Gramscian lenses, Nye's work would be an excellent example of policy prescriptions that would end the gaps and tensions within the globalist historic bloc and better serve the hegemonic project as a whole. His work provides us with a brilliant case of the role organic intellectuals play in the creation of ideas and mental images that give support and conscience to the historic bloc. The exact same comment could be applied to Nye's recent work on the Commission on Smart Power promoted by the Center of Strategic and International Studies. The Commission, which encompassed a number of intellectuals, politicians, former state officials and civil society representatives, ended up producing a final report with prescriptions for a better use of US power resources for future administrations (Armitage and Nye Jr 2007).[10]

Once again, we are not implying that Nye was intentionally or consciously trying to provide a globalist historic bloc with guidance for its hegemony. Most probably, Nye would not even agree with the existence of a globalist historic bloc and internal tensions over hegemony within it. We have no reason to doubt that Nye's advocacy of a US foreign power based on soft power is his sincere advice on a more adequate and effective course for conducting the country's foreign relations, based on his personal choices, on a genuine lack of interest to engage neo-Gramscian authors, on preferences to focus on states in detriment of non-state agents and on reaching a broader non-academic audience. Nye has all the merit of pointing limitations of declinists authors at the end of the 1980s, of identifying limits on the concept of power of mainstream IR theories and of opening space to debates on intangible aspects of power. Nevertheless, through the comparison between the concept of soft power and hegemony we could establish that soft power does not properly articulate behaviours, resources and strategy; conceals the relation between coercion and consent; misinterprets the spheres of political and civil society; and cannot articulate the struggle for values, principles and ideas in the international system. Our argument is that these flaws might have been avoided if the analogy between hegemony and soft power was fully pursued.

We acknowledge that the neo-Gramscian analysis might not appeal to most readers, but it served us well to present an alternative and provocative way of thinking. After all, being an organic intellectual is not a bad thing. For Gramsci, organic intellectuals provide cohesion and guidance to hegemony. If we leave out the Marxist terminology, we would all agree that Nye is an exemplar intellectual and that his work was passionately devoted to provide good, genuine and cautious advice to US foreign policy. As long as one believes in the righteousness of his principles and values, being an organic intellectual turns out to be quite a noble job. As Robert Cox reminds us, all theories have an embedded perspective derived from the social and political context in which they were developed (Cox 1981). The idea that power has a soft facet, disconnected from coercion, and that one of its sources is a set of universal values actually means that there is some kind of good power out there. As analysts, the framework provided by the concept of hegemony allows us to see that values, principles and ideas are not universals; they are in fact disputed, and the idea of a soft power is not a neutral concept but part of this struggle. As long as the analyst has this clarity of mind, there are no problems in making normative choices for specific sets of principles. In the end, as Nye argues, 'no country' and no one 'likes to feel manipulated, even by soft power' (Nye Jr 2004: 25).

Notes

1 The authors would like to thank Lorraine Macmillan, Chris Hill, Inderjeet Parmar and Joe Nye for their valuable comments and criticism.

2 In this regard, see especially chapters 3 and 6.

3 To Nye's credit, his book was written before the events of 9/11 had taken place. His critique of triumphalism predates the 'war on terror' and the invasion of Iraq, after which any critique of this type of grand strategy became almost redundant. Nye early identified signals of this triumphalist influence in the repudiation of the Kyoto Protocol and the International Criminal Court in the first months of the George W. Bush administration.

4 It is worth noting that the referred quotation can be found only in footnotes on 1990 and 2002 books. It was only taken to the main text in 2004.

5 For an introductory discussion on strategy see Baylis and Wirtz (2007).

6 A counter-argument is possible taking into account the previous idea that command power can create soft power resources. In this sense, the power, control and influence of the Catholic Church during centuries of European history could have made its values and principles legitimate, up to the point that they are still soft power resources nowadays.

7 As seen before, the structure of the three books is very similar. After some theoretical considerations on the concept of soft power, and its contemporary relevance, Nye proceeds with an analysis of US power resources in comparison with its closest competitors. In all three books there is a clear focus on state agents.

8 The most well known of Gramsci's works is the *Prison Notebooks*. This title shows exactly what the work is: notebooks written when Gramsci was in prison in Italy during the fascist regime. In its original format, the notebooks are composed of a series of reflections on different subjects, which do not follow any specific order. Never published during his lifetime, those reflections were later published according to two systems of classification: at first the Togliatti edition, which used common themes and subjects as criteria for classification, and later the Gerratana edition, which sorted the notes according to the chronological order in which they were written. There is also a National edition, which is based on the Gerratana edition with some disagreements over its classifications. Recently, Carlos Nelson Coutinho, a recognized specialist in Gramsci's work, was the first author to publish an edition of the *Prison Notebooks* as a synthesis of the previous criteria of classification: the notes were both sorted by theme and chronological order. It is to this edition that the references in this chapter are made.

9 'Every social group, coming into existence on the original terrain of an essential function in the world of economic production, creates together with itself, organically, one or more strata of intellectuals which give it homogeneity and an awareness of its own function not only in the economic but also in the social and political fields. (...) However, every "essential" social group which emerges into history out of the preceding economic structure, and as an expression of a development of this structure, has found (at least in all of history up to the present) categories of intellectuals already in existence and which seemed indeed to represent a historical continuity uninterrupted even by the most complicated and radical changes in political and social forms.' Those are, respectively,

the two kinds of intellectuals identified by Gramsci: the organic intellectuals and the traditional intellectuals (2001: 15–16).

10 A project with similar aims was the Princeton Project on National Security, hosted at Princeton University and that counted almost 400 participants under the direction of G. John Ikenberry and Anne-Marie Slaughter. Just as well, it could be characterized as the work of organic intellectuals (Ikenberry and Slaughter 2006).

Bibliography

Armitage, R.L. and Nye Jr, J.S. (2007) *CSIS Commission on Smart Power: A Smarter, More Secure America*, Washington, DC: The CSIS Press.

Baylis, J. and Wirtz, J. (2007) 'Introduction', in J. Baylis, J. Wirtz, C.S. Gray and E. Cohen (eds) *Strategy in the Contemporary World*, 2nd edn, Oxford: Oxford University Press.

Cox, R.W. (1981) 'Social Forces, States and World Orders: Beyond International Relations Theory', *Millennium: Journal of International Studies*, 10(2): 126–55.

—— (1983) 'Gramsci, Hegemony and International Relations: An Essay in Method', *Millennium: Journal of International Studies*, 12(2): 162–75.

—— (1987) *Power, Production and World Order,* New York: Columbia University Press.

—— (1994) 'Gramsci, Hegemony and International Relations: An Essay in Method', in S. Gill (ed.) *Gramsci, Historical Materialism and International Relations*, Cambridge: Cambridge University Press.

Gill, S. (1986) 'American Hegemony: Its Limits and Prospects in the Reagan Era', *Millennium: Journal of International Studies*, 15: 311–39.

—— (1990) *American Hegemony and the Trilateral Commission*, Cambridge: Cambridge University Press.

—— (ed.) (1994) *Gramsci, Historical Materialism and International Relations*, Cambridge: Cambridge University Press.

Gill, S. and Law, D. (1988) *The Global Political Economy: Perspectives, Problems and Policies*, Baltimore, MD: Johns Hopkins University Press.

—— (1989) 'Global Hegemony and the Structural Power of Capital', *International Studies Quarterly*, 33: 475–99.

Gramsci, A. (1971) *Selection from the Prison Notebooks: edited by Quintin Hoare and Geoffrey Nowell Smith*, London: Lawrence and Wishart.

—— (2001) *Cadernos do cárcere: Vol. 2*, Rio de Janeiro: Civilização Brasileira.

—— (2002) *Cadernos do cárcere: Vol. 3*, Rio de Janeiro: Civilização Brasileira.

Gruppi, L. (1978) *O conceito de hegemonia em Gramsci*, Rio de Janeiro: Edições Graal.

Ikenberry, G.J. (2001) *After Victory: Institutions, Strategic Restraint, and the Rebuilding of Order After Major Wars*, Princeton, NJ: Princeton University Press.

Ikenberry, G.J. and Slaughter, A.M. (2006) *Forging a World of Liberty Under Law: U.S. National Security in the 21st Century*, Princeton, NJ: The Woodrow Wilson School of Public and International Affairs, Princeton University.

Kennedy, P. (1987) *The Rise and Fall of the Great Powers: Economic Change and Military Conflict from 1500 to 2000*, New York: Random House.

Keohane, R.O. and Nye Jr, J.S. (1977) *Power and Interdependence*, Boston, MA: Little Brown.

Nye Jr, J.S. (1990) *Bound to Lead: The Changing Nature of American Power*, New York: Basic Books.

—— (2002) *The Paradox of American Power: Why the World's Only Superpower Can't Go it Alone*, New York: Oxford University Press.

—— (2004) *Soft Power: The Means to Success in World Politics*, New York: Public Affairs.

Przeworski, A. (1985) *Capitalism and Social Democracy*, Cambridge: Cambridge University Press.

Robinson, W.I. (1996) *Promoting Polyarchy: Globalization, US Intervention and Hegemony*, Cambridge: Cambridge University Press.

—— (2004) *A Theory of Global Capitalism: Production, Class, and State in a Transnational World*, Baltimore, MD: Johns Hopkins University Press.

Rupert, M. (1995) *Producing Hegemony: The Politics of Mass Production and American Global Power*, Cambridge: Cambridge University Press.

Sassoon, A.S. (1980) *Gramsci's Politics*, New York: St Martin's Press.

Van der Pijl, K. (1984) *The Making of an Atlantic Ruling Class*, London: Verso.

3   Soft power and strategy
Developing a 'strategic' concept of power

Edward Lock

In coining the term 'soft power', Joseph Nye has contributed one of the best known and most widely referred to concepts within the discourse of US grand strategy. Nye introduced this term in 1990 in his book *Bound to Lead*, and has since developed the concept within a series of publications (Nye 1990: 32, 2002, 2004, 2007, 2008). Nye's (1990: 8) earliest work on the subject challenged those who presumed that US power was in decline and argued instead that America's power was far more comprehensive than was evident if one merely examined traditional power resources such as military capability, economic wealth and geographic and population size. Nye's key point here was that, in an increasingly interdependent world, 'hard power' resources, including military and economic assets, were of less utility than they had been in earlier eras of international politics. Of growing importance in the modern era was, according to Nye (1990: 32), 'soft power', the power associated with attracting others and getting them 'to want what you want'.

If the value of a concept were to be measured by the breadth and frequency of its use, Nye's notion of soft power could only be considered a success. However, while popular usage of the term has bloomed, this concept has also drawn a significant volume of criticism. In both public and academic circles, critics of soft power have highlighted the existence of ambiguity regarding this term. When asked about the importance of America's soft power, for example, then Secretary of Defence Donald Rumsfeld claimed not to know what it was (cited in Nye 2006). In academic circles, the notion of soft power has been criticized for being too blunt (Lukes 2007), too soft (Ferguson 2003) and too vague (Bially Mattern 2007). In general, therefore, there has been a call for greater clarity regarding the concept, a call that has been acknowledged and repeated by Nye himself (2007: 163).

This chapter seeks to add to both the criticism of this concept and to the efforts that have been undertaken to clarify and extend it. In this chapter I argue that Nye's conception of soft power is problematic to the extent that it is 'unstrategic'. By this I mean to say that Nye's conception of soft power, at least in its early form, tended to ignore the role of the subject of power, thus resulting in the emergence of an unconvincing account of soft power. Furthermore, I argue here that the unstrategic conception of soft power produced by Nye results from the conflation of relational and structural forms of power that is evident in his work. Because these different forms of power are conflated, neither is articulated in a clear manner and the role of the subject of power in relation to both is under-explored.

It is important to note that more recently, and especially in his writings on power and leadership, Nye (2008) has begun to address these problems. More precisely, Nye has sought to distinguish between relational and structural forms of power and to acknowledge the role of the subject of power through his claim that the analyst of power must consider the roles of leaders, followers and the context within which those actors operate. While this most recent work represents an important step forward in the development of the concept of soft power, it is by no means a final one. This chapter seeks to build upon Nye's attempts to remedy these flaws in his earlier work by advancing a strategic conception of power. A strategic conception of power centres on the relational qualities of power but it situates those relations of power within broader social structures. Furthermore, when we understand strategic theory as a theory of interdependent decision making, a strategic conception of power must also encourage a profound concern for the role of the subject of power within power relations.

This chapter proceeds in three stages. In the first section I seek to demonstrate the unstrategic nature of Nye's concept of soft power. In particular, I begin by highlighting the conflation of relational and structural forms of power that is evident in some of Nye's work on soft power. I then demonstrate the limitations of Nye's accounts of each of these forms of power and the tendency within his work to downplay the role of the subject of power. The second section addresses this weakness in Nye's early work on soft power by advancing a strategic conception of power. In order to do so, I begin by considering Nye's more recent work on leadership before turning to the work of Michel Foucault in order to advance a strategic conception of power. The final section illustrates this strategic conception of power with regard to the foreign policy of the USA.

The 'unstrategic' nature of soft power

Before critiquing Nye's conception of soft power, it is worth considering his attempts to define this concept.[1] Throughout his sustained attempts to advance the notion of soft power, Nye has presented it as a supplement to that of hard power. This distinction is itself grounded in the assumption that 'everyone is familiar with hard power' (Nye 2004: 5). Hard power rests on an actor's capacity to get others to change their positions through either the making of threats or the proffering of incentives. In other words, hard power is the power associated with 'sticks' and 'carrots'. It is in this context that Nye asserts the importance of a third mechanism through which actors can gain the results that they want within politics. This third mechanism is that described by Nye as 'attraction'. Soft power is therefore exercised through the use of attraction; the co-option of others so as to get them to want what you want. Nye (2007: 162–3) suggests that this form of power is neither new nor restricted to the realms of international or even national politics. Instead, he asserts that in personal relationships, business relationships or indeed in the relationships between states, the mechanism of attraction represents an important tool that can be utilized by actors in their efforts to attain the outcomes that they desire.

Nye also seeks to clarify the distinction between hard and soft forms of power through his identification of the different resources upon which such forms of power depend. Again, Nye's assumption here is that the concept of hard power is relatively straightforward. The capacity to threaten a person or state would seem to rest in one's possession of the means of exercising physical violence; strength in the case of an individual, military forces in the case of a state. Similarly, it is clearly the possession of wealth – either in terms of money or other valuable resources – that is the necessary prerequisite for the exercise of hard power in terms of inducement. When it comes to the exercise of soft power, however, a state must rely upon a different range of resources, including 'its culture (in places where it is attractive to others), its political values (when it lives up to them at home and abroad) and its foreign policies (when they are seen as legitimate and having moral authority)' (Nye 2007: 164). Thus, soft power is defined by Nye as a capacity that can be exercised by an agent through the use of attraction. Furthermore, that capacity is dependant upon the agent's possession of certain cultural and political values as well as upon their foreign policy practices.

The result of Nye's earlier efforts at clarifying the concept of soft power is the advancement of a definition of soft power as an agent-focused form of power exercised through the mechanism of attraction. However, this apparently simple definition masks a great deal of ambiguity and a number of significant conceptual problems. More precisely, on closer inspection it becomes clear that the source of ambiguity regarding Nye's understanding of the mechanism of attraction results from his conflation of relational and structural forms of power. Furthermore, this ambiguity results in two additional problems. First, because these very different forms of power are conflated in Nye's work, neither is clearly articulated. Second, Nye's accounts of each of these forms of power tend to provide little conceptual space in which to consider the role of the subject of power. It is in this latter sense that we can regard Nye's conception of soft power as being unstrategic. As has been noted above, Nye's more recent work on this subject has begun to address these problems. However, it remains necessary to precisely identify these problems if we are to subsequently evaluate Nye's more recent efforts to remedy them.

To conclude that, especially in his early work on the subject, Nye tended to conflate relational and structural forms of power within his conception of soft power is by no means self-evident. After all, in seeking to clarify his intentions, Nye (2007: 163) has suggested that his goal has been to produce an agent-focused rather than a subject-focused concept of power; no mention is made of relational or structural forms of power. Regardless of such claims, however, the conflation of relational and structural forms of power becomes evident when we examine the inconsistent explanations of soft power within Nye's writings. Nye varies between two different accounts of soft power. On the one hand, there is the suggestion that soft power can be used to change the values held by others (Nye 1990: 32, 2002: 9, 2004: 5). It is in this context that Nye discusses the promotion of principles such as 'democracy'. To illustrate this point, Nye (2007: 165) refers to the potential use by the USA of film and television shows to promote democracy and the rule of law in China. On the other hand, however, Nye (2007: 164) has stated explicitly that principles such as democracy represent resources that a state such as the USA can utilize in order to attract others, but that it will only be able to do so where those principles or values are shared by others. In this case, soft power is not about changing the values held by others so that they are more similar to one's own, but instead about changing the policies of others where broad cultural and political values are already shared.

The problem here is that these two illustrations of soft power actually refer to very different forms of power. In the former case, it is an actor who exercises power by changing the values of another. Here, therefore, power exists within the context of a relationship between the two actors. In the latter case, what we are really referring to is a form of structural power or, in other words, the power that is 'exercised' by social structures such as shared norms or values. What is most important here is that, to the extent that we wish to conceive of soft power in terms of the exercise of the mechanism of attraction, both of these forms of power must be considered.

In order to understand this point it may help to consider a more mundane example; here, that of attraction between two teenage school children, A and B. We can easily imagine that, in their attempt to attract B, A might engage in certain practices, such as the purchasing and wearing of fashionable clothing. On examining this situation, the analyst of power may well decide that A has gained power through their attempts to exercise attraction. A may well feel a sense of empowerment as a result of their choice to wear fashionable clothing and, indeed, there may even be a discernible shift in the status of A and in their capacity to gain outcomes that they want within the context of the schoolyard. Alternatively, however, if the analyst of power were to consider this example from the perspective of A's parents, they may well conceive of A's behaviour in terms of their submission to social structures or norms that constitute and regulate the meaning of 'attractiveness'. If we adopt this perspective, we are less likely to view A as an agent exercising power and more likely to conceive of them as being subject to the power of social structures. Thus, the analyst of power seemingly has a choice to make. Should power be attributed to the individual who seeks to attract another by engaging in certain forms of behaviour or should they instead attribute power to the social structures that dictate what it means to be attractive?

This choice may seem relatively trivial when raised with regard to the infatuation of teenagers (though the situation would doubtless seem anything but trivial to the teenagers concerned). The very real importance of this choice becomes more evident when we consider the mechanism of attraction in the context of US foreign policy. It is in this context that a heated debate has occurred. On the one hand, analysts of power such as Nye have argued that the USA can exercise power more effectively within international politics if it promotes certain values and abides by certain norms. According to Nye, such acts of agency can make the USA more attractive and more powerful. On the other hand, neoconservatives in particular have railed against such arguments, contending instead that such a policy merely results in the submission of the USA to international norms (see, for example, Brooks and Wohlforth 2002: 31). In the example above, the teenager sees an act of agency intended to make them more attractive and more powerful whereas the parents see an exercise in conformity. In the case of the USA, Nye emphasizes the agency of Washington, whereas others see America being tied down by countless norms and rules.

My point here is not to attempt to settle this debate but is instead to highlight the importance within the concept of soft power of two very different forms of power, one associated with the agency of actors such as the USA and one associated with the social structures which determine what it means to be attractive. The importance of distinguishing between these two forms of power has been made clear by a number of recent works on the concept of power as it applies to the field of international relations (Barnett and Duvall 2005; Guzzini 2005), yet within Nye's work on soft power these two distinct forms of power are often conflated. The result of this conflation is the emergence within Nye's account of soft power of two problems. The first of these is that neither of these forms of power is adequately conceptualized and the second is that his accounts of soft power evidence a tendency to down-play the role of the subject of power within power relations. Each of these problems requires consideration.

Nye does not provide a compelling account of a relational form of power primarily because his work centres on the claim that one might adopt *either* an agent-centred concept of power *or* a subject-centred concept of power (see especially Nye 2007: 163). Nye draws the distinction between agent and subject because he seeks to develop a conception of power that is applicable in the context of US foreign policy making. More precisely, Nye (2002: 17) has sought to explain how the USA can maintain its preponderance of power within the international system. The trouble with pursuing an agent-focused concept of power is not that it precludes one from ever considering the role of the subject of power but instead that it predisposes us to shift our attention towards the agent and away from the subject, thus resulting in an oversimplified understanding of power. This problem is evident within Nye's work in terms of his tendency to describe soft power as something that is capable of being possessed by an agent, thus implying that it is a resource rather than a feature of a relationship. As a result, soft power becomes something almost tangible, something that can be 'enhanced', 'curtailed', 'produced' or 'squandered' (see Nye 2002: 72–3, 2007: 163). The suggestion that power is something that can be possessed is conceptually problematic (Reus-Smit 2004: 55), and it moves Nye dangerously close to those scholars who have defined power in terms of resources. Nye (2007: 164) explicitly warns against this so-called 'vehicle fallacy', but his determination to describe an agent-centred concept of power repeatedly leads him back in this direction.

If Nye's discussion of the relational component of soft power suffers from certain limitations, so too does his account of structural forms of power. This is particularly evident with regard to his discussion of structural power and its relationship to the soft power of the USA. The power associated with social structures such as common values, institutions or culture is clearly crucial to Nye's account of soft power. What is particularly troubling here, however, is that Nye's work often seems to suggest that such social structures can be possessed by a particular actor. Thus, for example, he speaks of America's universal values as representing a resource that can be deployed by the USA (Nye 2004: 11). While this position acknowledges that social structures are produced by agents, it ignores the fact that social structures are ontologically distinct from those actors and cannot be said to be possessed by them. What Nye ignores is that social structures are properties of a society rather than resources 'owned' by individual actors (Guzzini 1993: 465–6). Therefore, while we may often associate certain democratic principles with the USA, and even acknowledge that such principles may in part have originated within the USA, this does not mean that either the meaning or the legitimacy of such principles are or can be controlled solely by the USA.

If Nye's conflation and confusion of relational and structural forms of power leads him to advance conceptually limited accounts of each of these forms of power, it also leads to a second problem, namely his tendency to restrict the conceptual space in which consideration of the role of the subject of power may be undertaken. It is in this sense that Nye's early account of soft power may be criticized on the grounds that it is unstrategic. Before considering this problem in further detail it is necessary to clarify what is meant here by the term 'unstrategic'. After all, Steven Lukes (2007: 97) has criticized Nye's account of soft power precisely because he deems it to be too strategic in orientation. On closer inspection, however, it becomes clear that Lukes' argument rests on a flawed conception of strategy. Strategy, for Lukes, describes the means by which agents advance their interests in a zero-sum or conflictual context. Thomas Schelling has demonstrated convincingly that strategy should not be thought of in this way. Instead, Schelling argues that while the term 'strategy' sounds 'cold-blooded, the theory [of strategy] ... is not essentially a theory of aggression or of resistance or of war'; it is, instead, 'the conditioning of one's behaviour on the behaviour of others, that the theory is about' (Schelling 1980: 15). It is in this context that, according to Schelling (1980: 16), we might think of the theory of strategy as representing the 'theory of interdependent decision'. Thus, to argue that Nye's conception of soft power is unstrategic is to assert that his conception of power lacks an adequate account of the interdependence between the agent and subject of power.

My concern here is not that Nye chooses to focus empirically on the exercise of power by an agent rather than on the role of the subject of power. Indeed, when discussing the innumerable examples that are used to illustrate his understanding of soft power, Nye (2004) does indeed refer to the role of the other in terms of the interpretation of culture, values and communicative strategies. Instead, my concern is that Nye's attempts to conceptualize soft power threaten to dismiss any meaningful role for the subject of power. This is true with regard to relational forms of power, where Nye explicitly chooses an agent-centred instead of a subject-centred view of power, and structural forms of power, where Nye grants possession of (and agency with regard to) social structures to the USA but not to others.

Interestingly, the importance of allowing space within a conception of power for the agency of the subject is evident within many contemporary works on power, including accounts of both agent-focused and structural forms of power. With regard to the former, the key move is to consider agency as inherently forming part of a power relationship (Lukes 2005: 73; Reus-Smit 2004: 56). This moves us away from treating power as a mere resource and towards a consideration of power as a capacity that must necessarily exist within the context of a relationship between multiple actors. This point is made starkly by Foucault (1982: 220), who argues 'that "the other" (the one over whom power is exercised) [must] be thoroughly recognized and maintained to the very end as a person who acts'. Likewise, Barnett and Duvall (2005: 45) suggest that an agent-focused form of power must be conceived in the context of 'behavioural relations or interactions'. When seen in this light, therefore, Nye's conceptual separation of agent and subject is likely to encourage flawed analyses of US power.

If the subject of power is granted conceptual space within many of the more convincing accounts of a relational form of power, the same is true in many accounts of structural power. The general point here is clear: while social structures constitute (and constrain) certain agents, they are also themselves products of the practices of agents (Giddens 1984: 28–9). The untenable alternative to this position is one of structural determinism whereby we treat subjects as 'cultural dupes' incapable of agency (Clegg 1989: 138). Turning again to the mechanism of attraction, which is central to Nye's concept of soft power, we can appreciate that the possibility of attraction rests upon the existence of social norms defining what it means to be attractive. These norms, while constraining and enabling the practices of agents are also constituted by those practices.

What is crucial, however, is that we cannot presume that such social norms represent a possession or resource of those whom are deemed attractive. It is exactly this mistake that is made by Nye when he suggests that certain values and norms represent power resources of the USA. Nye's insistence that certain norms or values represent the resources of the powerful serves to create a false distinction between agents and subjects and their respective relationships to social structures. Janice Bially Mattern (2007) also notes this problem in Nye's work, though she addresses it from another angle. Janice Bially Mattern (2007: 103) criticizes Nye for advancing an ontological contradiction through his treatment of attraction as occurring through a process of social construction on the one hand, and naturally on the other. Nye (2007: 163) has challenged this criticism by suggesting that it is entirely appropriate to treat the attractiveness of, for example, the principle of democracy as being 'natural' in the short term even while acknowledging that, in the long term, such attractiveness may fade. This response is less than convincing. What is produced here is a fundamental distinction between, on the one hand, an empowered USA that has, through an exercise of agency, raised the principle of democracy to its current exalted status and, on the other hand, those actors who are now subject to the 'natural' attraction exerted by democracy. Such an account is troubling; both on empirical grounds and in terms of the exceptional status granted to the USA (something that is itself redolent of the rhetoric of the Bush administration). Unlike the USA, other states are treated here as mere subjects of the power of social norms regarding the attractiveness of democracy. The role of such subjects as agents in their own right is dismissed here, thus adding to the unstrategic nature of Nye's conception of soft power.

Developing a strategic account of soft power

The challenge that has been set by the previous section is to develop an account of power that builds upon Nye's notion of soft power without repeating the twin errors that result from his conflation of relational and structural forms of power. The first such error is that by conflating these two distinctive forms of power Nye fails to produce a convincing account of either. The second is that Nye tends to dismiss the role of the subject of power, either by drawing an overly simplistic distinction between agent and subject or by conceiving of social structures as the possessions of the powerful.

The challenge of incorporating both relational and structural forms of power within a single account, and without advancing simplistic accounts of either, is by no means a simple one to overcome. Indeed, a number of prominent works on the concept of power within international relations (IR) have concluded that we need to disaggregate rather than combine the two forms of power mentioned above if we are to understand either (Barnet and Duvall 2005; Guzzini 2005). If we were to adopt this approach in the analysis of the exercise of soft power through the mechanism of attraction, we would be forced to examine either a given set of power relations (such as the attraction of A to B) or a given system of structural power (such as a system of norms regarding the meaning of attraction). What would be lost here is precisely the interplay between these two elements of power that is of most interest within the notion of soft power.

Nye's most recent work on leadership and power has begun to remedy some of the weaknesses of his earlier work by advocating the analysis of leaders, followers and the context in which the power relationship between the two exists. By considering the role of followers as well as leaders, Nye's work has begun to take seriously the role of the subject of power. Furthermore, Nye has begun to explicitly distinguish between relations of power and the social structures that both enable and constrain such relations. Nye (2008: 32–7) recognizes the role of the subject of power most obviously in his lengthy discussion of the relationship between leaders and followers. Nye also addresses the relationship between agency and structure in the context of leadership, particularly through his discussion of the relationship between leaders and the cultural contexts in which they operate. Thus, building on Edgar Schein's work on organizational culture, Nye (2008: 92) argues that while 'the culture of a group sets the framework for leaders', so too 'leaders create cultures when they create groups and organizations'.

Nye has thus sought to address the two concerns raised in the previous section, yet within his discussion of each of these issues lies room for greater precision and clarity. On the one hand, for example, when discussing the relationship between leaders and followers, Nye (2008: 35–6) notes that 'followers often have the power to help lead a group'. Similarly, when discussing the relationship between leaders and (organizational) culture, Nye (citing Schein, 2008: 92) concludes that 'managing culture is one of the most important things that leaders do. If leaders do not "become conscious of the cultures in which they are embedded, those cultures will manage them." ' What emerges from Nye's discussion of these issues, therefore, is some measure of ambiguity. In defence of Nye, it must be noted that the relationships that he is examining – power relations and the relationship between agency and structure – present thorny intellectual problems that have challenged numerous scholars of power (Haugaard 2002). However, there is no avoiding the uncertainty raised by his attempt to explain these relationships. If followers can also lead, how are we to understand leadership? What do we mean by the term 'manage' if we are to accept both that leaders manage culture and that cultures manage leaders?

The remainder of this chapter seeks to advance and then illustrate a strategic conception of power, one which more clearly explains the relationships between actor and subject on the one hand, and agent and structure on the other. In pursuing this objective, it is useful to turn to the work of Michel Foucault. To do so on the grounds that Foucault (1980; 1994) produced important work on the concept of power may appear as justification enough. However, what is truly important with regard to Foucault's work on power is that there is much to be learned from his writings regarding the possible features of a strategic account of power. Foucault's articulation of a strategic account of power began in the final stages of his *Discipline and Punish*, and was continued in a series of later works, including *The Will to Knowledge* (1978), 'The Subject and Power' (1982) and *Society Must Be Defended* (2004). Within such writings, Foucault's objective was to challenge the 'juridical' conception of power which, according to him, represented the prevailing account of power within the Western social sciences. The juridical model conceives power as flowing down from a sovereign who sits above society and exercises power in the form of repression (Foucault 1978: 85–9). In this sense, power has systemic properties that are structured around a central point, namely the sovereign. Furthermore, power's exercise can best be attributed to that sovereign and best be described in terms of the placement of constraints upon members of society.

Foucault's (2004: 15) first step in breaking free of this conception of power is to conceive of politics – and of power – in terms of a reversal of Clausewitz's famous dictum that war is the continuation of politics through other means. By asserting that politics should be conceived of as the continuation of war by other means, Foucault (1978: 92) seeks to encourage us to conceive of power in a most important manner; as a function of force relations. This moves us away from attributing power to an individual or institution and towards an analysis of power relations between multiple individuals. Foucault (1982: 217) does not deny the disequilibria among those engaged in power relations: 'let us not deceive ourselves; if we speak of the structures or the mechanisms of power, it is only insofar as we suppose that certain persons exercise power over others'. However, what he does seek to suggest is that power 'is nevertheless always a way of acting upon an acting subject or acting subjects by virtue of their acting or being capable of action' (Foucault 1982: 220). Put simply, Foucault's point is that the existence of power implies the existence of a subject that is, at least in theory, capable of resistance. In other words:

> ... a power relationship can only be articulated on the basis of two elements which are each indispensable if it is really to be a power relationship: that 'the other' (the one over whom power is exercised) be thoroughly recognized and maintained to the very end as a person who acts; and that, faced with a relationship of power, a whole field of responses, reactions, results, and possible inventions may open up.
>
> (Foucault 1982: 220)

This understanding of power generates the need to analyse power relations less in terms of the resources of a single actor, and more in terms of an 'antagonism of strategies' (Foucault 1982: 210–11).

How then, can Foucault's strategic conception of power aid us in remedying some of the problems identified in Nye's account of soft power? Before considering this question in further detail, it is worth noting that there are enough similarities between these two accounts of power to suggest that some attempt at integration may be fruitful. Both scholars have sought to describe a form of power that is effective precisely because its effects are elusive. Nye highlights the value of generating consent for one's policies through the exercise of soft power not in terms of this being somehow more ethical than the exercise of, for example, military force (Nye 2007: 169–70), but instead because it is a particularly efficient form of power. Similarly, Foucault (1978: 86) has argued that power 'is tolerable only on condition that it mask a substantial part of itself. Its success is proportional to its ability to hide its own mechanisms.' Furthermore, both scholars are interested in explaining a form of power that operates not merely by presenting the subject of power with incentives or disincentives, but instead by changing how subjects understand the world in which they live. For Nye (2008: 29), this involves shaping the preferences subjects, whereas for Foucault (1982) this involves the constitution of certain types of subjects. It is because of such similarities that a consideration of Foucault's strategic conception of power promises to supplement rather than negate the notion of soft power.

Foucault's work on power offers insight into the nature of relational and structural forms of power (including the place of the subject of power within the context of each) and into the relationship between these forms of power. Such an account of power forces us to conceive of agency in terms of its position within relations of power. Foucault's account of power as constituting force relations nicely captures the point made persuasively by Schelling (1980: 16), namely, that strategy ought to be conceived in terms of interdependent decisions. This prevents us from being able to dismiss conceptually the role of the subject of power; rather the proper subject of analysis here is the relationship between the strategies of multiple actors. Effective strategy often (though not always) requires one to anticipate and then seek to condition the behaviour of one's adversary. It is in this sense that Foucault's distinction between the exercise of (direct and physical) violence and the exercise of power becomes relevant. 'A relationship of violence acts upon a body or upon things; it forces, it bends, it breaks on the wheel, it destroys, or it closes the door on all possibilities', whereas 'what defines a relationship of power is that it is a mode of action which does not act directly and immediately on others. Instead it acts upon their actions: an action upon an action, on existing actions or on those which may arise in the present or the future' (Foucault 1982: 220). In so doing, however, we need to appreciate that, even for the powerful, involvement in a relationship of power requires 'the conditioning of one's behaviour on the behaviour of others' (Schelling 1980: 15). This is true because within power relations there can be no final or complete dismissal of the subject who acts.

This may appear to be a rather abstract point, yet it has practical implications. The key point made above is that the successful exercise of power, by definition, requires the subject of power to decide to act in a manner consistent with one's intention. It is at this moment of decision that the subject of power becomes an actor rather than a mere object. This matters because it is conceivable that even the making of the most severe threat may not result in a successful exercise of power. Thus, for example, while we might often assume that threatening someone with death will leave that individual with no real decision to make, all we need to do to appreciate the error of such an assumption is to consider the case of a soldier manning a checkpoint faced with a suicide bomber. In such a situation, the capacity for action of the subject of power becomes absolutely obvious. If we turn to a situation where an actor seeks to exercise power through the mechanism of attraction rather than coercion, the scope for agency available to the subject of power appears even larger. Interestingly, Foucault's (1982: 222) descriptions of a relationship of power in terms of an 'agonism', a 'reciprocal incitation' and state of 'permanent provocation' also seem peculiarly appropriate to a description of a relationship of attraction. In seeking to attract another individual, one must engage in an attempt to anticipate what that individual finds attractive. The interdependent nature of such agency is obvious here. One is seeking to exercise power over another through the conditioning of one's own behaviour based on one's expectations about how that other interprets 'attractiveness'.

The strategic nature of this account of agency becomes clearer if we draw upon the example of a wrestling match. Clausewitz (1976: 75) famously referred to war as being akin to a wrestling match due to the clashing of forces that takes place in either contest. Alternatively, Foucault's reference to the 'agonism' that is central to a strategic power relationship 'is based on the Greek ἀγώνισμα meaning "a combat". The term would hence imply a physical contest in which the opponents develop a strategy of reaction and of mutual taunting, as in a wrestling match' (Foucault 1982: 222, footnote 3 [translator's note]). We can certainly identify the agency of one wrestler within such a contest, but that agency cannot be adequately explained or understood without reference to the other wrestler. The exercise of strength and power by one wrestler within such a contest is fundamentally dependent upon and, indeed, shaped by the resistance that the agency of the other provides. Again, what is obvious here is the interdependence of the agents engaged in the contest. Thus, despite the fact that a wrestling match is necessarily an example of zero-sum behaviour, we must still conceive of the exercise of power within this context in terms of a clashing of interdependent strategies.

A strategic conception of power also alters our understanding of social structures. In general terms, we might define social structures as intersubjective norms regarding meaning. More specifically, within power relations defined in terms of an 'antagonism of strategies', social structures might be understood as providing the 'terrain' upon which such strategies are developed. It is in this sense that Guzzini (2000), drawing upon the work of Pierre Bourdieu, uses the notion of 'fields' to describe the realm of political behaviour constituted by particular sets of social structures or norms. Thus, Guzzini (2000: 166) describes fields as 'the playgrounds where agents realize individual strategies, playing within, and thereby openly reproducing, the rules of a given game.' Karin Fierke (1998: 17), drawing on Wittgenstein's notion of 'language games', makes a similar point by suggesting that it is within such games that agents engage in strategic political action and manoeuvre.

Two points warrant particular attention here. On the one hand, such norms and rules must be conceived as both constraints that proscribe certain forms of behaviour, and, on the other, as constituting certain behaviour as meaningful. It is in this sense that we can appreciate Foucault's suggestion that power is both restrictive and productive. Wrestling rules and norms, for example, certainly dictate those forms of behaviour that are either formally proscribed or informally frowned upon. At the same time, however, norms regarding techniques, moves and strategies also enable actors to engage in behaviour that can be recognized as wrestling. If we return to the example of attraction in the school yard, we can appreciate in more detail why it is that the social norms regarding fashion both enable A to exercise power within their relationship with B and constrain A by determining what it means to be attractive. Likewise, the USA is both empowered and constrained by norms that constitute international legitimacy in terms of liberal and democratic principles.

The understanding of structural power advanced here also challenges Nye's (2004: 7) suggestion that social structures represent resources that can be possessed and exercised by an agent in a manner that is analogous to the ownership and deployment of wealth or military force. Unlike objects such as tanks which possess a tangible material reality, social structures are incapable of being possessed. Social structures consist of norms or rules regarding meaning and are therefore intersubjective. As we shall see below, this ontological status holds important implications with regard to the relationship between agents and social structures. Furthermore, being intersubjective, social structures are incapable of being possessed by a particular actor. It is true, as scholars such as Foucault (1989) and Bourdieu (1994) have attempted to show, that one of the primary effects of social structures is to differentiate between types of subjects and to empower some and not others. Clearly, for example, norms regarding both status and legitimacy empower the USA more than they do certain other states. However, while social structures may advantage some more than others, because they are inherently linked to meaning, and because meaning is intersubjective, they cannot be possessed by a particular actor (Guzzini 2005: 498). Instead, such social structures are constituted through the practices of both those who are advantaged and those who are disadvantaged by their structuring effects.

If a strategic conception of power helps us to address some of the problems with regard to Nye's accounts of both relational and structural forms of power, it also helps us to appreciate the relation between them. As has been noted above, it is this issue which represents one of the most potentially important aspects of Nye's account of soft power. The question, at least as far as Nye is concerned, is how US policymakers can construct certain social structures which will constitute America as an attractive state, thereby empowering the USA within the context of its relations with others. In order to begin to address this question, we must consider in more detail the ontological status of social structures. As has been noted above, social structures can be thought of as constituting a field (or fields) in which the (interdependent) strategies of actors are pursued. This terrain consists of the intersubjective norms and rules that constitute meaning and therefore enable actors to engage in power relations. However, the practices of such actors can also reconstitute these social structures, thereby changing them and the effect that they may have in the future. This is possible because social structures are norms regarding meaning, and meaning itself cannot be finally fixed due to its dependence upon language (see, for example, Campbell 1998; Fierke 1998; Jackson 2005). It is because of this 'play of meaning' that social structures – rules or norms regarding, for example, the meaning of attractiveness – can be reinterpreted and reconstituted.

To say that change is possible is not to say that it is easy. To change a social structure, such as an international norm regarding attraction, requires far more than a mere individual intention to do so. Two initial constraints on the potential for change are worth noting here. First, an attempt to alter certain rules must be understood by others if it is to become socially significant, thus returning us to the inherent limitations of undertaking socially meaningful action. Second, even if such an attempt is understood, it must be accepted by others. In short, because social structures or norms are intersubjective rather than subjective, changes to them must also take place at a social rather than an individual level.

Intriguingly, there is a certain resonance between this claim regarding the play of meaning within social structures and the claim made by strategic theorists regarding the role of uncertainty in war (Reid 2003a, 2003b). Clausewitz is famous, among other things, for emphasising the importance of unpredictability in war (Gray 1999: 94). According to Clausewitz, it is 'the play of chance and probability within which the creative spirit is free to roam' (cited in Reid 2003b: 67). This play of chance and probability even applies to the physical terrain upon which war is fought (Clausewitz 1976: 109; Luttwak 2001). If the landscapes upon which wars occur provide such potential for uncertainty and reinterpretation, so too do the social structures that constitute the terrain upon which power relations are played out. Furthermore, the antagonistic relationship of strategies that exists within relations of power (or attraction) means that meaning, and thus the character of social structures themselves, represents that which is to be fought over as well as that which defines how two actors fight.

To briefly summarize the limited account of a strategic conception of power discussed above, it is possible to argue that power must be conceived of in relational terms (rather than as a property of an agent). Agency exists within such a relationship, but it is an agency of a curious kind. The agency of one actor within a power relationship is ultimately dependent upon the existence and agency of that actor that we may, by way of convenience, label as the subject of power. Thus, even if we were to focus our empirical analysis of power on the practices of a particular actor, our analysis would necessarily refer to the subject of power due to the interdependent nature of relations of power. Furthermore, to the extent that we might seek to analyse social structures that, among other things, serve to define the meaning of attractiveness, we must acknowledge the inherent ambiguity of those social structures, and the play of chance and probability that such ambiguity opens up.

Applying a strategic account of soft power

There is no disguising the unfinished nature of the account of power discussed in the previous section. This final (and necessarily brief) section seeks to add some much needed clarity to this conception of power by considering how the application of this strategic conception of soft power might benefit our attempts to understand the power of the USA.

The first advantage offered by the adoption of a strategic conception of power concerns our understanding of the relational element of power. More precisely, a strategic conception of power helps us to avoid the common error of assuming that power is something that is possessed by states such as the USA. Nye is less guilty than many others of making this error (see, for example, Mead 2004; Joffe 2006), yet it creeps into his work at times. This may result from his determination to develop an agent-centred conception of soft power that is tailored to the practical requirements of policy makers. Nye (2004: 105–25) avoids this error most consistently when discussing the specific details of Washington's foreign policy, such as those regarding its use of public diplomacy. Other aspects of his work remain less immune to this error, however, especially those in which he seeks to 'measure' the power of the USA relative to others (Nye 2002: 17–35, 2004: ch. 3). At such times Nye comes closest to treating power as something that is possessed by agents.

What then is wrong with the power-as-possession thesis? Put simply, the more that we treat power as a possession of actors, the more we are likely to then seek to identify what attributes or resources an actor has that make it powerful. The dangers here are twofold. First, to equate power with certain resources is to perpetuate the 'vehicle fallacy' that scholars (including Nye) have repeatedly warned against (Reus-Smit 2004: 50–1). The problem here is obvious; actors with great power resources do not always exercise power over others in terms of getting them to do what it is that they want them to do. Second, the assumption that power is possessed by one actor implies that we can successfully evaluate the exercise of power by the USA simply by examining what it is the USA does and without even considering those over whom US power is exercised. Those who approach the analysis of US power with the intention of improving US foreign policy would do well, therefore, to note Colin Gray's (1999: 18–19) warning that 'strategic history demonstrates the prevalence of the error of neglect of the enemy'.

While the errors considered above are evident in elements of Nye's work on soft power, they are more bluntly evident in the post-Cold War writings of some neoconservative scholars. What stronger notion of power-as-possession can one get than, for example, Stephen Brooks and William Wohlforth's (2002: 33) assertion that American power represents an 'iron fist' to be wielded by Washington? Their work also provides an example of scholarship that suffers from the 'vehicle fallacy'; at the heart of their article lies an attempt to measure the power of the USA in terms of the various resources that it possesses. The limitations of such an approach are immediately evident when one compares the almost giddy celebration of American military superiority apparent in the article to the very real challenges faced by the American military in its attempts to construct a stable Iraq (Herring and Rangwala 2004; Baker and Hamilton 2006). Furthermore, the ignoring of the relational nature of power and the problems that follow from this are nowhere more clearly demonstrated than in neoconservative writings on the pursuit of primacy. To assert that USA power is not merely the means by which foreign policy is pursued but also the very end pursued through that foreign policy is to demonstrate a most blatant misunderstanding of the concept of power. Thus, calls by scholars such as Charles Krauthammer (1990/91) and William Kristol and Robert Kagan (1996) for the pursuit and maintenance of unipolarity again ignore the fact that power is exercised in the context of relationships; it is not a mere possession of actors.

The adoption of a strategic conception of power would aid us in avoiding the problems referred to above because it requires us to consider the relationship of power between agent and subject. Again, this relationship is best characterized in terms of an agonism of interdependent strategies. To acknowledge this interdependence is not for a moment to suggest some measure of equality. Thus, to say that our analysis of US power ought to incorporate consideration of the subject of that power is not to make an ethical claim regarding the rights of the other. Instead, it is to make the practical claim that the exercise of power over another is likely to be less successful to the extent that we ignore the fact that the other is an agent capable of action. Such an approach moves us away from the making of general claims regarding the primacy, dominance or preponderance of the USA and towards the analysis of specific relationships and the (interdependent) strategies that the US pursues within them.

The second advantage offered by the adoption of a strategic conception of power relates to our understanding of structural forms of power. Such an understanding of power requires the rejection of the notion that social structures or norms can be possessed by a particular agent. Recall that Nye (2004: 11) asserts that universal values such as those regarding democracy represent resources of the USA. Though he goes on to qualify this position, we can immediately see the similarity between this claim and that of Kristol and Kagan (1996: 27), who championed the promotion of the American principles of democracy, free markets and respect for liberty. Chris Reus-Smit (2004: 55) highlights the errors of this position through reference to the reactions of Indian leaders to British efforts at promoting just such principles: 'they took the ideas of liberalism and democracy they imbibed in the imperial heartland and fashioned them into anti-imperialism and nationalism.' A strategic conception of power forces us to appreciate the intersubjective – rather than the subjective – nature of social structures such as norms and values. It encourages us to consider how the practices of multiple actors serve to constitute certain structures, and not merely how such structures benefit certain actors.

A strategic conception of power also encourages us to avoid the assumption that social structures are fixed or natural. Again, if we recall that Nye (2007: 163) has argued that it is reasonable to take for granted the (near) universal attractiveness of democracy, we can see similarities between his position and that of those close to the Bush administration who have also claimed that American values are, by their very nature, universal (see, for example, Rice 2000: 49). The great danger in making this assumption is that we ignore the socially constructed nature of social structures and thus limit our capacity to imagine resistance to such structures or how such resistance may be overcome. This danger has been most obvious in relation to the early experiences of the Bush administration with regard to democracy promotion in Iraq: because members of the administration had so frequently claimed the universal acceptance of certain values there was little conceptual space in which planning could take place for the promotion of such values within Iraq (Fukuyama 2006: 115). A strategic conception of power envisions social structures as terrains upon which political contestation takes place. Crucially, however, because of the play of meaning that is inherent within intersubjective structures, the nature of these terrains cannot be conceived as being either natural or necessarily permanent. Therefore, while social structures may constitute and regulate the practices of certain actors, they are themselves capable of being challenged, reinterpreted and reconstituted by those very actors. Rather than merely acknowledging the existence of prominent social structures, a strategic conception of power encourages us to ask how certain structures have come to be powerful, what practices might be employed to promote such structures and where and how such structures are or maybe challenged.

If a strategic conception of power helps us to avoid these specific problems, it also differs from prevailing accounts of power in terms of tone. The adoption of a strategic conception of power demands humility, both from the analyst of power and from the foreign policy practitioner. Once we conceive of relational power in terms of an agonism of interdependent strategies, we are forced to acknowledge both the insufficiency of simplistic measures of power in terms of the resources of particular actors and the potential challenges associated with analysing complex and specific power relations. Similarly, when seeking to analyse the effects of social structures (such as norms regarding what it means to be attractive) we must acknowledge the potential for actors to challenge and reconstitute those structures and to thereby render our analyses of them redundant. Humility is essential in our analysis of power not because such a posture is somehow ethically superior to hubris, but instead because it represents a practical necessity when we understand power correctly. To return to Nye's conception of soft power, it is well worth noting the presence within his work of exactly such a sense of humility. This represents a true strength of Nye's work. It also affirms the possibility of achieving the objective that is pursued within this chapter; that is the critique and development, rather than the mere replacement, of Nye's conception of soft power.

Note

1 Again, it is important to note that the critique presented in this section focuses on Nye's earlier attempts to define soft power – his more recent work on leadership (Nye 2008) is considered below.

Bibliography

Baker, J.A. and Hamilton, L.H. (co-chairs) (2006) *The Iraq Study Group Report: The Way Forward – A New Approach*, New York: Vintage.

Barnett, M. and Duvall, R. (2005) 'Power in International Politics', *International Organization*, 59(1): 39–75.

Bially Mattern, J. (2007) 'Why Soft Power Isn't So Soft: Representational Force and Attraction in World Politics', in F. Berenskoetter and M.J. Williams (eds) *Power in World Politics*, London: Routledge.

Bourdieu, P. (1994) *Academic Discourse: Linguistic Misunderstanding and Professorial Power*, Cambridge: Polity.

Brooks, S. and Wohlforth, W. (2002) 'American Primacy in Perspective', *Foreign Affairs*, 81(4): 20–33.

Campbell, D. (1998) *Writing Security: United States Foreign Policy and the Politics of Identity*, rev. edn, Manchester: Manchester University Press.

Clausewitz, C. (1976) *On War*, indexed edn, M. Howard and P. Paret (ed. and trans.), Princeton, NJ: Princeton University Press.

Clegg, S.R. (1989) *Frameworks of Power*, London: SAGE.

Digeser, P. (1992) 'The Fourth Face of Power', *Journal of Politics*, 54(4): 977–1007.

Ferguson, N. (2003) 'Power: Think Again', *Foreign Policy*, March/April: 18–24.

Fierke, K. (1998) *Changing Games, Changing Strategies: Critical Investigations in Security*, Manchester: Manchester University Press.

Foucault, M. (1977) *Discipline and Punish: The Birth of the Prison*, trans. A. Sheridan, New York: Pantheon.

—— (1978) *The Will to Knowledge: The History of Sexuality, Volume I*, London: Penguin.

—— (1980) *Power/Knowledge: Selected Interviews and Other Writings, 1972–1977*, C. Gordon (ed.), C. Gordon, L. Marshall, J. Mepham and K. Soper (trans.), Harlow: The Harvester Press.

—— (1982) 'The Subject and Power', in H.L. Dreyfus and P. Rabinow (eds), *Michel Foucault: Beyond Structuralism and Hermeneutics*, Hemel Hempstead: The Harvester Press.

—— (1989) *Madness and Civilisation: A History of Insanity in the Age of Reason*, London: Routledge.

—— (1994) *Power: Essential Works of Foucault, 1954–1984*, J.D. Faubion (ed.), London: Penguin.

—— (2004) *Society Must Be Defended*, D. Macey (trans.), London: Penguin.

Fukuyama, F. (2006) *After the Neocons: America at the Crossroads*, London: Profile Books.

Giddens, A. (1984) *The Constitution of Society*, Cambridge: Polity.

Gray, C. (1999) *Modern Strategy*, Oxford: Oxford University Press.

Guzzini, S. (1993) 'Structural Power: The Limits of Neorealist Power Analysis', *International Organization*, 47(3): 443–78.

—— (2000) 'A Reconstruction of Constructivism in International Relations', *European Journal of International Relations*, 6(2): 147–82.

—— (2005) 'The Concept of Power: A Constructivist Analysis', *Millennium: Journal of International Studies*, 33(3): 495–521.

Herring, E. and Rangwala, G. (2004) *Iraq in Fragments: The Occupation and Its Legacy*, London: Hurst.

Jackson, R. (2005) *Writing the War on Terrorism: Language, Politics, and Counter-Terrorism*, Manchester: Manchester University Press.

Joffe, J. (2006) *Überpower: The Imperial Temptation of America*, New York: W. W. Norton.

Kristol, W. and Kagan, R. (1996) 'Toward a Neo-Reaganite Foreign Policy', *Foreign Affairs*, 75(4): 18–32.

Krauthammer, C. (1990/91) 'The Unipolar Moment', *Foreign Affairs*, 70(1): 23–33.

Lukes, S. (2005) *Power: A Radical View*, Second Edition, Basingstoke: Palgrave Macmillan.

—— (2007) 'Power and the Battle for Hearts and Minds: On the Bluntness of Soft Power', in F. Berenskoetter and M.J. Williams (eds) *Power in World Politics*, London: Routledge.

Luttwak, E. (2001) *Strategy: The Logic of War and Peace*, rev. edn, Cambridge, MA: Belknap Press.

Mead, W.R. (2004) *Power, Terror, Peace, and War: America's Grand Strategy in a World at Risk*, New York: Vintage.

Morriss, P. (1987) *Power: A Philosophical Analysis*, Manchester: Manchester University Press.

Nye, J.S. (1990) *Bound to Lead: The Changing Nature of American Power*, New York: Basic Books.

—— (2002) *The Paradox of American Power: Why the World's Only Superpower Can't Go It Alone*, Oxford: Oxford University Press.

—— (2004) *Soft Power: The Means to Success in World Politics*, New York: Public Affairs.

—— (2006) 'Think Again: Soft Power', *Foreign Policy*, 1 March. Available at: http://yaleglobal.yale.edu/article.print?id=7059 (accessed 28 April 2008).

—— (2007) 'Notes for a Soft Power Research Agenda', in F. Berenskoetter and M.J. Williams (eds) *Power in World Politics*, London: Routledge.

—— (2008) *The Powers to Lead*, Oxford: Oxford University Press.

Reid, J. (2003a) 'Foucault on Clausewitz: Conceptualising the Relationship Between War and Power', *Alternatives*, 28(1): 1–28.

—— (2003b) 'Deleuze's War Machine: Nomadism Against the State', *Millennium: Journal of International Studies*, 32(1): 57–85.

Reus-Smit, C. (2004) *American Power and World Order*, Cambridge: Polity.

Rice, C. (2000) 'Promoting the National Interest', *Foreign Affairs*, 79(1): 45–62.

Schelling, T. (1980) *The Strategy of Conflict*, Cambridge, MA: Harvard.

4   The unbearable lightness of soft power

Christopher Layne

Introduction

In the immediate aftermath of the 9/11 attacks, there was an outpouring of goodwill toward the USA from abroad. This sympathy for the USA dissipated quickly, however, as public opinion around the world registered its disapproval of the George W. Bush administration's essentially unilateral decision to invade Iraq in March 2003, and the policies it employed in prosecuting the so-called War on Terror – including torture, renditions and the incarceration of suspected terrorists at the US naval base in Guantanamo Bay, Cuba. The backlash of world public opinion against the USA during the Bush administration became a major foreign policy issue during the 2008 campaign.

The tenor of the Democratic Party's critique of the Bush administration's foreign policy was that it had alienated the world by acting unilaterally rather than multilaterally, by-passing international institutions, flouting international law and norms, and disregarding the interests and opinions of other states.[1] Indeed, this judgment of Bush's foreign policy was not merely an issue of partisan politics – it resonated widely in American foreign policy circles.[2] As *New York Times* reporter David E. Sanger put it, Bush 'knew about hard power but had given little thought to the virtues of soft power, the power of America to shape events through the allure of its culture and example' (Sanger 2009: 457). The Obama administration came to office promising to repair the damage done by its predecessor to America's global standing.

Unlike the Bush administration, the new administration has pledged, as senior officials have said – including President Barack Obama himself – to listen to the opinions of others as well as to lead.[3] The new administration promised to eschew the alleged unilateralism of its predecessor. As Secretary of State Hillary Rodham Clinton said, although the new administration would work to 'strengthen America's global leadership' it recognized that 'America cannot solve the most pressing problems on our own, and the world cannot solve them without America. The best way to advance America's interest in reducing global threats and seizing global opportunities is to design and implement global solutions.'[4] As President Obama said in his Inaugural Address, under his administration, instead of relying excessively on military power, the USA would emphasize diplomacy and cooperation with allies. 'Recall', he said, 'that earlier generations faced down fascism and communism not just with missiles and tanks, but with sturdy alliances and enduring convictions.' Instead of using the hard fist of American power to run roughshod over others, the USA, Obama said, would act on the principle that its security depends on others' perceptions of the justness of its policies, the power of its example and its ability to refrain from imposing its will on others. In a word (or two), the Obama administration came to office determined to restore America's soft power. President Obama reaffirmed this commitment in his June 2009 Cairo address that sought to improve the Islamic world's perceptions of the USA. Moreover, the Obama administration is – at least rhetorically – taking soft power to a new level by transforming it into (in typical American fashion) a new and improved version: 'smart power'.

The origins of soft power

The idea of soft power was formulated by Joseph S. Nye, Jr – a noted Harvard scholar who also held important foreign policy appointments in the Jimmy Carter and Bill Clinton administrations – in a widely discussed 1990 book, *Bound to Lead* (Nye, 1990). Nye's purpose in writing *Bound to Lead* was to attack the so-called declinists – scholars of American foreign policy and international political economy – who, in the 1980s, contended that America's relative military and economic power were diminishing.[5] Nye not only claimed that the declinists were wrong about US hard power, but also that they overlooked a unique source of US geopolitical influence: its soft power. Predicting that in an interdependent, post-Cold War world coercive ('hard') power would be of decreasing utility, he argued that co-optive power – 'getting others to do what you want' – and the soft power resources upon which it rested (cultural attraction, ideology and international institutions) would play an increasingly important role in US foreign policy (Nye 1990: 188). Nye (1990: 191) believed that the USA had 'more co-optive power than other countries in the international system'. At least in part, Nye advanced the concept of soft power in reaction to the 1980s fears that the USA was losing its lead in hard power.

Bound to Lead introduced the concept of soft power, but Nye did not fully flesh out the concept either there or in subsequent work that alluded to soft power (Nye, 2002). Nye (2004) returned to the subject and provided a detailed elaboration of his original ideas on soft power by more precisely defining what it means and describing how it operates. He says soft power is a nation's ability to get others to do what it wants without using either coercive military or economic pressure, or offering material inducements (Nye 2004: x).[6] Soft power 'arises from the attractiveness of a country's culture, political ideals, and policies' (Nye 2004: x). Nye (2004: 5–6) states unequivocally that soft power involves neither the use of carrots nor sticks; rather it is 'leading by example and getting others to do what you want'. In other words, soft power is the ability to shape others' preferences (Nye 2004: 5). According to Nye (2004: 6), the key attribute of soft power is the ability to attract because 'attraction often leads to acquiescence'. The factors that generate this attractiveness are a state's culture, values, political ideals and policies (Nye 2004: x).

Nye, of course, focused on the sources of *American* soft power. He claimed that America's cultural attractiveness, its democratic institutions and values, and commitment to multilateralism would draw other states into Washington's orbit and legitimate US policies. Although Nye does not quite say so, soft power really reflects the injection of business school ideas about marketing into the American foreign policymaking process. Soft power is a means of marketing the American 'brand'.[7] Indeed, Nye has stated that soft power's effectiveness can be evaluated by employing the same tools that marketing executives employ to measure the impact of advertising campaigns: 'Whether a particular asset is an attractive soft power resource can be measured through polls or focus groups. Whether that attraction in turn produces desired policy outcomes has to be judged in each particular case' (Nye 2008: 96). As Nye conceived it, soft power is fundamentally about improving the USA's image among populations in other countries. Its premise is that the better America's image in the world, the more allies it will have, the more support its policies will receive from other states, and the more secure it will be.

Conceptualizing soft power

Although Nye does not cast soft power as a theory, it needs to be subjected to empirical testing to determine the validity of its claims and the robustness of its causal logic. In fact, Nye does advance hypotheses about how soft power is supposed to work also specifies its causal mechanisms.

Nye's case for soft power, however, is marred by some important weaknesses. Given the influence that soft power has had on US foreign policy debates, it is surprising that it has not been rigorously tested and its weak soft points exposed to scrutiny. Space constraints do not permit a full testing of soft power in this chapter. In part, this is because soft power touches on multiple literatures about international relations (IR) theory and foreign policy decision making. Here, it is only possible to outline some of soft power's conceptual vulnerabilities and to demonstrate that the empirical support for the theory is weak. This chapter, therefore, should be regarded as the starting point for a more intense discussion of soft power, not as the final word.

A good place to start analyzing soft power is Nye's claim that soft power is based on attractiveness and seduction (Nye 2004: x, 5). He explicitly analogizes soft power to the effect of attraction and seduction in interpersonal relationships. This is a dubious analogy, however. Individual decision makers are people but states are not. The argument that states can be attracted and seduced by policies of another state the same way lovers are seduced by their partners is not compelling. Foreign policy decision making is mediated by domestic political institutions and bureaucracies and filtered through the prism of the national interest. There is very little evidence that states (or the policymakers who act in their name) make decisions because they 'like' another state or its leaders. A good historical illustration (and a cautionary one for the Obama administration) is President Woodrow Wilson's tumultuous public reception when he visited Europe after World War I. Wilson was lionized by masses of people in Western Europe who adored him for his liberal ideals and vision of a new – just and peaceful – world order. However, this public adulation – the attraction to Wilson both as a man and as a symbol of American ideals – did not carry over into the negotiations at Versailles where the French leader Georges Clemenceau and British Prime Minister Lloyd George each proved to be tenacious defenders of his state's national interests.

Nye ties soft power to international legitimacy, and, especially the roles of shared values and norms as the yardsticks of legitimate state behaviour (in this latter respect, soft power intersects with the work of many constructivists in IR theory). As he says, soft power rests on an 'attraction to shared values and to the justness and duty of contributing to the advancement of these values' (Nye 2004: 7, 11). To illustrate his argument, he attributes the zone of peace in post-war Western Europe, and in the trilateral world, to 'shared values about what constitutes acceptable behavior among similar democratic states' (Nye 2004: 20). In this respect, soft power is basically about legitimacy: 'Legitimacy is central to soft power. If a people or nation believes American objectives to be legitimate, we are more likely to persuade them to follow our lead without using threats or bribes. Legitimacy can also reduce opposition to – and the costs of – using hard power when the situation demands' (Armitage and Nye 2007: 6). Legitimacy, in turn, is linked to multilateralist policies that commit the USA to acting through international institutions. As Nye (2004: 11) puts it, 'If a country's culture and ideology are attractive, others more willingly follow. If a country can shape international rules that are consistent with its interests and values, its actions will more likely appear legitimate in the eyes of others. If it uses institutions and follows rules that encourage other countries to channel or limit their activities in the ways it prefers, it will not need as many costly carrots and sticks.'

Nye's depiction of how soft power operates raises several questions. First, the causal mechanisms through which soft power is supposed to operate are fuzzy. For example, is legitimacy the consequence of multilaterlism, of shared values or both? Does soft power bring about the outcomes Nye attributes to it or are these caused by other factors: for example, the role of institutions and the impact of democracy on inter-state relations? Is soft power a distinct independent variable or merely a proxy for the independent variables specified by these other approaches? How can Nye's claims for soft power be falsified? This leads to a closely related second point. Nye's argument for soft power is essentially congruent with other IR theories: institutionalism, the democratic peace theory and constructivist claims about the role of norms. From an analytical standpoint, the question arises: what is the difference between soft power and these approaches? In other words, what is soft power's value added? Finally, the utility of the soft power concept is undermined by the fact that Nye's definition of the term is maddeningly inconsistent. As Leslie Gelb (2009: 69) points out, Nye has expanded the definition beyond 'pure' attraction (without coercion or inducements) to include both economic statecraft – used as both a carrot and as a stick – and even military power.

Nye's own illustrations of how soft power (purportedly) works demonstrate how poorly specified are its causal mechanisms. Even if one accepts that soft power exists and can affect a state's foreign policy, it is hard to trace the relationship between soft power and policy outcomes. For example, Nye (2004: 48–9) claims that soft power enabled the USA to achieve its policy objectives in fostering democracy and free markets in Western Europe following World War II. And, indeed, during the Cold War, the USA deliberately wielded soft power resources to win the allegiance of intellectual elites in Western Europe by using the Central Intelligence Agency to covertly support publications, conferences and cultural events (Saunders 1999; Berghahn 2001). However, it is not obvious that these efforts had any real significance in tying Western Europe to the USA. In contrast to the murky effects of soft power, it is much easier to trace the effect of the carrots and sticks that Washington offered to Western European governments: military protection from the Soviet threat and economic assistance through the Marshall Plan. Moreover, to the extent that Western European governments were motivated to bandwagon with the USA in the immediate aftermath of World War II, it was because the economic assistance they received from the USA enabled them to turn back challenges to their hold on political power mounted by the Communist parties in places such as France and Italy. Nye (2004: 39) also asserts that following World War II, America's soft power dissuaded Western Europe from balancing against preponderant USA. In fact, however, in the late 1940s Britain did fear US hegemony and attempted to balance against the United States, and in the early 1960s under President Charles de Gaulle, France also sought to create a geopolitical counterweight to American power (Layne 2006a, 2006b).

According to Nye (2004: 49), soft power was an important factor in America's victory over the Soviet Union in the Cold War. And, indeed, as he points out, the USA did promote numerous exchange programs during the Cold War that sought to expose members of the Soviet elite to American values in the hope that they would return home and become – as many did – advocates of liberal reforms. In a similar vein, Nye (2004: 17) also argues that by convincing East Europeans of America's moral superiority over the Soviet Union, US soft power helped to undermine Moscow's grip on the Warsaw Pact nations. Nevertheless, it is difficult to demonstrate that American soft power had any causal significance in bringing about the Cold War's end. Although the causes of the Soviet Union's collapse continue to be debated vigorously, it is easier to demonstrate the impact of material factors – the Reagan defence build up, the Soviet Union's economic and technological backwardness, and the sclerosis of the Soviet system itself – than it is to show the causal significance of ideational factors like soft power. (Bialer 1986; Aslund 1989; Schweizer 1996).

This critique of soft power does not mean that ideas are unimportant in international politics. They are important. For example, there is a vast literature that shows how ideology has influenced American foreign policy.[8] But when ideas impact policy, it is usually at the level of policymaking elites. According to Nye, however, soft power is measured by using polls and focus groups to assess its impact on a nation's public opinion. This is fine as far as it goes. This is a long way, however, from establishing that soft power's impact upon public opinion in a target state will actually affect that state's foreign policy. Operationally, as Nye conceives it, soft power is a two-step process. Step 1 employs soft power to affect public attitudes in the target state. Step 2 requires that the target state government's policymaking will respond to the soft power-induced views of the public.

The problem with Nye's conception of how soft power operates is that public opinion does not make foreign policy, the state's central decision makers do. And there is little reason to believe that public opinion affects their calculations (Lobell et al. 2009) significantly. There are at least two reasons why it is difficult to establish the causal link between public opinion and foreign policy outcomes that Nye posits. First, public attitudes are notoriously transient. The effects of soft power can be observed through polling one day but vanish the next. Second – and much more problematic – for soft power to 'work', there must be a demonstrated causal connection between public opinion and state policy. This is often very difficult to establish – even in democracies. The reason – which is downplayed by liberal theories of governance – is that states (especially strong ones) are autonomous actors that are only constrained minimally by 'civil society'.

Liberal political theory, of course, is hostile to the idea that the state exists autonomously from its host society.[9] However, liberal theory notwithstanding states, especially strong states, possess considerable autonomy (although the state's autonomy may be uneven and vary with respect to specific policy areas) (Krasner 1978: 58; Skocpol 1985: 17–18). As the political scientist Theda Skocpol (1985: 9) observes, 'States conceived as organizations claiming control over territories and people may formulate and pursue goals that are not simply reflective of the demands or interests of social groups.' The state's autonomy derives from three factors: (1) its necessity; (2) the multiplicity of key functions the state performs; and (3) its control over an identifiable territory (Mann 1984). The state is necessary because all societies require rules (especially rules that protect life and property). The state's necessity is a lever that it can use to pursue its own interests. The state performs multiple important functions, especially in the spheres of economics, maintenance of internal order and defence against external aggression, which invest it with autonomous power.[10]

Even in liberal democratic polities the state can be autonomous.[11] This should be most apparent in those policy realms that are pre-eminently within the state's province, such as foreign policy and national defence. A state – even a liberal state – that enjoys relative autonomy with respect to its external policy can be expected to respond (more or less) rationally to the constraints imposed by the international system, and to be relatively impervious to the effect of others' soft power in formulating its own foreign policy. One of soft power's key weaknesses is that it rests on a simplistic view of the foreign policy decision making process.

The state's central decision makers (who are, effectively, the state) are often powerful enough to pursue foreign policies that are at variance with public opinion – even in liberal democracies.[12] As Richard Merritt and Dina Zinnes (1991: 255) put it, 'the foreign policy elites who carry out the foreign policies of countries throughout the world use the same means such as diplomacy and protocol, control information, claim expertise and the need for secrecy, and are not particularly controlled by … democratic representatives'. Simply put, contrary to the mythology of liberalism, even in democracies there is no true marketplace of ideas. Or, to put it a bit differently, it is not a competitive marketplace because the state has the instruments to dominate it.

There is considerable empirical evidence supporting this point. As numerous studies have demonstrated, states are adept at manipulating public opinion by managing information flows and manipulating discourse. Indeed, going back to the Spanish-American War, few governments have been as skilful in using these techniques to rally support as that of the USA. As Eugene Secunda and Terence Moran (2007: 7) observe 'the U.S. public should better comprehend how U.S. presidents and their administrations exploit the media and execute marketing strategies to win support for their war policies' (see also Thompson, 1992). After 9/11, and especially during the run-up to the March 2003 invasion of Iraq, the Bush administration provided a textbook example of how the state can use its power to shape public opinion and sell its preferred policies even to a sceptical public (Kaufmann, 2004; Cramer, 2007; Thrall, 2007).

The fact that, in the realm of foreign policy the state controls public opinion rather than being controlled by it is a fact that undermines the causal logic of soft power. Because the state does have considerable autonomy in the realm of foreign policy, it should be expected that on issues that are of high salience to the policymaking elite – especially in the realm of national security – the decision making processes of strong states (democracies and non-democracies) will approximate the unitary rational actor model (Allison 1971). This is because national under these conditions, top-level decision makers assume the key roles and push other government officials and interest groups to the margins of decision making. This means that soft power is peripheral to policy decisions in the arena of high politics.[13] One could illustrate this with numerous examples, but two will suffice.

During the NATO Intermediate Nuclear Forces deployment in the early and mid-1980s, West German public opinion opposed the emplacement of Pershing II missiles in the Federal Republic of Germany and was viscerally anti-American. Under the leadership of Chancellor Helmut Kohl, however, the West German government went ahead with the deployments anyway (Layne 1984). More recently, the 2006 US Congressional elections – which resulted in sweeping gains for the Democratic party – were widely interpreted as a rejection of the Bush administration's Iraq policy and a signal that the American public wanted the USA to disengage from the war. Instead of winding down the American military commitment in Iraq, however, the Bush administration ignored both public and Congressional opinion and implemented its 'surge' strategy by *increasing* US troop levels in Iraq. These two cases illustrate the fact that in the realm of foreign policy and national security, governments tend to be insensitive to public opinion. This is a major theoretical problem for those who believe soft power is an important foreign policy tool.

A final problem with soft power as a conceptual approach to IR and foreign policy analysis is that its definition is unclear. When he first articulated the idea of soft power, Nye narrowed its scope and stressed repeatedly that soft power is about the influence of ideas and culture and not about dangling carrots and sticks in front of other states to affect their behaviour. The definition of soft power has expanded, however. This is especially true with respect to its use in the arena of policymaking. As policymakers, foreign policy analysts and pundits – including Nye himself – have come to use the term, soft power now encompasses a wide array of instruments including: multilateral diplomacy; foreign aid; developmental assistance, the provision of international public goods; the exportation of democracy; nation-building (Armitage and Nye 2007; Campbell and Flournoy 2007). Today, when scholars and policymakers talk about soft power, they use the term in this sense. Indeed, the term soft power these days is so expansive that it can be said to include just about everything including the kitchen sink (and military power). As Leslie Gelb (2009: 69) puts it, 'Soft power now seems to mean everything.' Nye himself has played a major role in this process by advancing the notion of smart power. Smart power – which can be dubbed Soft Power 2.0 – has superseded Soft Power 1.0 in the US foreign policy lexicon.

Soft power in US foreign policy

Soft power and its associated concepts have resonated both with those who make American foreign policy policies and those who write about it. Soft power is widely viewed an effective means of preserving American hegemony by legitimizing US dominance and reassuring other states that the USA will not abuse its preponderant power. Soft power stresses the need for the USA to act multilaterally through international institutions and the attractive power of America's democratic ideals and political institutions.

When the Cold War ended, leading US neorealist scholars predicted that unipolarity would quickly give way to multipolarity as other states balanced against American hegemony (Layne 1993; Waltz 1993). This prediction rested on both strong theoretical and empirical foundations. After all, since the beginning of the modern international system (circa 1500), successive bids for hegemony – the Hapsburgs (Charles V, Philip II), France (Louis XIV, Napoeleon) and Germany (Wilhelm II, Adolph Hitler) – were each defeated by countervailing coalitions. The lesson seemed clear: the fate of hegemons is to fail.

Since the Soviet Union's collapse, starting with the George H.W. Bush administration, it has been the policy of every US administration to preserve unipolarity, and maintain the USA's post-Cold War hegemony. Given the historical record, it might have seemed that such a grand strategy would elicit counter-hegemonic balancing by other states. But – contrary to the predictions of neorealists – American preponderance has not been counterbalanced – at least not yet.[14] Drawing on neorealism, hegemonic stability theory, balance of threat theory, and liberal IR theory, a number of prominent IR theorists – *American* ones – have advanced several explanations of why US hegemony has endured for nearly two decades without any major challenge, and to suggest that America can prolong its primacy far into the future. Soft power plays a key role in these explanations.

Liberal IR theorists and balance-of-threat realists attribute America's successful hegemony to the fact that it is a 'benevolent' hegemon. Other states, they say, will acquiesce in US hegemony if America displays self-restraint by exercising its predominance multilaterally through international institutions. Moreover, America's 'soft power' – the purportedly singular attractiveness of America's political and economic institutions, and its culture – is said to attract other states into Washington's orbit (Ikenberry and Kupchan, 1990; Ikenberry 1998/9, 2002a,b; Mastanduno 1997; Nye 1990, 2002; Walt 2002, 2005).[15] The leading advocates of soft power clearly view it – coupled with multilateralism – as means to bolstering the USA's hegemony. As Richard Armitage and Joseph Nye (2007: 5) assert, 'The goal of U.S. foreign policy should be to prolong and preserve American preeminence as an agent for good. Achieving this goal is impossible without strong and willing allies and partners who can help the United States to determine and act on priorities.'

A good example of how soft power is viewed as an instrument for preserving US hegemony is Fareed Zakaria's (2008) widely noted recent book, *The Post American World*. Actually, the title of Zakaria's book is a textbook example of literary bait and switch, because he argues that by employing soft power – especially multilateral diplomacy – the USA can keep its grip on preponderant power. Far from the USA being in decline, Zakaria (2008: 218) claims, the world is moving America's way with respect to modernization, globalization, human rights and democracy. That is, international politics is being shaped by American soft power.

In this world, Zakaria (2008: 219, emphasis added) argues, America has the opportunity to 'remain *the* pivotal player in a richer, more dynamic, more exciting world.' All that USA needs to do to maintain its paramount role in world politics is to renounce the unilateralism and blunderbuss diplomacy that characterized the Bush administration. Instead, the USA needs only to revert to its (purported) tradition of working through multilateral institutions and relying on diplomacy and persuasion. Zakaria (2008: 234) argues the USA can place itself at the centre of the international system for a long time to come because there is 'still a strong market for American power, for both geopolitical and economic reasons. But even more centrally, there remains a strong ideological demand for it'. The USA can remain the pivot of international politics by accommodating the desire of rising powers for validation, avoiding the coercive imposition of its preferences on the rest of the world and engaging in 'consultation, cooperation, and even compromise' (Zakaria 2008: 233). Zakaria (2008: 233–4) makes clear that when it comes to bolstering US primacy, soft power is even more important than hard power.

In essence, Zakaria claims that soft power helps to legitimize the United States' hegemony. In advancing this argument, he draws upon the rich American IR literature that contends that the USA can defuse other states' fears of its hegemonic power by voluntarily exercising self-restraint and foregoing unilateral actions. As Ikenberry (1998/9: 76–77) puts it, 'American hegemony is reluctant, open, and highly institutionalized – or, in a word, liberal. This is what makes it acceptable to other countries that might otherwise be expected to balance against hegemonic power, and it is also what makes it so stable and expansive'. That is, by exercising its preponderance through multilateral institutions and accepting externally imposed restraints on its power, and practicing foreign policy self-restraint, the USA can demonstrate to others that its hegemony is benign, because it is based on mutual consent, and give and take. (Ikenberry 2002a: 10; Walt 2005).

US policymakers believe that the USA is a benevolent hegemon because its primacy is legitimized by its soft power. As National Security Adviser Sandy Berger argued in a 1999 speech, 'We are accused of dominating others, of seeing the world in zero-sum terms in which any other country's gain must be our loss. But that is an utterly mistaken view. It's not just because we are the first global power in history that is not an imperial power. It's because for 50 years, we have consciously tried to define and pursue our interests in a way that is consistent with the common good – rising prosperity, expanding freedom, collective security' (Berger 1999). More recently, President George W. Bush employed the rhetoric of hegemonic benevolence in his January 2004 State of the Union speech by declaring, 'We have no desire to dominate, no ambitions of empire.'[16] And the Bush administration's 2002 *National Security Strategy of the United States* claimed that the rest of the world will accept US hegemony because rather than using its 'strength to press for unilateral advantage', the USA seeks to 'create a balance of power that favors human freedom: conditions in which all nations and all societies can choose for themselves the rewards and challenges of political and economic liberty' (Bush, 2002: Introduction). Like Berger, Bush simply was echoing his father, President George H.W. Bush, who stated in his January 1992 State of the Union speech, 'A world once divided into two armed camps now recognizes one sole and preeminent superpower: the United States of America. And they regard this with no dread. For the world trusts us with power – and the world is right. They trust us to be fair and restrained; they trust us to be on the side of decency. They trust us to do what's right.'[17] Or so American policymakers, influenced by their belief in soft power, would like to believe.

For foreign policy analysts such as Nye, Walt, Ikenberry and Zakaria, soft power is linked inextricably to multilateral diplomacy. However, the belief that others will view the USA hegemony as legitimate if it acts multilaterally is doubtful. The very hallmarks of international politics – anarchy, self-help and competition – mean that, in the realm of security, unilateralism is always the default option of great powers. As John Mearsheimer (2002: 33) writes: 'States operating in a self-help world almost always act according to their own self-interest and do not subordinate their interests to the interests of other states, or to the interests of the so-called international community. The reason is simple: it pays to be selfish in a self-help world.' Smart policymakers in other states know this and understand the implications with respect to US behaviour.

Prophylactic multilateralism cannot inoculate the USA from counter-hegemonic balancing. The reality of the USA's enormous power cannot be hidden by the veil of multilateralism. Moreover, what the feisty Brooklyn Dodger Manager Leo Durocher said about baseball is also true in international politics: nice guys finish last. The USA did not attain hegemony by being nice, but rather by assertively – and often aggressively – using its power. Although the USA may employ a discourse that professes its regard for others' interests and a commitment to multilateralism, whenever it chooses to do so it can use its power unilaterally to others' detriment. If other states did not understand this before (though many of them did), the March 2003 US invasion of Iraq dispelled any remaining illusions on this point. For much of the world, the invasion shattered one of the important foundations upon which the notion of benevolent US hegemony is based: the perception that the United States is a status quo power. Since the Cold War's end, notes Walt (2005: 23), 'The United States has not acted as a "status quo" power: rather, it has used its position of primacy to increase its influence, to enhance its position vis-a-vis potential rivals, and to deal with specific security threats' (see also Sestanovich 2005).

The claim of soft power proponents that the USA – until the George W. Bush administration – preferred to act multilaterally is myth – not fact. Although that administration was more inept diplomatically than many of its predecessors, the substance of its policy was the same: the USA acts multilaterally when it can (i.e. when others support US policies), and unilaterally when it decides that it must, which is much of the time.[18] Following World War II, the USA created a web of security and economic institutions to solidify its hegemony in the non-Soviet world and promote its grand strategic ambitions. Some scholars – John Ikenberry (2000) is a leading example – depict this as an example of benevolent US soft power, but the USA undertook these policies to advance its hard power – geopolitical – interests. Specifically, it did so to avail itself of its allies' strategic resources (and keep them from drifting into the Soviet sphere). However, the USA never intended that it should itself be constrained by these institutions – and it seldom has been.[19]

All post-1945 US administrations 'have believed that the only way' the USA could attain its most critical grand strategic goals 'was to keep others from having too much influence' on its policies (Sestanovich 2005: 13). In the Suez, Berlin and Cuban missile crises, and during the Vietnam War, the USA acted unilaterally. Similarly, according to Stephen Sestanovich, it also did so during the Euromissile crisis of the early 1980s and during the negotiations on German reunification.[20] And although the US-led NATO interventions in Bosnia in 1995 and Kosovo in 1999 may have appeared to be – and certainly were depicted rhetorically by Washington as – multilateral actions, they were not. As Walt (2005: 46) observes,

'America's European allies complained during both episodes, but could do little to stop the United States from imposing its preferences upon them'. In truth, whenever they felt that US interests required doing so, preceding administrations acted no less unilaterally than did the Bush administration in deciding (foolishly) to invade Iraq in March 2003.[21]

There is no compelling reason to believe that multilateralism legitimizes US hegemony. There is a big gap between the way soft power advocates depict American foreign policy behaviour and the way the USA actually acts. Other states know that the USA (like all dominant great powers) habitually acts unilaterally when it feels that its interests require it to do so. Hence, they are unlikely to be reassured that US hegemonic power is benign. In other words, soft power is not very effective as means of preventing other states from opposing the policies of a hegemonic USA.

The fact that the USA is a liberal democracy is another reason why American scholars and policymakers believe the USA is a benevolent hegemon. John Ikenberry and Charles Kupchan (1990: 52) have argued that the liberal democratic nature of the USA's domestic political system legitimates US hegemony, simultaneously reassures others of its benevolence and attracts other states into the US orbit. These claims, however, rest on dubious reasoning. Certainly, there is a considerable literature purporting to show that the quality of international politics among democracies differs from that between democracies and non-democracies; that is, democracies cooperate with each other, constitute a 'pluralistic security community', accord each other respect and conduct their affairs based on shared values and norms (transparency, give and take, live and let live, compromise and peaceful dispute resolution [Deutsch 1957; Risse-Kappen 1995; Brown *et al.*, 1996]). These ideas comport with the Wilsonian ideology that shapes US foreign policy and which finds expression in the idea of soft power, which is a quintessentially liberal perspective. However, there is powerful evidence that democracies do not behave better toward each other than toward non-democracies.

The mere fact that the USA (allegedly) possesses soft power because it is a democracy does not mean that others will not fear its hegemonic power. There are two key reasons why this is so. First, the term 'democracy' itself is subjective; democracy has many different – contested – meanings (Oren, 1995; Collier and Levitsky 1997). Proponents of the democratic peace theory and liberal approaches theories tend to play fast and loose with the definition of democracy in order to preserve their theories from falsification. Second, theories that posit a special democratic (or liberal) peace are contradicted by the historical record. When important geopolitical interests are at stake, realpolitik – not regime type – determines great power policies (Layne 1994). Contrary to liberal theory, democracies (and liberal states) have threatened to use military force against each other to resolve diplomatic crises and have even gone to the brink of war. Indeed, democracies have not just teetered on the brink; they have gone over it. The most notable example of a war among democracies occurred in 1914 when democratic Britain and France went to war against democratic Germany.[22] Today, the fact that power in the international system is so heavily concentrated in the USA's favour means that whenever it believes its interests are threatened, the USA will act like hegemons typically have acted, notwithstanding that it is a democracy.[23]

When it comes to the purported attractiveness of US soft power, the fact that the USA shares democratic values in common with other states is overrated. Take the US relationship with Europe, for example. As soft power proponents never tire of saying, the USA and NATO Europe constitute a pluralistic security community united by shared values (Deutsch 1957; Risse-Kappen 1995). This relationship should be a strong case for the USA's soft power but it is not. US soft power proponents are worried about the slippage in the USA's popularity in Europe. As Kurt Campbell and Michele A. Flournoy (2007: 20) claim, 'During the Cold War, the United States could count on the goodwill of Western publics when the chips were down, but increasingly, there are serious questions as to whether many in Europe and elsewhere are rooting for to succeed, much less willing to lend us a helping hand.' This is a dubious claim that overlooks a long history of transatlantic discord that includes the 1956 Suez crisis, Vietnam, the Euromissile deployment crisis and serious divisions between the USA and Europe over detente and relations with the Soviet Union.

The course of transatlantic relations in recent years also raises serious empirical doubts about the claims of soft power proponents. For example, during its second term, the Bush administration – with Secretary of State Condoleeza Rice in the lead – tried hard to mend relations with the 'Old Europe' that had been damaged by the March 2003 US invasion of Iraq. Most observers of US foreign policy gave Rice high marks for efforts. Yet, this soft power diplomacy yielded scant results. NATO Europe continued to rebuff American entreaties to commit more forces to the effort in Afghanistan. At the alliance's April 2009 summit even Barak Obama – whom the Europeans regard as the embodiment of the virtues of soft power – was unable to persuade the European members of NATO to significantly increase their commitment to the war in Afghanistan. During both the Bush adminisration's second term and during the Obama administration, the USA and the Old Europe have remained badly divided not only over Afghanistan but also over future NATO expansion, the deployment of missile defences in Poland and the Czech Republic, and policy toward Russia (especially Europe's increasing dependence on Russian energy supplies). So even though the USA has reverted to a soft power strategy with respect to the Old Europe, this has not brought about any noticeable *substantive* improvement in relations between the USA and key European powers such as France and Germany.

The impact of soft power on US relations with the so-called New Europe is also questionable. For example, Nye (2004: 10) claims that the new East Central European members supported the US effort in Iraq (by deploying troops in token numbers) because of American soft power; specifically, the attraction of US democratic values. In fact, however, soft power had little, if anything, to do with the New Europe's (tepid) support for America's Iraq policy. Officials and policy analysts in the region are very candid in expressing the basis of their support: East Central Europe fears the resurgence of Russian power and looks to the US security guarantee represented by NATO as protection.[24] Fear of Russia – not soft power – explains why these states stay on the USA's good side.

Contrary to what its proponents claim, soft power does not transform the USA into a benevolent hegemon. In international politics, benevolent hegemons are like unicorns: they do not exist. This is a point that many in the US foreign policy establishment deny. For example, a recent Center for a New American Security report laments that, 'Gone are the days when the United States was widely viewed as a benign superpower that would use its extraordinary military might and political influence for the greater good' (Campbell and Flournoy 2007: 26). For them, the USA's 'hegemony problem' can be cured by acting multilaterally; revitalizing international institutions and doing good works (for example, spreading democracy, helping poor countries develop economically, combating global environmental and health problems) (Campbell and Flournoy 2007: 34–6). This policy prescription does not, however, address the root cause of the USA's hegemony problem. In today's world, other states dread both the over-concentration of geopolitical weight in the USA's favour, and the purposes for which it may be used. As Paul Sharp (2004: 314) writes, 'No great power has a monopoly on virtue and, although some may have a great deal more virtue than others, virtue imposed on others is not seen as such by them. All great powers are capable of exercising a measure of self-restraint, but they are tempted not to and the choice to practice restraint is made easier by the existence of countervailing power and the possibility of it being exercised.' Contrary to what US scholars and policymakers believe, soft power does not insulate the USA from a counter-hegemonic backlash. Other states understand that Washington's self-proclaimed benevolence is inherently ephemeral, but the hard fist of US power is tangible.

Who has soft power? Challenging America's soft power monopoly

US soft power proponents apparently believe that America's dominance in the realm of soft power parallels its preponderance in the realm of hard power. Indeed, it is difficult not to conclude that they assume that soft power is a unique attribute of the USA's power. Fareed Zakaria is a good example of this outlook. Bolstering his argument that there is a 'strong market' for US soft power, he (2008: 234) approvingly quotes a Singaporean scholar who claims: 'No one in Asia wants to live in a Chinese-dominated world. There is no Chinese dream to which people aspire.' However, another Singaporean, the scholar-diplomat Kishore Mahbubani, makes a very powerful argument to the contrary: in today's world, it is Asia – especially China – that increasingly wields the greatest amount of soft power, not the USA.

Mahbubani (2008: 133–40) contends that Asia's soft power has far more appeal than America's because Asia enjoys more true freedom than the West. Arguing that the West inappropriately defines freedom in absolute rather than relative terms, he defines human freedom as including freedom from want, freedom of security (absence of political instability), freedom to choose one's employment and freedom to think. Using China as an illustration, Mahbubani argues that Asians today are enjoying these freedoms in far greater abundance than ever before in their history.[25] He (2008: 229–34) believes that because of the attractiveness of its model of economic development, China is beating the USA at the soft power game in Asia.

Mahbubani's bottom line is that Asia is a juggernaut. The West can either accommodate a rising Asia or be steamrolled by it. As Mahbubani puts it, 'The time to restructure the world order has come. We should do it now' (Mahbubani, 2008: 235). Here, he offers a powerful counterargument to the widely held belief in US foreign policy circles that the USA is best-placed to use soft power to revamp the international system's governing institutions. As Mahbubani (2008: 235–7) sees it, the impetus for reform will come from a rising China, which will have soft power and legitimacy advantages over the USA. Given what he terms the incompetence of the USA and EU as global leaders, the West should accept the democratization of global governance to accommodate Asia's increased clout in the international system.[26] International institutions – the UN, the IMF and the World Bank – should be revamped to reflect the emerging distribution of power in Asia's favour. 'The West knows,' Mahbubani (2008: 242) claims, 'that the amount of political and economic space it occupies in the world is shrinking. The logical consequence is that the Western domination of several global institutions will have to diminish – not a prospect that many Western countries will relish'. Mahbuhani, however, clearly relishes the West's decline. Global leadership, he (2008: 237–8) says, historically is provided by emerging powers – today, China – and the West had better get used to this transition.

There are two reasons to believe the efficacy of America's soft power is declining. First, the US model of political and economic development is likely to be challenged by alternatives. This is not just the view of those like Mahbubani who welcome Asia's – and China's – rise. In its *Global Trends 2025* report, the National Intelligence Council noted that the superior economic performance of authoritarian governments such as China's might discredit both democracy and economic liberalism (NIC 2008: 8–9, 87). Given the prevailing belief in US foreign policy circles that American values are universal and that the US model of economic and political development has worldwide applicability, the rise of alternative models would undermine the USA's soft power. As the NIC observes:

> The state-centric model in which the state makes the key economic decisions and, in the case of China and increasingly Russia, democracy is restricted, raises questions about the inevitability of the traditional Western recipe – roughly liberal economics and democracy – for development. Over the next 15–20 years, more developing countries may gravitate toward Beijing's state-centric model rather than the traditional Western model of markets and democratic political systems to increase the chances of rapid development and perceived political stability.
>
> (2008: 13–14)

These concerns were percolating even before the current global and financial crisis struck with full-force in fall 2008. The crisis has made these worries about the future of US soft power even more acute. The global financial and economic crisis has discredited one of the pillars of US soft power: American free market capitalism and, more generally, liberalism (economically and institutionally) itself. As former US Deputy Treasury Secretary Roger Altman (2009: 2) puts it, the meltdown has 'put the American model of free market capitalism under a cloud'.

The second reason why US soft power is declining in effectiveness is because Mahbubani is right: the USA is not the only country that posses soft power. China, especially, has become increasingly adept at developing its own soft power based on its culture, diplomacy and the attractiveness of its own system as an alternative to the American model of political and economic development (Kurlantzick 2007).[27] As a 2007 report by the Center for a New America Security noted, 'Rather than seeking to weaken or confront the United States directly, Chinese leaders are pursuing a subtle, multifaceted, long-term grand strategy that aims to derive as many benefits as possible from the existing international system while accumulating the economic wherewithal, military strength, and soft power resources to reinforce China's emerging position as at least a regional great power' (Campbell and Flournoy 2007: 17). Indeed, the Center for a New American Security acknowledges that China – a non-democracy – may have more soft power than the USA and finds that this fact 'is a troubling indictment of our current course' (Campbell and Flournoy 2007: 18).

The fact that China weathered the economic storm far better than the USA, has positioned it to expand its role in the developing world (Altman 2009: 12). Even before the meltdown, China was taking advantage of America's preoccupation with the War on Terror to project its soft power into East and Southeast Asia.[28] China also is making inroads in Latin America, Africa and Central Asia by providing aid and development assistance and through weapons sales.[29] Similarly, China is using its financial clout to buy up huge quantities of raw materials and natural resources worldwide, and thereby bringing states into its political orbit. Finally, China's willingness to extend economic assistance to other states without interfering in their internal political arrangements is beginning to affect change in prevailing international norms.[30]

US soft power and multilateral institutions

Many in the US foreign policy establishment believe that international institutions are a critical transmission belt for the exercise of the USA's soft power. Unsurprisingly, there is widespread agreement that the USA should take the lead in revamping and updating the international institutional structures it created after World War II. As Kurt Campbell and Michele Flournoy argue, 'It is in the best interests of both the United States and the world community to have more effective international institutions to deal with problems that can only be addressed through collective action' (Campbell and Flournoy, 2007: 34). Scholars and foreign policy analysts like Stephen G. Brooks and William C. Wohlforth, and Fareed Zakaria, believe that international institutions can help perpetuate American dominance (Brooks and Wohlforth 2008; Zakaria 2008). By strengthening international institutions, they say, the USA can 'lock-in' the hegemonic order that it built after World War II and thereby ensure that it persists after unipolarity ends.[31] Brooks and Wohlforth also maintain that unipolarity affords the USA a 20-year window of opportunity to recast the international system in ways that will bolster the legitimacy of American power and advance US security interests (Brooks and Wohlforth 2008). Ironically, however, it is in the very arena of international institutions where a truly post-American world may be taking shape, and the erosion of US soft power is first being felt.

Although there is a consensus that international institutions need to be overhauled, pressures for reform are pushing in the opposite direction than the one prescribed by Brooks and Wohlforth, because the impetus for change is coming from China and the other emerging powers. This became evident during the run-up to the April 2009 London meeting of the G20 when China and other rising powers argued both that international institutions need to be revamped to give them more of a voice, and also that the international privileges heretofore enjoyed by the USA and Europe need to be rolled-back. These developments highlight a weakness in the institutional 'lock-in' and '20 years' opportunity' arguments: if they perceive that the USA is declining, the incentive for rising powers such as China is to wait a decade or two and reshape the international system themselves. This illustrates a very important point about soft power: it potency is closely tied to hard power. Moreover, because of the perception that its hard power is declining, and the hit its soft power has taken because of the meltdown, there is a real question about whether the USA retains the credibility and legitimacy to take the lead in institutional reform. As *Financial Times* columnist Martin Wolf says, 'The ability of the west in general and the U.S. in particular to influence the course of events will also be damaged. The collapse of the western financial system, while China's flourishes, marks a humiliating end to the "unipolar moment". As western policy makers struggle, their credibility lies broken. Who still trusts the teachers?'[32] For the USA, in other words, declining hard power goes hand-in-hand with declining soft power.

'New and Improved': From Soft Power 1.0 to Smart Power (or Soft Power 2.0)

Following the tried and true path of American marketing mavens, the creators of the original soft power have introduced a (purportedly) new and improved version: 'smart power'. Smart power marries hard and soft power (hard power plus soft power = smart power).[33] Thus smart power is:

> [A]n approach that underscores the necessity of a strong military, but also invests heavily in alliances, partnerships, and institutions at all levels to expand American influence and establish the legitimacy of American actic Providing for the global good is central to this effort because it helps Amer

reconcile its overwhelming power with the rest of the world's interests and values.

(Armitage and Nye 2007: 7)

Smart power is viewed by the US foreign policy establishment as means of enabling the United States to prevail in the contest with Islamic fundamentalism. As such it involves policies that are not much different from those of the Bush administration's agenda of nation-building, democratization and development.

According to policymakers and analysts, basing US strategy on smart power is not altruistic. Rather, they contend, it is a matter of enhancing US security because when people in other countries lack economic opportunity or are denied avenues for political participation, the result is failed states that cause instability and conflict – and become safe havens for Islamic fundamentalist terror groups like al-Qaeda (Campbell and Flournoy 2007: 35). US policymakers increasingly recognize that military force alone is insufficient to enable the USA to prevail in conflicts such as Iraq, Afghanistan and Pakistan. Thus, as Secretary of Defense Robert M. Gates (2008) has said, US efforts must also address 'economic development, institution building, the rule of law, promoting internal reconciliation, good or at least decent governance [and] public services ...'. Reduced to its fundamentals, smart power is about promoting democracy and good governance, and economic development in the expectation that by doing so the USA can remove the grievances that fuel terrorism and the kind of instability that causes states to fail.[34]

Labeling a policy as 'smart' power does not necessarily make it so. It is evident that US policymakers have failed to learn some important lessons about the limits of the USA's power. When it comes to spreading democracy and good governance, and promoting economic development, there is considerable evidence that the USA lacks the capacity to achieve these objectives. With respect to democracy promotion, as former national security adviser Brent Scowcroft correctly has observed: 'The reason I part with the neocons is that I don't think in any reasonable time frame the objective of democratizing the Middle East can be successful. If you can do it, fine, but I don't think you can, and in the process of trying to do it you can make the Middle East a lot worse.'[35]

Democracy and nation-building are hard tasks, and Washington's track record is not encouraging. Since the Cold War's end, the USA – without any notable success – has engaged in democracy promotion and nation-building in Panama, Somalia, Haiti, Bosnia, Kosovo, Iraq and Afghanistan. US efforts to assist post-Soviet Russia's democratization – a key American aim since the Cold War's end – also have been disappointing. The lesson to be learned from these efforts is that the barriers to transplanting democracy successfully on foreign soil are formidable, which comes as no surprise to those scholars – 'transitologists' – who study democratic transitions.

The USA, of course, did succeed in imposing democracy on Germany and Japan after World War II. These two cases, however, are singular exceptions to the general rule that democratic transitions imposed by an outside power's military occupation invariably fail. Unique circumstances enabled the USA to attain its goal of transforming Germany and Japan politically – circumstances that do not exist in Iraq, Afghanistan or the Middle East generally. Among transitologists there is widespread agreement about the factors that conduce to successful democratic transitions: a modern market-based economy; absence of hostility between ethnic or religious groups; a political culture that is hospitable to democracy; and a vibrant civil society. Another important factor is the capacity of state institutions to perform their tasks effectively. When these metrics are employed, it is obvious that countries such as Iraq and Afghanistan (and Pakistan) are poor candidates for democracy transplants.

The US strategy of trying to bring democracy – or at least good governance – to places like Iraq and Afghanistan has also run up against both the law of unintended consequences, and the old adage that one should be careful for what one wishes. Rather than advancing US interests, the Bush administration's Middle Eastern regime change and democratization strategy backfired by making things worse – not better – in the region. The Obama administration's strategy in Afghanistan is likely to do the same. Here, the consequences of the USA's post-9/11 policy are consistent with the historical pattern of US attempts to foster regime change abroad – a pattern that long predates Iraq. Analysing the history of such American efforts, Stephen Kinzer (2006: 6) observes that 'it is clear that most of these operations actually weakened American security. They cast whole regions of the world into upheaval, creating whirlpools of instability from which undreamed-of threats arose years later'.

This comes as no surprise to those who study the process of democratization, which often results in the creation of *ill* liberal democracies. Notwithstanding their 'democratic' credentials, such regimes usually are unstable and prone to adopt ultra-nationalist and bellicose external policies. As Edward D. Mansfield and Jack Snyder (2005/06: 39) have pointed out, 'Pushing countries too soon into competitive electoral politics not only risks stoking war, sectarianism and terrorism, but it also makes the future consolidation of democracy more difficult'. Far from promoting peace in the Middle East, the US policy of 'unleashing Islamic mass opinion through sudden democratization might raise the likelihood of war' (Mansfield and Snyder 2005/06: 41). Moreover, in a volatile region like the Middle East, it is anything but a sure bet that newly democratic regimes would align themselves with the USA. And, if new democracies in the region should fail to satisfy the political and economic aspirations of their citizens – precisely the kind of failure to which new democracies are prone – they easily could become even dangerous breeding grounds for terrorism than are the authoritarian, or autocratic/theocratic regimes now in power in the Middle East.

As Katarina Delacoura (2005: 975) points out, far from bringing peace, stability and true democracy to the region, 'democratization in the Arab world may have a number of outcomes unpalatable for the US'. The electoral victory of the radical Hamas organization in the February 2006 Palestinian elections – coupled with the strong showing of the fundamentalist Islamic Brotherhood in Egypt's 2005 parliamentary elections – prove the point. Indeed, the Bush administration was so upset with the victory of Hamas, that it reportedly discussed with Israel a policy to destabilize the Palestinian Authority in order to force Hamas out of power.[36] Similarly, neither the Bush administration nor its successors can be pleased with geopolitical results of the democratization effort in Iraq. By empowering Iraq's Shiite majority – and, more important, Shia elites with close and long-standing ties to Tehran – the perverse effect of American policy has been to greatly enhance Iranian power in the region.

When it comes to development, smart power is just as flawed a concept as it is with respect to democracy promotion. As the noted developmental economist William Easterly (2007: 331) has observed, external attempts to develop other nations' economies invariably fail because experts really don't know what it takes for outsiders to 'cause' development in other countries. With respect to development, so-called smart power is nothing more than old wine in a new bottle. It traces its provenance back to the 'Charles River' school of modernization theory that was influential during the 1950s and early 1960s. Although ostensibly a response to the Cold War communist challenge – especially in the underdeveloped Third World – the Charles River school was firmly rooted in the USA's own distinctive national identity, its ideology and its sense of national purpose.

Modernization theory conceived of economic development as a means of extending America's vision of economic political and global liberalism. By exporting this vision to areas of the world potentially vulnerable to the communist model of development it was argued, the USA would be able to defeat communism and bolster its own security. Modernization theory posited that economic growth and political reform were linked; development would lead to democratization. Resting on the foundations of a purportedly objective, rational social science, modernization theory held that there was a single model of development – based on America's own experience – that was applicable to all nations. Modernization theory, in other words, employed a 'one size fits all' world view that 'folded a world of diversity and complexity into a common, simple schema' (Latham 2003: 13). The Charles River School 'wanted to direct the process of development in other nations by proposing that those nations follow the mythic American example. The modernization theorists believed they were doing the world a favor by aiding "them" to become more like "us"' (Gilman 2003: 15). In Vietnam, the USA sought – with disastrous consequences – to test its approach to nation-building by deploying modernization theory as an antidote to revolutionary, anti-colonial warfare (Hatcher 1990).

One would have thought that Vietnam discredited the USA's pursuit of nation building – and the reputation of modernization theory – forever. Clearly, this is not the case. The overlap between modernization theory and smart power are striking. They share similar assumptions, rhetoric and objectives. There is a simple explanation of why nation building remains at the centre of the US foreign policy agenda. As Michael Adas (2006: 409) notes, the 9/11 attacks led to the 'restoration of the mix of nation-building projects and violent interventions that had been widely deemed discredited since the humiliating retreat from Vietnam'. The so-called War on Terror (repealed by the Obama administration in name, but not in fact) has been invested with the same stark ideological dimensions as was the Cold War. Just as during the Cold War, the 'backwardness' of the Third World was seen by US policymakers as a breeding ground for communism and revolutionary nationalism, so today failed states and the 'backward' Islamic regions of the Middle East, and Central and South Asia are seen as incubators for Islamic extremists. Here, however, smart power is just as likely to lead to foreign policy disaster for the USA in Iraq, Afghanistan and Pakistan as did its Charles River Cold War version in Vietnam.

Conclusion

Since Joseph Nye first coined the term in 1990, soft power has become a widely used idea in discussions of American foreign policy. As a concept, soft power is beguiling but as a theoretical construct it is not robust. Indeed, on close examination, soft power is just a pithy term for multilateralism, institutionalism, the democratic peace theory and the role of norms in international politics. In other words, it is liberal internationalism. Although 'soft power' has had an impact on the discourse of American foreign policy, it does not offer any independent contribution to understanding either international politics or America's external policy.

Soft power is a weak reed upon which to base US foreign policy. Soft power focuses on changing the atmospherics of American diplomacy through better marketing, public diplomacy, and being nice to others. A good example is President Obama's June 2009 Cairo speech, which was designed to improve the US image in the Islamic world. By all accounts, the address was successful in this regard. Yet, as the most perceptive observers noted, this display of soft power would do little to improve US relations with the Islamic world, especially in the Middle East.

To do that, the USA will need to adopt policies – especially with respect to the Israel/Palestinian issue – that comport with the national interests of the key Islamic states in the region. As the editorial reaction of one newspaper in the region said, 'To win our hearts, you must win our minds first, and our minds are set on the protection of our interests.'[37] What is true in the Middle East is true of other regions of the world as well. As already noted, the soft power approach of Secretary of State Condoleeza Rice (during the Bush administration's second term) and of the Obama administration has failed to bridge the gap in national interests between the USA and its key European allies on issues such as Afghanistan, Russia, NATO expansion and missile defences. International politics is not a popularity contest. Contrary to what soft power proponents believe, sprucing up the USA's attractiveness and its image will not win the USA either more allies, or more acquiescence to American policies. States act on the basis of their interests and America's alleged soft power has little or no effect on their foreign policy decisions.[38] Other states will follow the USA's lead only because of self-interest, or because the USA is able successfully to coerce or induce them to do so.

Nye's original definition of soft power focused on the attractive power of a state's culture and values, and explicitly stated that soft power excludes both coercion and inducement. It is clear, however, that soft power has never existed in this pristine form. During the heyday of the USA's post-World War II hegemony, US dominance in international politics rested firmly on the foundation of the USA's hard power. The willingness of other states to acquiesce in US hegemony was not a function of 'legitimacy' but a consequence of the USA's preponderance. Legitimacy is simply a discourse term that hegemons use to rationalize their privileged position in the international system, and that others use when they lack the hard power to actually constrain a hegemon's policies.[39]

There is always a paradox to hegemony: it both entices and repels. Other states fear the threat that is inherent in a hegemon's hard power. However, a hegemon can entice other states into its orbit (or, minimally, cause them to refrain from counter-hegemonic balancing) by providing military and economic public goods that benefit confer system-wide benefits. Militarily, the hegemon is responsible for stabilizing key regions and for guarding the global commons (Posen 2003). Economically, the hegemon provides public goods by opening its domestic market to other states, supplying liquidity for the global economy and providing a reserve currency (Kindleberger, 1973; Gilpin 1975, 1981). Other states are always calculating whether the threat of over-concentrated power is outweighed by the benefit of consuming the public goods that the hegemon provides. This is why, as many analysts understand – both soft power proponents (including Nye) and sceptics – there is a close correlation between a state's hard power and its soft power.

Whether the USA will be able to continue to act as a hegemon by providing these collective goods is an open question. Militarily, the burgeoning fiscal crisis may compel it to retrench strategically in coming years. Economically, it already is doubtful that the USA is still a hegemon. Indeed, at the April 2009 G20 meeting in London, President Barack Obama acknowledged the USA no longer is able to play this role, and the world increasingly is looking to China (and India and other emerging market states) to be the locomotives of global recovery.[40] Additionally, the USA's liberal preferences have suffered a set back. Institutions have failed to produce a coordinated response to the financial and economic crisis: through the actions of national governments, the state has been brought back in to economic policy, and states have responded to the crisis by adopting nationalistic policies rather than through international cooperation.[41]

The future of US soft power is problematic precisely because America's hard power is declining. As a result, there is mounting evidence that other states are beginning to ponder the creation of new international institutions and policies that will supplant the post-1945 international order that the USA created. Even before the current financial and economic meltdown, the dramatic ongoing shift in the distribution of global economic – and ultimately geopolitical – power from the Euro-Atlantic world to Asia was prompting calls that international institutions be reformed to reflect the diminished clout of the 'West' – especially of the USA.[42]

Although it still is early days, steps in this direction already are being taken. For example, China has become increasingly vocal in suggesting that there is a need to rethink the role of the dollar as the international economic system's reserve currency.[43] The emergence of the G20 and its displacement of the G8 at the April London economic summit, and China's new weight in the IMF, underscore that China and India, and other emerging economies are gaining muscle in international institutions at the expense of the USA (and Europe). Moreover, China and Russia are in the vanguard of creating new institutions as alternatives in to the structures the USA erected after World War II. In the area of security, these include the Shanghai Cooperation Organization and the Moscow-sponsored Collective Security Treaty Organization. In the realm of economics, this includes not only the G20 but also the June 2009 meeting of the so-called BRIC (Brazil, Russia, India and China) states in Yekaterinburg, Russia, the purpose of which was, as Russian President Demitri Medvedev said, 'to create the conditions for a more just world order' and to 'build an increasingly multipolar world order'.[44] It would seem that the foundations of the America-dominated international order are beginning to crack. The cracks will grow wider as the waning of US power begins to accelerate over the next decade or two. Simply put, the (already-visible) decline of US hard power will spur a concomitant slippage in its 'soft power.'

Soft power is nothing more than a catchy term for the bundle of liberal internationalist policies that have driven US foreign policy since World War II, and which are rooted in the Wilsonian tradition. Beyond the fact that soft power is not efficacious in terms of producing outcomes, its affect on American foreign policy is pernicious. Soft power is just a polite way of describing the ideological expansionism inherent in US liberal internationalism. That expansionism led to disasters like Vietnam and Iraq, and is pushing the USA headlong into another quagmire in Afghanistan. Dressing up liberal internationalism as 'smart power' does not make it wise or intelligent. Whatever it is called, it is causing the USA to become imperially overstretched and accelerating the decline of American power. The diminution of US power, and the rise of new great powers such as China will lead inexorably to a restructuring of the international order. Adjusting to a changing international environment will not be easy for a state like the USA, which has been accustomed to being on top of the hard power league tables for a long time, and which also believes its values are universal.[45] If the USA is to have any chance to reorient its foreign policy and grand strategy it will need to abandon both the illusions of soft power and the myths of liberalism which underpin them. Rather, the USA will need to practice prudence and restraint to conserve its hard power resources, and to find ways of using its diminished hard power more effectively in a multipolar world that will no longer be dominated by America's power, ideals, or the institutions it built after World War II. This is a major challenge and it remains to be seen whether the USA can adapt to the shifting balance of world forces.

Notes

1 As Campbell and Flournoy (2007: 17–18) argue, 'The emphasis on American exceptionalism in recent years has engendered an attitude that the United States should not be expected to abide by various international conventions, treaties, or legal structures, even though our nation played a critical role in negotiating them.' They also point to the George W. Bush administration's violation of international law with respect to torture and conclude that, 'These blatant departures from the rule of law have tarnished the image of the United States as a leading supporter of international human rights and legal norms.'

2 For example, see Campbell and Flournoy (2007); Armitage and Nye (2007).

3 Quoted in Helene Cooper, 'Obama Will Face a Defiant World on Foreign Visit', *New York Times*, 29 March 2009, p. A1.

4 Statement of Senator Hillary Rodham Clinton, Nominee for Secretary of State, Senate Foreign Relations Committee, 13 January 2009, pp. 2–3.

5 The most celebrated declinist argument was Paul Kennedy's (1987) *The Rise and Fall of the Great Powers*, which made the case that 'imperial overstretch' was undermining the economic foundations of US power and, hence, would result ultimately in America's loss of its geopolitical dominance. In addition to Kennedy, a number of other scholars made similar claims, including: David Calleo (1982, 1987), James Chace (1981), Robert Gilpin (1981, 1986) and Samuel P. Huntington (1987).

6 Nye (2004: 5) adds an important qualifier when he says, 'sometimes you can get the outcomes you want without *tangible* threats or payoffs' (emphasis added). As discussed below, carrots and sticks may not always be tangible or apparent but can, nonetheless, influence other states' behavior.

7 For a similar argument that soft power is about a state's 'brand,' see Kurlantzick (2007).

8 For example, see Hunt (1987); Layne (2006a); McDougall (1997); and Williams (1961).

9 For a discussion of liberalism's hostility to the state as an autonomous actor, see Evans *et al.* (1985). Some liberals extend the argument further, and regard the state as the generator of both international and domestic violence. Hence, the solution to violence, at home and abroad, is political decentralization and democratization (Rummel 1997).

10 In Mann's (1984: 210) words: 'The state is not merely a locus of class struggle, an instrument of class rule, the factor of social cohesion, the expression of core values, the centre of social allocation processes, the institutionalization of military force ... it is a different socio-spatial organization. As a consequence we can treat states as *actors*, in the person of state elites, with a will to power and we can engage in [a] "rational action" theory of state interests. ...'

11 As Eric Nordlinger (1981: 1) said of democracies: 'The preferences of the state are at least as important as those of civil society in accounting for what the democratic state does and does not do; the democratic state is not only frequently autonomous insofar as it regularly acts upon its preferences, but also markedly autonomous in doing so even when its preferences diverge from the demands of the most powerful groups in civil society.'

12 These points are developed in Gowa (1995).

13 On this point, see Theodore Lowi (1967). Lowi argues that democracies make better foreign policies during crises because decisionmaking tends to be tightly concentrated, and the influence of interest groups, and social forces, is reduced correspondingly.

14 For discussion of why – at least in the short-term – neorealists were wrong in their predictions that other states would balance against the USA and push the distribution of power from unipolarity to multipolarity, see Layne (2006b).

15 'Unipolar stability' realists advance a different explanation for the success of the USA's hegemonic grand strategy. They claim both that the present unipolar distribution of capabilities in America's favour is so overwhelming as to be insurmountable, and also that other states will not balance against the USA because they receive important security and economic benefits from American hegemony (Wohlforth 1997, 2002; Brooks and Wohlforth 2002, 2008)

16 'President's State of the Union Message to Congress and the Nation,' *New York Times*, 21 January 2004.

17 'State of the Union: Transcript of President Bush's Address on the State of the Union,' *New York Times*, 29 January 1992.

18 A related charge against the George W. Bush administration is that it blundered when, immediately after 9/11, President Bush told the rest of the world that it had but two choices: they could either support the USA unquestioningly, or oppose it and incur its wrath. Blunder or not, the administration hardly was the first to engage in such bullying tactics. During the height of the Cold War, for example, Secretary of State John Foster Dulles argued that it was 'immoral' for the non-aligned bloc to remain neutral in the contest between the USA and the Soviet Union.

19 Anyone who has delved into the primary sources of American post-World War II diplomacy knows that when US diplomats speak of 'consulting' with allies, what they really mean is that Washington will inform them of the policies it already has decided to pursue. Even during the 1950s – the supposed high-water mark of US multilateralism – key American policymakers made no secret of their unilateralist preferences. Belying NATO's mythical image as the institutional acme of multilateralism, US unilateralism was very much on display in relations with Western European states. When consulting the Western Europeans, Secretary of State Dean Acheson said, the trick was to find a way to communicate with them 'without limiting US freedom of action unduly' (Acheson to Bruce, 19 September 1952, *FRUS 1952–54*, V:325). Similarly, Secretary of State John Foster Dulles told West German Chancellor Konrad Adenauer that Washington could not commit to a prior consultation formula that would tie its hands (Dulles to Adenauer, 29 November 1957, *FRUS 1955–57*, IV:212). As Dulles told the National Security Council: 'It was harder for the United States than for other NATO nations to agree to full consultation on all policy matters, because of the world-wide commitments and interests of the United States. ... We do not want to be in a position where we are unable to act promptly if necessary for the reason that we are obliged to consult with the NATO Council before taking action' (Memorandum of Discussion, 348th Meeting of NSC, 12 December 1957, *FRUS 1955–57*, IV:216).

20 As Sestanovich says of the George H.W. Bush administration's 'consultation' of US allies during the negotiations on German reunification: 'From the president on down, it usually amounted to respectful listening, followed by actions that paid little or no attention to what other governments said' (Sestanovich 2005: 17).

21 The important objection to the Bush administration's Iraq policy is not that it was unilateral, but that it was unwise (and would have been just as unwise even if pursued 'multilaterally').

22 For the argument that 1914 in the West was a war among democracies, see Layne (2001). For a supporting argument, see Oren (1995).

23 Of course, the fact that the USA purportedly is a democratic hegemon does nothing to cause non-democratic states (either second-tier major powers, or lesser-ranking regional powers) to regard US primacy as benevolent. By definition, the soft power that accrues to the USA by virtue of the fact that it is a democracy cannot affect non-democratic states because public attitudes toward the USA will not affect policy in non-democratic states. Indeed, far from finding US soft power attractive, because the USA seeks to export its domestic institutions and values abroad – often by pursuing regime change – and categorizes other states as 'threats' because of their domestic political systems and ideologies, it is perceived by such states as a danger to them. Given that states and regimes want to survive, it is unsurprising that states perceiving a US threat to their interests and to regime survival seek to defend themselves – often

by adopting asymmetric strategies, including acquiring weapons of mass destruction, and supporting terrorism.

24 During a December 2008 trip to Bucharest, senior Romanian national security officials made this clear to me. They also said that Romania, and the other East Central European states, also look to the USA as a counterweight against France and Germany.

25 Although for the West the 'idea that freedom can be relative and can indeed take many forms is alien', for Asians 'if they compare their lives today with their lives a few decades ago – they have achieved much greater freedom' (Mahbubani 2008: 134).

26 Mahbubani (2008: 114) argues that the 'role and purpose' of the major multilateral international institutions 'has been distorted by the Western powers'. For his critique of Western competence in managing the international system, see Chapter 5.

27 As Armitage and Nye (2007: 25) observe, 'With Washington preoccupied in the Middle East, China has deftly stepped into the vacuum left by the United States, primarily to pursue its own economic interests, but possibly also to pursue its long-term strategic goals of becoming a global power rather than simply a regional one. China has taken a two-pronged approach, strengthening its hard power resources while simultaneously expanding its soft power influence. The most visible example of China's growing soft power is Beijing' embrace of, and at times leadership in, multilateral organizations where the US role has diminished or is absent altogether, particularly in China's own backyard.'

28 See Guy Dinmore, Anna Fifield and Victor Mallet, 'The Rivals: Washington's Sway in Asia is Challenged by China', *Financial Times*, 18 March 2005, p. 11; Jane Perlez, 'Across Asia, Beijing's Star is in Ascendance', *New York Times*, 28 August 2004.

29 See Isabel Gort and Jamil Anderlini, 'China Puts Up $10bn for Central Asia Loans', *Financial Times*, 17 June 2009, p. 5; Simon Romero and Alexei Barrionuevo, 'Deals Help China Expand Sway in Latin America', *New York Times*, 16 April 2009, p. A1; 'Friends of Opportunity', *Economist*, Volume 389, Issue 8608, 29 November 2008, pp. 41–2; Tom Burgis, 'Beijing to Boost Spending in Africa Fund', *Financial Times*, 17 March 2009, World News, p. 8; William McNamara, 'China Eyes Developed Mines Assets', *Financial Times*, 6 January 2009.

30 As C. Fred Bergsten, Charles Freeman, Nicholas Lardy and Derek Mitchell point out, 'China's growing influence on accepted international norms and principles need not be explicit to have an impact. To date, the Chinese development model has gained currency simply because of China's apparent success, and the attractiveness of China's hands-off standards-free policy to authoritarian leaders and even some populations tired of perceived heavy-handedness and condescension form Western aid donors' (Bergston *et al.* 2008: 225).

31 See Ikenberry (2000) and Keohane (1984).

32 Wolf, 'Seeds of Its Own Destruction', *Financial Times*, 8 March 2008.

33 'Smart power is the combination of hard and soft power', Joseph S. Nye, Jr in 'The U.S. Can Reclaim "Smart Power"', *Los Angeles Times*, 21 January 2009.

34 With respect to democracy, smart power holds that the practical aspects of democracy require a more patient, bottom-up approach' to transplanting democracy than Bush's grand vision of democratizing the Middle East (Campbell and Flournoy 2007: 36). This bottom up approach – which is woven into General David Petraeus' new approach to counter-insurgency – runs counter to what social scientists know about state-building. States, and political systems, are built from the top down, not the bottom up. With respect to development, 'It is difficult to dismiss the counter terrorism rationale for development aid out of hand. As we bring hope to others that they can, by their efforts,

improve the quality of their families' lives, they are likely to invest more in their future and be less prone to violence and extremism. In the short term, development also helps to counter the terrorist recruitment narrative that depends on a United States that is weak-willed, but on an American that is hard-hearted. Today's central question is not simply whether we are capturing or killing more terrorists than are being recruited and trained, but whether we are providing more opportunities than our enemies can destroy and where we are addressing more more grievances than they can record' (Armitage and Nye 2007: 40). As Secretary Gates (2009: 29) puts it, 'Where possible, what the military calls kinetic operations should be subordinated to measures aimed at promoting better governance, economic programs that spur development, and efforts to address the grievances among the discontented from among whom the terrorists recruit. It will take the patient accumulation of quiet successes over a long time to discredit and defeat extremist movements and their ideologies.' Taking the long view, smart power proponents argue that, 'The most sustainable rational for global development over time is this: American leaders ought to commit to global development because it reinforces basic American values, contributes to peace, justice, and prosperity, and improves the way we are viewed around the world. Investing in development contributes to American security at home by promoting stability abroad' (Armitage and Nye 2007: 41).

35 Quoted in Jeffrey Goldberg, 'Breaking Ranks', *The New Yorker*, 31 October 2005.

36 Steven Erlanger, 'U.S. and Israelis Are Said to Talk of Hamas Ouster', *New York Times*, 14 February 2006.

37 Quoted in 'Let's be Friends,' *The Economist*, 6 June 2009, p. 44. As the *Financial Times'* chief Middle Eastern correspondent noted, notwithstanding President Obama's eloquence, the Cairo speech 'also poses risks for the US president. For while his words masterfully addressed the conflicting pressures the US faces in the region, he will soon discover that translating them into coherent policies is far more challenging if not impossible' (Roula Kalaf, 'US President Cracks the Code to Win over Islam', *Financial Times*, 5 June 2009.

38 As Leslie Gelb (2009: 219) puts it, 'soft power is foreplay, not the real thing.' As he notes, soft power proponents 'overlook the fact that ... good acts alone will rarely cause leaders to alter their assessments of their own national interests or do what they don't want to do, which is what power is all about.'

39 Whether international legitimacy matters, and, if so, how much – and how much legitimacy considerations constrain the USA – are contested issues. For the argument that hegemony is an attribute accorded by other states to the dominant power – that is, hegemony is a based on legitimacy, not hard power – see Clark (2005). As Brooks and Wohlforth (2008: 172) point out, however, legitimacy is only a weak constraint on US policy, because, in part, hegemons – precisely because of their hard power – are able to define international norms and institutional rules. Thus, 'power can help build, maintain, and mold legitimacy'.

40 As President Barack Obama said, 'If there is going to be renewed growth it can't just be the United States as the engine, everybody is going to have to pick up the pace.' He also observed that 'in some ways the world has become accustomed to the United States being a voracious consumer market and the engine that drives a lot of economic growth worldwide. And I think that in the wake of this crisis, even as we're doing stimulus, we have to take into account our own deficits' (quoted in David E. Sanger and Mark Landler, 'In Europe, Obama Faces Calls for Rules on Finances', *New York Times*, 1 April 2009).

41 In particular, recent developments in the European Union suggest that global meltdown has dealt liberalism a blow. The EU's key members (Britain, France and Germany) are seeking economic security by adopting self-help policies rather than putting multilateral cooperation first. This is a reminder that we still live in a world of nation states, and that even in economics nationalism is the default option. Or, as German Chancellor Angela Merkel recently put it, 'International policy is, for all the friendship and commonality, always also about representing the interests of one's own country' (quoted in Nicholas Kulish and Judy Dempsey, 'Merkel Is Set to Greet, and Then Resist, Obama', *New York Times*, 29 March 2009). Recent examples of European states putting self-interest ahead of cooperation include the French government requiring Puegot and Renault to invest in their factories in France – not elsewhere in Europe – in exchange for government loans; European governments – especially Britain – pressuring banks to repatriate capital from overseas subsidiaries in other EU member states; German reluctance to raise taxes or resort to deficit spending to stimulate the rest of Europe; and Germany and France blocking a proposed EU rescue of financially stricken East Central European states and passing the buck for doing so to the IMF. Even in Europe – where war is said to be 'unthinkable' and liberalism is supposedly entrenched – some observers worry openly that the Continent could revert to the dark days of the late 1920s and 1930s. See Gideon Rachman, 'Euroscepticism is Yesterday's Creed', *Financial Times*, 2 March 2009; William Drozdiak, 'In Europe, Breaking Up Is So Easy to Do', *Washington Post*, 1 March 2009; and Philip Stephens, 'Wanted: Leaders to Face the Demons of Europe's Past', *Financial Times*, 19 February 2009. For a historian's argument that Europe is always just a step away from backsliding to war, political extremism, and ethnic violence, see Mark Mazower, *Dark Continent: Europe's Twentieth Century* (New York: Knopf, 1997).

42 'The time to restructure the world order has come,' Kishore Mahbubani (2008: 235) has written, 'We should do it now.' Given what he terms the 'incompetence' of the USA and European Union as global leaders, the West should start by democratizing global governance to accommodate Asia's increased clout (2008: 235–7). International institutions – the United Nations, the International Monetary Fund and the World Bank – should be revamped to reflect the emerging distribution of power in Asia's favor. 'The West knows,' Mahbubani (2008: 242) claims, 'that the amount of political and economic space it occupies in the worked is shrinking. The logical consequence is that the Western domination of several global institutions will have to diminish – not a prospect that many Western countries will relish.'

43 David Barboza, 'China Urges New Money Reserve to Replace The Dollar', *New York Times*, 23 March 2009; Jamil Anderlini, 'China Wants to Oust Dollar as International Reserve Currency', *Financial Times*, 24 March 2009; and Andrew Batson, 'China Takes Aim at Dollar', *Wall Street Journal*, 24 March 2009. China's proposals are attributable partly to its fear that value of its huge dollar holdings will be eroded by the USA's bleak long-term fiscal prospects. Michael Wines, Keith Bradsher and Mark Landler, 'China's Leader Says He Is "Worried" over U.S. Treasuries', *New York Times*, 13 March 2009.

44 'Not Just Straw Men', *The Economist*, 20 June 2009, pp. 63–5; Andrew E. Kramer, 'Emerging Economies Meet in Russia', *New York Times*, 17 June 2009; Isabel Gorst, 'Emerging Powers Want Fair Global Economic Order', *Financial Times*, 17 June 2009; Michael Hudson, 'Washington Is Unable to Call All the Shots', *Financial Times*, 15 June 2009.

45 The belief that American values are universal is intrinsic to soft power. As Nye asserts (2004: 11), 'When a country's culture includes universal and its policies promote

values and interests that others share, it increases the probability of obtaining its desired outcomes because of the relationships of attraction and duty it creates.'

Bibliography

Adas, M. (2006) *Dominance By Design: Technological Imperatives and America's Civilizing Mission.* Cambridge, Mass.:Belknap.

Allison, G. (1971) *The Essence of Decision: Explaining the Cuban Missile Crisis*, Boston, MA: Little, Brown.

Altman, R. (2009) 'The Great Credit Crash, 2008: A Geopolitical Setback for the West,' *Foreign Affairs*, 88:1: 2–14.

Armitage, R.L. and Nye, Jr, J.S. (2007) *CSIS Commission on Smart Power: A Smarter, More Secure America*, Washington, DC: Center for Strategic and International Studies.

Aslund, A. (1989) *Gorbachev's Struggle for Economic Reform*, Ithaca, N.Y.:Cornell University Press.

Bialer, S. (1986) *The Soviet Paradox: External Expansion, Internal Decline*, New York: Columbia University Press.

Berger, S. (1999) 'American Power: Hegemony, Isolationism or Engagement,' Council on Foreign Relations, 21 October 1999. Available at: http://www.cfr.org/publication/3600/american_power/html. Accessed 12 January 2010.

Berghahn, V.R. (2001) *America and the Intellectual Cold Wars in Europe*, Princeton, NJ: Princeton University Press.

Bergston, C.F., Freeman, C., Lardy, N. and Mitchell, D. (2008) *China's Rise: Challenges and Opportunities*, Washington, DC: Brookings Institution.

Brooks, S.G. and Wohlforth, W.C. (2002) 'American Primacy in Perspective,' *Foreign Affairs*, 81(4): 20–33.

—— (2008) *World Out of Balance: International Relations and the Challenge of American Primacy*, Princeton, NJ: Princeton University Press.

Brown, M.E., Lynn-Jones, S.M. and Miller, S.E. (eds) (1996) *Debating the Democratic Peace*, Cambridge, MA: MIT Press.

Bush, G.W. (2002) 'Introduction', *National Security Strategy of the United States of America*, Washington, DC: White House.

Calleo, D. (1987) *Beyond American Hegemony*: The Future of the Western Alliance, New York: Basic Books.

—— (1982) *The Imperious Economy*, Cambridge, Mass.: Harvard University Press.

Campbell, K.M. and M.A. Flournoy (2007) *The Inheritance and the Way Forward*, (Washington, D.C.: Center for a New American Security).

Chace, J. (1981) *Solvency: The Price of Survival*, New York: Random House.

Clark, I. (2005) *Legitimacy in International Society*, Oxford: Oxford University Press.

Collier, D. and Levitsky, S. (1997) 'Research Note: Democracy with Adjectives: Conceptual Innovation in Comparative Research', *World Politics*, 49(3): 430–51.

Cramer, J.K. (2007) 'Militarized Patriotism: Why the Marketplace of Ideas Failed Before the Iraq War', *Security Studies*, 16(3): 489–524.

Delacoura, K. (2005) 'US Democracy Promotion in the Arab Middle East Since 11 September 2001', *International Affairs*, 81(5): 963–979.

Deutsch, K. (1957) *Political Community in the North Atlantic Area*, Princeton, NJ: Princeton University Press.

Easterly, W. (2007) 'Was Development a Mistake? *American Economic Review*, 97(2): 328–332.

Evans, P.B., Rueschemeyer, D. and Skocpol, T. (1985) 'On the Road to a More Adequate Understanding of the State', in P.B. Evans, D. Rueschemeyer and T. Skocpol (eds) *Bringing the State Back In*, Cambridge: Cambridge University Press.

Gates, R.M. (2008) Speech Delivered at Center for International and Strategic Studies, Washington, DC, 26 January 2008. Available at: www.defenselink.mil/speeches/speech.aspx?speechid=1211. Accessed 12 January 2010.

—— (2009) 'A Balanced Strategy', *Foreign Affairs*, 88(1): 28–40.

Gelb. L. (2009) *Power Rules: How Common Sense Can Rescue American Foreign Policy.* New York: Harper

Gilman, N. (2003) *Mandarins of the Future: Modernization Theory in Cold War America*, (Baltimore, MD: Johns Hopkins University Press.

Gilpin, R. (1975) *U.S. Power and the Multinational Corporation: The Political Economy of Foreign Direct Investment*, New York: Basic Books.

—— (1981) *War and Change in International Politics*, Cambridge: Cambridge University Press.

—— (1986) *The Political Economy of International Relations*, Princeton, NJ: Princeton University Press.

Gowa, J. (1995) 'Democratic States and International Disputes', *International Organization*, 49(3): 511–22.

Hatcher, P. (1990) *Suicide of an Elite: American Internationalists and Vietnam*, Stanford, CA: Stanford University Press.

Huntington, S.P. (1988) 'Coping with the Lippmann Gap', *Foreign Affairs*, 66(3): 453–477.

Ikenberrry, G.J. (1998/9) 'Institutions, Strategic Restraint, and the Persistence of Postwar Order', *International Security*, 23(3): 43–78.

—— (2000) *After Victory: Institutions, Strategic Restraint, and the Rebuilding of International Order After Major Wars*, Princeton, NJ: Princton University Press.

—— (2002a) 'Introduction', in G.J. Ikenberry (ed.) *America Unrivaled: The Future of the Balance of Power*, Ithaca, NY: Cornell University Press.

—— (2002b) 'Democracy, Institutions, and American Restraint', in G.J. Ikenberry (ed.) *America Unrivaled: The Future of the Balance of Power*, Ithaca, NY: Cornell University Press), pp. 213–38.

—— and Kupchan, C.A. (1990) 'The Legitimation of Hegemonic Power', in D.P. Rapkin (ed.) *World Leadership and Hegemony*, Boulder, CO: Lynne Reiner, pp. 49–69.

Kaufmann, C. (2004) 'Threat Inflation and the Marketplace of Ideas: The Selling of the Iraq War', *International Security*, 29(1): 5–48.

Kagan, R. (2003) *Of Paradise and Power: America and Europe in the New World Order*, New York: Knopf.

Kennedy, P. (1987) *The Rise and Fall of the Great Powers: Economic Change and Military Power from 1500 to 2000*, New York: Random House.

Keohane, R. (1984) *After Hegemony: Cooperation and Discord in the World Political Economy.* Princeton, NJ: Princeton University Press.

Kindleberger, C.P. (1973) *The World in Depression, 1929–1939,* Berkeley, CA: University of California Press.

Kinzer, S. (2006) *Overthrow: America's Century of Regime Change from Hawaii to Iraq*, New York: Times Books.

Kurlantzick, J. (2007) *Charm Offensive: How China's Soft Power is Transforming the World*, New Haven, CT: Yale University Press.

Krasner, S.D. (1978) *Defending the National Interest*, Princeton, NJ: Princeton University Press.

Jervis, R. (1978) 'Cooperation Under the Security Dilemma', *World Politics*, 30(2): 167–214.

Joffe, J. (1995) 'Bismarck or Britain: Towards an American Grand Strategy After Bipolarity', *International Security*, 19(4): 94–117.

Latham, M. (2000) *Modernization as Ideology: American Social Science and 'Nation Building' in the Kennedy Era*, Chapel Hill, NC: University of North Carolina Press.

—— (2003) 'Introduction', in D.C. Engerman, N. Gilman, M.N. Haefele and M. Latham (eds) *Staging Growth: Modernization, Development, and the Global Cold War*, Amherst, MA: University of Massachusetts Press, pp. 1–22.

Layne, C. (1984) 'Toward German Reunification?', *Journal of Contemporary Studies*, 7(4): 7–37.

—— (1993) 'The Unipolar Illusion: Why New Great Powers Will Rise', *International Security*, 17(4): 5–51.

—— (1994) 'Kant or Cant: The Myth of the Democratic Peace', *International Security*, 19(2): 5–49.

—— (2001) 'Shell Games, Shallow Gains, and the Democratic Peace', *International History Review*, 23(4): 799–813.

—— (2006a) *The Peace of Illusions: American Grand Strategy from 1940 to the Present*, Ithaca, NY: Cornell University Press.

—— (2006b) 'The Unipolar Illusion Revisited', *International Security*, 31(2): 5–41

Lowi, T. (1967) 'Making Democracy Safe for the World', in J.N. Rosenau (ed.) *Domestic Sources of Foreign Policy*, New York: Free Press, pp. 295–331.

Mahbubani, K. (2008) *The New Asian Hemisphere: The Irresistible Shift of Global Power to the East*, New York: PublicAffairs.

Mann, M. (1984) 'The Autonomous Power of the State', *Archives europeenes de sociologie,* 28(2): 185–213.

Mansfield, E. and Snyder, J. (2005/06) 'Prone to Violence: The Paradox of the Democratic Peace', *The National Interest*, 82: 39–45.

Mastanduno, M. (1997) 'Preserving the Unipolar Moment: Realist Theories and U.S. Grand Strategy', *International Security*, 21(4): 49–88.

McDougall, W.(1997) *Promised Land, Crusader State: The American Encounter with the world since 1776.* Boston, Mass.: Houghtan Mifflin.

Mearsheimer, J. (2002) *The Tragedy of Great Power Politics*, New York: W.W. Norton.

Merritt, R.L. and Zinnes, D.A. (1991) 'Democracies and War', in A. Inkeles (ed.) *On Measuring Democracy: Its Consequences and Concomitants*, New Brunswick, NJ: Transaction Publishers.

National Intelligence Council (2008) *Global Trends 2025: A Transformed World*, Washington, DC: US Government Printing Office.

Nordlinger, E. (1981) *On the Autonomy of the Democratic State*, Cambridge, MA: Harvard University Press.

Nye, Jr, J.S. (1990) *Bound to Lead: The Changing Nature of American Power*, New York: Basic Books.

—— (2002) *The Paradox of American Power: Why the World's Only Superpower Can't Go It Alone*, New York: Oxford University Press.

—— (2004) *Soft Power: The Means to Success in World Politics*, New York: Public Affairs.

—— (2008) 'Public Diplomacy and Soft Power,' *The Annals of the American Academy*, 616:-

Oren, I. (2005) 'The Subjectivity of the 'Democratic Peace': Changing U.S. Perceptions of Imperial Germany', *International Security*, 20(2): 147–85.

Posen, B.R. (2003) 'Command of the Commons: The Military Foundation of U.S. Hegemony', *International Security*, 28(1): 5–46.

Risse-Kappen, T. (1995) *Cooperation Among Democracies: The European Influence on U.S. Foreign Policy*, Princeton, NJ: Princeton University Press.

Rummel, R.J. (1997) *Power Kills: Democracy as a Method of Nonviolence*, New Brunswick, NJ: Transaction Books.

Sanger, D. (2009) *The Inheritance: The World Obama Confronts and the Challenges to American Power*, New York: Harmony.

Saunders, F.S. (1999) *The Cultural Cold War: The CIA and the World of Arts and Letters,* New York: The New Press.

Schweizer, P. (1986) *Victory*. New York: Atlantic Monthly Press.

Secunda, E. and Moran, T. (2007) *Selling War to America: From the Spanish-American War to the Global War on Terror*, Westport, CT: Praeger.

Sestanovich, S. (2005) 'American Maximalism', *National Interest*, 79: 13–23.

Sharp, P. (2004) 'Virtue Unrestrained: Herbert Butterfield and the Problem of American Power', *International Studies Perspectives*, 5(3): 300–15.

Skocpol, T. (1985) 'Bringing the State Back In: Strategies of Analysis in Current Research', in P.B. Evans, D. Rueschemeyer and T. Skocpol (eds) *Bringing the State Back In*, Cambridge: Cambridge University Press.

Thompson, J.A. (1992) 'The Exaggeration of American Vulnerability: The Anatomy of a Tradition', *Diplomatic History*, 16(1): 23–43.

Thrall, A.T. (2007) 'A Bear in the Woods? Threat Framing and the Marketplace of Ideas', *Security Studies*, 16(3): 452–88.

Walt, S.M. (2002) 'Keeping the World 'Off-Balance', in G.J. Ikenberry (ed.) *America Unrivaled: The Future of the Balance of Power*, Ithaca, NY: Cornell University Press, pp. 121–54.

—— (2005) *Taming American Power: The Global Response to U.S. Primacy*, New York: W.W. Norton.

Waltz, K. (1993) 'The Emerging Structure of International Politics', *International Security*, 18(2): 44–79

—— (2000) 'Structural Realism After the Cold War', *International Security*, 25(1): 5–41.

Williams, W.A. (1988) *The Tragedy of American Diplomacy*. New York: W.W. Norton.

Wohlforth, W.C. (1997) 'The Stability of a Unipolar World', *International Security*, 24(1): 5–41.

—— (2002) 'U.S. Strategy in a Unipolar World,' in G.J. Ikenberry (ed.) *America Unrivaled: The Future of the Balance of Power*, Ithaca: Cornell University Press, pp. 98–120.

Zakaria, F. (2008) *The Post-American World*, New York: W.W. Norton.

5   *The Power Game*, soft power and the international historian[1]

Till Geiger

Introduction

From the beginning of the novel, *The Power Game*, the reader is aware that the US undersecretary of state for security affairs, Peter Cutler, is forced to resign for having jeopardized an American military raid meant to prevent the transfer of nuclear technology from Pakistan to Iran. The novel traces the events leading to this tragic outcome particularly Cutler's protracted battle to persuade the fictional Kent administration to rely primarily on American soft power in its attempts to stop nuclear proliferation. When diplomacy fails to achieve the desired outcome, the administration decides to use military force to prevent the sale of nuclear technology from Pakistan to Iran. In this context, Cutler faces a moral dilemma, as the planned American raid might kill a friend from his student days at Princeton, the Pakistani nuclear engineer Ali Aziz, who is now in charge of the nuclear installation to be attacked. While being a firm believer in the necessity of Pakistan possessing atomic weapons to balance the nuclear arsenal of its larger neighbour, India, Aziz has been horrified by the plans of the new Pakistani regime to sell nuclear technology to Iran, and has, at great personal risk, provided the American intelligence services with vital information about the Pakistani nuclear programme. In the end, Cutler sends Aziz a cryptic message warning him of the impending raid. Aziz does not heed the warning of his friend and dies during the American raid, as do a number of American commandos having accomplished their mission (Nye 2004b).

In reply to the question of whether his novel represents an allegory of soft power, Joseph Nye has rejected any attempt to read the novel as 'a fictionalized version of my book about soft power'. Instead he has suggested that the book is

> a story about decline and fall. Peter Cutler starts out with good intentions, but in the process he becomes corrupted by power.
>
> (Soutphommasane and Chau 2005)

Essentially a *Bildungsroman*, Nye's Washington novel charts Cutler's rise from humble beginnings as the son of a minister from Maine who becomes a professor of international relations (IR) at Princeton and his subsequent downfall having become corrupted by the malign influence of power. Caught in backroom intrigues, Cutler loses his moral bearings while endlessly fighting his corner against rivals within the administration and becoming increasingly estranged from his wife, children and university colleagues in Princeton. In the end, he succumbs to an extramarital affair. Forced out of his job, he considers suicide only to find redemption on his favourite fishing lake near the family cabin in Maine.

The Power Game is another manifestation of Nye's writings on soft power; although the novel is targeted at a wider audience than merely the community of IR scholars. While the intended audience of Nye's books on soft power are policymakers and the interested public, it is harder to identify the target readership of this novel. The bulk of the novel is devoted to recounting the bureaucratic infighting in Washington. Indeed, the book has been praised for its insight into the inner workings of the American government (Arthur 2004). Reflecting Nye's experience as practitioner as well as an analyst, this emphasis can be read as an attempt to provide his readers with an insight into the intricate nature of the domestic American foreign policymaking process. In this sense, the novel is another form of engagement with current American foreign policy albeit in fictional form. Despite its non-academic format, Nye regards the novel as important intervention in the debate about the future of American foreign policy.[2]

The novel effectively posits the question of the morality of American foreign policy and the exercise of power, be it hard, soft, sticky or smart.[3] Even though *The Power Game* is about the relationship of power to morality, Nye '... drew this novel as one in which soft power doesn't prevail. Peter Cutler advocates soft power but he doesn't win,' (Soutphommasane and Chau 2005). In the novel, soft power becomes one of the alternative policy tools or governance techniques which the fictional Kent administration might deploy to prevent the sale of nuclear weapons and technology to Iran. The choices faced by the Kent administration's national security team are not unlike the decisions American foreign policymakers have to make frequently. Any decision in the novel has implications that cannot easily be undone once a government has embarked on a certain course of action. Through its narrative focus on foreign policymaking, the form of the novel enables Nye to engage with the question of how a government might deploy soft power to achieve its policy objectives, rather than persuading his readers to recognize the importance of soft power as in his political writing on soft power per se. The novel is of such interest to me as a historian of the transatlantic relationship in the early Cold War, because its narrative engages with the question of how governments deploy power (including soft power) in ways which have significant resonance with the research of international historians and are more difficult to explicate 'in theory'.

Consequently, this chapter will explore these resonances. The first section will examine how the conceptualization of soft power in Nye's writings has been shaped by the narrative forms he has used to discuss the concept. Arguing that his novel, *The Power Game*, is merely another form of Nye's exploration of American (soft) power, the analysis in this section will challenge Nye's recent attempts in his scholarly writing to see soft power as primarily the result of public diplomacy shifting the focus to other forms of soft power, their construction and historical contingency. Drawing on the uses of soft power in *The Power Game*, the following sections will examine three examples of soft power in the novel: the exercise of soft power through multilateral international cooperation; foreign aid as generating soft power capital or resource; and soft power arising through the experience of having studied in the USA and encountered American society.

Soft power: conceptualization, narrative form and history

> Most academic disciplines have their own conventions determining the form of academic writing within the discipline. For example, articles in history journals are more likely to begin with something that evokes the particularity of their subject matter – for example, an anecdote or salient quotation from contemporary sources – than with discussions of theory or historical interpretation.
>
> (Sewell 2005: 4)

In contrast to historians, social scientists tend to start articles or books by exploring the relevant theory relating to a particular question. Written by an international historian, this chapter draws on the plot of Nye's novel as a way into its subject matter: the use of soft power by governments. Through this approach, this chapter side-steps the issue of what constitutes soft power. Arguably, Nye himself uses both the form of the novel and the general non-fiction books targeted at the policymaking community, to explore aspects of American (soft) power that are difficult to capture in a theoretical treatise on the topic. While the imprecision of the concept may annoy IR scholars, its vagueness may make it an appealing concept in the wider discussions of American foreign policy, and can also be embraced to explore American (soft) power in new productive ways which might enrich the debate on the concept's usefulness.

The point about the content of the form can be extended to Nye's writing on soft power. By using the form of non-fiction books and articles directed at the policymaking community and a wider audience, he can partly evade the conventions of social science writing. This is demonstrated by the fact that in contrast to the convention of IR texts, Nye opens his 2004 book, *Soft Power*, with the following anecdote:

> In 2003, I was sitting in the audience at the World Economic Forum in Davos, Switzerland, when George Carey, former Archbishop of Canterbury, asked Secretary of State, Colin Powell why the United States seemed to focus only on its hard power rather than its soft power. I was interested in the question, because I had coined the term 'soft power' a decade or so earlier. Secretary Powell correctly replied that the United States needed hard power to win World War II, but continued, 'And what followed immediately after hard power? Did the United States ask for dominion over a single nation in Europe? No. Soft power came in the Marshall Plan. ... We did the same thing in Japan.' Later in the same year, I spoke about soft power to a conference

> cosponsored by the U.S. Army in Washington. One of the speakers was Secretary of Defense Donald Rumsfield. According to a press account, 'The top military brass listened sympathetically' to my views, but when someone in the audience later asked Rumsfield for his opinion on soft power power, he replied 'I don't know what it means.'
>
> (Nye 2004c: ix)

Nye uses this anecdote to suggest that the concept of soft power has not only entered the foreign policy discourse in recent years, but has also been misappropriated by policymakers, thus forcing its creator to clarify its meaning. Nye (2004c: 1–2) goes on to conceptualize power by using analogy likening power to the weather and love, and appealing to our experiential knowledge of power before exploring the concept of soft power through the discussion of examples. Originally, Nye defined soft co-optive power as 'getting others to want what you want' arising from certain soft power resources such as cultural attraction, ideology and international organizations (Nye 1990a, 31–2, 1990b, 2004c: 44–68). While Nye has consistently used this definition, he has deployed the concept rather differently to intervene in debates about American grand strategy since early 1990s. In *Bound to Lead*, Nye (1990a: 29–35) used the concept of soft power to dispel the popular belief in America's decline as an international power. In this context, he argued that soft power significantly extended America's hard power resources, even though they may have declined relative to other powers. A decade on, in *The Paradox of American Power*, Nye argued against the converse conclusion that as the world's only superpower, the USA did not need the support of other countries to maintain its position within the international system. By restricting its hard power through international cooperation, the USA would increase its overall influence (Nye 2002).

As this discussion suggests, Nye's definition of soft power is protean and arguably imprecise. For example, Nye's definition of soft power excludes foreign aid because of its conditionality relying on inducement to further foreign policy objectives. Nevertheless, Nye (2004c: 48) argues that the Marshall Plan was crucial in creating the transatlantic alliance immediately qualifying this statement by noting the importance of American popular culture. Nye (2004c: 61) goes on to suggest that Western Europeans accepted American ideas and values regarding federalism, democracy and open markets because of far-sighted policies such as the Marshall Plan. As Nye's observations suggest, the exercise of hard power such as foreign aid cannot always be separated from the exercise and generation of soft power. In *The Soft Power* and his most recent book, *The Power to Lead*, Nye (2004c: 32, 147, 2008a: 83) acknowledges the importance of combining hard and soft power in order to effectively influence the thinking and actions of others by invoking the new concept of smart power.

Throughout his writing on the topic, Nye repeatedly acknowledges that policymakers are hard to persuade of the importance and efficacy of soft power. In contrast to more tangible forms of power, soft power is intangible and to some degree defies measurement except by proxies such as the expenditure on public diplomacy. Indeed, Nye (2004c: 99–135, 2008b) has increasingly focussed on public diplomacy as the means by which governments might generate and wield soft power in the world. Moreover, he continually stresses that mobilization of soft power depends on circumstances and context, which are often beyond the control of foreign policymakers, particularly in a democracy. As a consequence, policymakers face the possibility that despite considerable investment in soft power resources, circumstances or other decisions may nullify the potential advantages in terms of persuading others. Nevertheless, Nye urges policymakers to devote more resources to cultivating soft power resources through public diplomacy. At the same time, he does not provide a compelling case that soft power can be easily generated through such spending, or that such expenditure would be more effective than increased spending on military power or foreign aid. Indeed, Nye suggests that soft power is at the bottom of the power pyramid, below military and economic power. Therefore, it is hardly surprising that American policymakers pay in Nye's view insufficient attention to soft power and its creation or production. However, such neglect may have major implications for America's standing in the world, if Nye (2004c) is correct in suggesting that recent changes in international relations and the economy have increased the importance of soft power.

However, this emphasis on public diplomacy may be misplaced, because such policies have to be contextualized. For example, the large-scale foreign aid to Western Europe (and Japan) under the Marshall Plan and later the Mutual Security Program was accompanied by an unprecedented programme of American public diplomacy in the late 1940s and 1950s. As the Truman administration reduced economic aid during the Korean War, public diplomacy became an increasingly important aspect of fighting the Cold War (Matsuda 2007). Besides the efforts of the United States Information Service, American private foundations (with covert financial support by the American government) spearheaded such efforts to combat anti-Americanism in Western Europe. Such efforts were primarily directed at Western European elites (Pells 1997: 37–93; Berghahn 2001). However, such expenditure on public diplomacy was only a fraction of the earlier economic aid.

As Nye himself argues, Marshall aid contributed to American soft power through accelerating the already existing process of the Americanization of Western European societies in the immediate post-war period. Over the last two decades, historians have studied the deliberate transfer of American models, values and practices to Western European and Japanese businesses, economies, societies and cultures. While this process of Americanization began in the late nineteenth century, the transmission and adoption of American management models and production methods accelerated in the post-1945 period, when successive American administrations encouraged this transfer through their technical assistance programmes and by funding numerous productivity missions from Western Europe and Japan to the USA.[3] To a lesser extent, economic historians have analysed the degree to which Western European governments adopted American ideas about economic development and economic policymaking in particular (Berghahn 1986). However, these studies have largely neglected the transfer of American governance techniques to Western Europe (Geiger 2008). While acknowledging the importance of the Marshall Plan as a conduit for American ideas, the literature on Americanization stresses the rather selective adoption of such models, values and practices resulting in their hybridization (Zeitlin 2000). Despite their selective adoption, the attractiveness of American models, values and practices contributed to the acceptance by Western European governments of the American vision for a new liberal international economic order after 1945. However, the acceptance of American economic aid limited the choices of Western European governments in terms of economic and social reform (Lehmann 2000: 15).

While not an exercise in soft power, American economic aid increased American soft power considerably by transforming Western European economies and societies in the immediate post-war period. The substantial financial aid induced Western European countries to accept American leadership of the international economic order. Through this acceptance, Western European governments helped to extend American power and co-produced American hegemony in the post-1945 period (Krige 2006: 4–9). In the case of Japan, the combination of American military government rule, foreign aid and public diplomacy led to a dependency and to an uncritical subordination to American power (Matsuda 2007). Therefore, American soft power is not just the innocent product of the attractiveness of American values, democracy and capitalism, but rather arises from the USA's superior power resources and its ability to augment its power by constantly renegotiating the terms of domination and subordination (Krige 2008). This transformation of IR and the consequential American dominance endured, because these bargains partly became institutionalized in multilateral international organizations, which became the sites of renegotiation of American hegemony. This analysis suggests that the construction of these institutional arrangements depended on particular historical circumstances. At the same time, existing institutional arrangements limited, to some degree, the potential for alternative institutional arrangements to emerge. Indeed, the history of successful international cooperation may explain the endurance of certain institutional arrangements such as NATO, which no longer fulfil their original purpose and which are arguably no longer in the interest of the USA (Sjursen 2004; Menon 2007: 50–99).

In exploring American power, this chapter uses Nye's (2002: 16) definition of hegemony as '… a situation where one country has significantly more power resources or capability than others'. Drawing on Foucault's concept of the liberal governmentality, this chapter will treat soft power, on the one hand, as an argument for liberal internationalism which can be instrumentalized as a technique/tool/governmental rationality for extending power, and on the other hand, as embodied in certain practices, systems and institutions, but also persons and material goods.[5] In this sense, the ability to mobilize soft power to co-opt other governments constitutes a potentially important policy instrument for American foreign policymakers in their efforts to preserve American preponderance in the world.[6] At the same time, soft power cannot be deployed in isolation, but only as part of a combination of hard, sticky and soft power (Wilson 2008: 114–16). As soft power and its potential usefulness as a policy tool depends on the circumstances, Nye's novel and examples drawn from history allow me to explore the contingent nature of American soft power.

American soft power and multilateral international cooperation

After managing to cajole his opposite numbers in other government departments into agreeing upon an American position, Peter Cutler in *The Power Game* heads a delegation to a meeting of western governments in London to discuss international controls on the transfer of sensitive technology to countries developing nuclear capabilities. In the protracted struggle to reach a policy consensus in Washington, Cutler starts to neglect his family and cancels the annual fishing trip with his college friends from Princeton. The cancellation of the trip is an early sign that he is losing touch with the moral principles embodied in the American landscape, not to say wilderness, and in its democratic traditions arising from the spirit of the pioneers. In the novel, the discussions with America's partners on extending the controls on transfer of nuclear technology prove difficult forcing Cutler to make some concessions in order to reach a compromise in multilateral negotiations. However, the fruits of his hard negotiating nearly unravel when, distracted by his extramarital affair, he forgets to approve a vital reporting cable allowing his rivals in Washington to undermine the agreement reached in multilateral negotiations (Nye 2004b: 128–59).

This section from *The Power Game* illustrates clearly the process involved in the renegotiation of international agreements. Even when countries support the same policy objective, this process of renegotiation is contingent on the institutional framework. Multilateral export control regimes emerged in the immediate post-war period. In the late 1940s and 1950s, Congress insisted that successive American administrations limit the export of strategic goods to the Soviet bloc and threatened to withdraw economic aid from any Western European government engaging in such trade. At the same time, Western European governments continually argued that the proposed American export controls were overly restrictive, undermining their economic interests and recovery. While Western European governments accepted the necessity of restricting the exports of strategic goods and advanced technology, they persistently disagreed with American negotiators over the scope of such export controls, which resulted in constant lengthy negotiations and unsatisfactory compromises within the Coordinating Committee for Multilateral Export Controls, better known by its acronym as CoCom (Funigiello 1988: 27–48).[7] Despite the persistent tensions between the USA and its Western allies over strategic export controls, Western countries created a separate multilateral export control regime in the 1970s in order to prevent further nuclear proliferation by controlling the export of sensitive material including dual-use technology to countries suspected of using such materials to acquire nuclear weapons (Nuclear Suppliers Group 2005). If multilateral export control regimes owed their origins to the exercise of coercive American power, such regimes have now become institutionalized and accepted as forms of international cooperation (and arguably a form of soft power) (Nye 1990b: 65–6). Moreover, Western governments have tended to create additional new multilateral arrangements to address newly emerging policy concerns rather than trying to address problems through existing institutions.

Multilateralism became one of the hallmarks of American foreign policy after 1945. The willingness of the USA to be bound by the rules of international multilateral organizations legitimized American foreign policy around the globe, but particularly in the eyes of Western European governments (Ikenberry 1992; Goldstein 1993; Ruggie 1993). As already noted, the USA used the coercive power of Marshall aid to promote Western European integration (Hogan 1987). For example, the Western Europeans reluctantly complied with the obligation to establish the Organisation for European Economic Co-operation (OEEC) to distribute American economic aid and to coordinate Western European reconstruction efforts. At the same time, the British and French governments colluded to restrict the powers of the OEEC to direct the economies of member states (Milward 1984: 168–211). Knowing the importance attached by American policy-makers to Western European integration, the British foreign minister Ernest Bevin initiated the Brussels Treaty Organisation partly to ensnare the USA in an entangling Western military alliance (Baylis 1993). Indeed, Western European governments embraced the international multilateral institution in the immediate post-war period (Geiger 1996). Western European governments soon discovered that they could protect their interests more effectively through international cooperation. While diminishing the power of the nation state in some respects, Alan Milward (1992a) has convincingly argued that negotiating institutional arrangements allowed countries to secure concessions from their partners thereby reducing the social cost of opening their economies. Moreover, multilateral institutional arrangements enabled Western European governments to balance American power. For example, Western European governments resisted the attempt of the USA, with some support from Britain, to subsume the OEEC into the North Atlantic alliance, following the outbreak of the Korean War, in order to plan the economic aspects of western rearmament (Milward 1992b; Geiger 1996).

Multilateral cooperation does restrict American coercive power, but can enhance not only American soft power, but also ultimately hard power. Given the asymmetrical distribution of power between the USA and its allies, Western European governments have used European multilateral institutions not only to balance American power, but also to influence it. The willingness of successive American administrations not only to permit and tolerate, but also at times, to encourage the formation of alternative loci of countervailing power remains one of the more remarkable features of post-war American foreign policy. Arguably, this support for independent Western European institutions increased American soft power. For smaller Western European governments, the importance of the USA for Western Europe became a powerful argument to curtail any ambition by the larger member states to dominate the European integration process.

Given the often lengthy process of negotiation required, multilateral institutional arrangements and practices create a certain path dependency once they have been established. As the former German foreign minister, Joschka Fischer, has pointed out, American soft power effectively prevents the emergence of alternatives to global capitalism. Citing Nye, he goes on to argue that the attractiveness of the American model arises from its technological lead and model of mass consumerism. If a nation wants to participate in the global economy, it has to accept (indeed, has had to accept) rules governing international trade and finance largely agreed by the developed countries (Fischer 2006: 85). Fischer's observation highlights an aspect of soft power that Nye neglects: namely that international multilateral agreements such as the Kyoto Protocol on Climate Change can empower other countries to seize the initiative, engage in agenda-setting and influence the institutional practices which once established will be hard to overturn later. However, Nye sees the failure by the Bush administration to accept the Kyoto Protocol merely in terms of the decision's impact in reducing American soft power (Nye 2004c: 64–5). Therefore, he overlooks the fact that multilateral institutions and arrangements are not only capable of acquiring, but do actually acquire considerable soft power if seen as legitimate by a large group of countries. Depending on the circumstances, the soft power of such multilateral institutions or agreements can be substantial, making it hard for other governments, including even the USA with its formidable hard and soft power, to challenge these arrangements.

Foreign aid and soft power

When American intelligence learns in *The Power Game* that the movement of the nuclear weapons from Pakistan to Iran is imminent, Cutler is charged with trying to dissuade the Pakistani regime by threatening the withdrawal of Western economic aid and development loans. On his way to Karachi, Cutler visits Tokyo to enlist the support of the Japanese government. Over tea, the Japanese foreign minister Takashi, and his deputy Sato tell Cutler that such a threat might undermine the goodwill Japan has been building up in the region, because of its dependence on imported oil from the Middle East. However, they agree to Cutler's request in return for his promise to permit the exports of potentially sensitive Japanese technology to the Middle East. While Cutler is happy to give such a promise, American diplomats in Tokyo point out to him that his vague undertaking will be interpreted by his Japanese counterparts as a firm commitment (Nye 2004b: 179–82, 190–1).

This episode in *The Power Game* highlights another facet of international multilateral cooperation, indeed of diplomatic relations more generally. In agreeing to bring its foreign policy into line with a shared foreign policy objective, policymakers of one country may do so in the expectation of winning certain concessions from other parties to the agreement, as in this example.

Such expectations may form part of an (implicit) understanding which has never been fully articulated. In this case, the willingness to agree to coordinate foreign policies may be interpreted as evidence of the soft power of the other country. At the same time, the unarticulated nature of such understandings may give rise to conflicts and even lead to major confrontations in rare cases. Rather than presuming that other countries necessarily share their interests and values, foreign policymakers need to be aware of the unarticulated expectations of their counterparts in other countries to anticipate such problems.

Arguably, the Cold War developed out of the disappointed expectations of such implicit understandings arising from the wartime conferences between American and Soviet leaders to respect the other's sphere of influence (Trachtenberg 2008). As a consequence, Stalin and the Soviet leadership promoted the division of Germany and Europe in the immediate post-war period (Roberts 2007). For the Soviet leadership, this understanding did not necessarily extend to traditionally British interests in the Near and Middle East.[8] Therefore, Soviet foreign policymakers might reasonably have expected the USA not to oppose Soviet demands for stationing of Soviet troops in Iran and for free passage through the Dardanelles. Abandoning their stated commitment to internationalism through the United Nations, American policymakers regarded such demands as expansionist and started to contain what they saw as Soviet expansionism. As a consequence, the relationship between the two superpowers continued to deteriorate with the mutual misperceptions on both sides contributing to the deepening conflict (Gaddis 1972: 353–61). By constructing the Soviet Union as their opponent in the nascent Cold War, American diplomats engaged in consolidating the USA's influence in Western Europe while attempting to paint the Soviet Union as intransigent, and blocking 'benign' American initiatives such as the Marshall Plan (Cox and Kennedy-Pipe 2005). During the Berlin airlift crisis, American policymakers resisted attempts to find a diplomatic solution to the crisis in spring 1949 in order to complete the North Atlantic Treaty negotiations and the creation of a separate West German state (Eisenberg 2004). The paradox remains that both sides accepted and respected each other's spheres of influence in Europe throughout the Cold War. This tacit understanding led to the uneasy but peaceful co-existence of the two blocs by the late 1950s, begging the question whether the Cold War had in fact to become such a deep and protracted conflict involving the costly arms race of the 1950s and 1960s. However, the other tacit understanding about the unwinnability of a thermonuclear war prevented the latest crisis from escalating to an all-out armed global conflict. From a post-Cold War perspective, some historians have questioned whether in their defence of American values, freedom and democracy, American national security policymakers did indeed pursue a more morally justifiable foreign policy than their Soviet counterparts post-Stalin (Ribuffo 2004: 62–6).

Within the emerging Western bloc, many Western European policymakers shared the commitment of their American counterparts to a new multilateral liberal international economic order. At the same time, Western policymakers questioned whether their war-torn economies would be able to liberalize their international trade and payments without lengthy adjustment periods. Despite their serious concerns, British politicians agreed to make the pound convertible as part of the American loan agreement in 1946. American policymakers made sterling convertibility a condition in an attempt to ensure the early implementation of the Bretton Woods agreements on the new international financial order. However, the American loan proved insufficient to both pay for Britain's imports and bolster her currency reserves sufficiently to maintain convertibility in the summer of 1947. The inevitable crisis forced the British government to suspend sterling convertibility after merely six weeks in August 1947, thus reinforcing the sense of an ever-deepening economic crisis in Western Europe. By the time of the sterling crisis, the Truman administration had recognized that, in order to restart intra-European trade, Western European governments would have to be permitted to discriminate against dollar imports for the foreseeable future, and to achieve international convertibility gradually as part of a concerted effort (Milward 1984: 462–77).

As noted earlier, many American policymakers went further in calling for the economic integration of Western Europe. Western European governments publicly endorsed such calls agreeing to study the possibility of creating a Western European customs union. Despite needing further American financial assistance, British policymakers remained nevertheless determined to defend Britain's preferential trading arrangements with other Commonwealth countries and the Sterling Area (Newton 1984). Disappointed with the general lack of progress, the head of Economic Cooperation Administration, Paul Hoffman, implored Western European governments in November 1949 to liberalize their trading relations and set up a regional multilateral payments system, the European Payments Union (EPU). Fearing that such an arrangement would undermine the Sterling Area, the British government continued to resist the American plans for several months, despite considerable American pressure and being isolated within the OEEC. Given that vital British interest seemed to be at stake, most historians have been puzzled by the Attlee government's decision to join the proposed EPU in May 1950. By consenting to the American proposals, British policymakers hoped to convince their American counterparts to assume a stronger leadership role with the North Atlantic alliance and spearhead Western rearmament efforts. In their attempts to maintain Britain's (imagined) position as America's leading ally in Western Europe, British ministers felt this position might be undermined by the French government's announcement of the Schuman Plan on 5 May 1950 calling for the creation of a common European market for coal and steel. Not necessarily realizing the complex motives behind the British decision, American Marshall Plan officials offered the British government additional financial support to address their immediate concerns about the implications of EPU membership for British currency reserves (Geiger 2004: 75–80; Geiger and Toye 2008). By making concessions over Western European economic integration, the British government hoped that American policymakers would regard Britain's continued global military presence more favourably. In this context, British policymakers viewed with some concern American ideas about military integration with the North

Atlantic alliance. While endorsing military cooperation in principle, they rejected the notion that they should integrate their armed services into a joint Western European military force (Geiger 2008). Despite different understandings of the agreements reached at the London North Atlantic Council (NAC) meeting in May 1950, both governments presented the outcome as reflecting their understanding of Western military cooperation.

Before these different conceptions of military cooperation could lead to any major disagreements, the outbreak of the Korean War radically altered the Western policy agenda. In the months following the North Korean invasion of the Southern Korean peninsula, war hysteria prevailed in the corridors of power in Washington. As a consequence, American policymakers failed to understand why their Western European counterparts did not share their sense of urgency about the global situation. President Truman and American diplomats entreated their Western European allies to embark on massive rearmament programmes. Not convinced of the immediate danger of a Soviet attack, Western European governments continued to insist that their economic reconstruction efforts had to remain their first priority and would reduce the attractiveness of communism in their countries. British defence planners also remained sceptical that the North Korean invasion would be the prelude to another world war. Nevertheless, British ministers decided to send troops to Korea, but remained reluctant to increase the defence budget substantially. In order to persuade the British and other Western European governments to increase their defence expenditure, the Truman administration offered considerable American military aid to support Western European rearmament efforts. On this promise of substantial American military aid, British ministers announced the government's intention to expand its planned defence budget by one-third over three years. However, American officials regarded this increase as insufficient and continued to put pressure on British ministers to enlarge the rearmament programme further. Moreover, the Truman administration now made military aid conditional on the completion of a burden-sharing exercise within the North Atlantic alliance. Following the rout of the United Nations forces after the intervention of Chinese forces, the British government acceded to American pressure and announced further increases in its rearmament programme in order to maintain influence over the American conduct of the war in Korea, and foreign policy more generally. At the same time, the Truman administration embarked on a massive mobilization effort for the Cold War. As part of this effort, American government and defence contractors increased their purchases of raw materials for military production and strategic stockpiling, leading to massive increases in world prices. Increased raw material prices triggered a severe economic downturn and marked increased unemployment in Western Europe.

The economic crisis prompted Western European governments to demand a review of national defence efforts at the Ottawa North Atlantic Council meeting in September 1951. During the autumn, the Temporary Council Committee (TCC) assessed the political and economic ability of member states to sustain their current levels of military expenditure. To the dismay of most member governments, the

TCC review found that they could afford to increase their rearmament efforts. However, the massive protests by their allies convinced American policymakers that in order to gain approval for a strengthening of the alliance's organizational structure through the creation of a permanent secretariat, the American government would have to tolerate their allies reducing their rearmament programmes as well as agree to provide substantial military aid to prevent even deeper cuts in Western military efforts. Indeed, this development allowed Britain not only to curtail the pace of rearmament in Britain, but also to adopt a more capital-intensive defence strategy based on an increased nuclear capability. This new British defence strategy went against American thinking on the division of military roles within the alliance. However, propping up an important ally had become more important for the American policymaking community in the outgoing Truman administration. Nevertheless, a more acute awareness of the different conceptions of Western defence cooperation and the implicit associated understandings by American policymakers would have avoided the conflict that pitted the USA against its Western European allies in autumn 1951 (Maier 1992; Geiger and Sebesta 1996, 1998; Hammerich 2003, 1998; Geiger 2008).

For all parties, any international accord will involve some cost which each country will try to mitigate through the terms of agreement. In the fictional example in *The Power Game*, the Japanese government tries to offset the considerable costs of the multilateral action in terms of expending the social power capital, that it had built up through foreign aid or public diplomacy efforts over a long period of time, by obtaining concessions for its high-technology exports. Even if multilateral agreements create a basis for coordinated action, the other historical examples demonstrate that the associated costs of multilateral accords required further bargaining on both a bilateral and multilateral basis. Depending on the circumstances, American foreign policymakers found it difficult to persuade other governments to follow their lead in such negotiations. At the same time, other governments sought to cultivate their own 'special' relationship with the USA in order to advance their own national interests and influence the American policymaking agenda. In this context, the ability of American foreign policymakers to influence other governments depended on striking the right balance between multilateral and traditional bilateral diplomacy as well as between hard, sticky and soft power.

In all episodes discussed in this section, American policymakers might have interpreted the willingness of other governments to agree to American proposals as reflecting American soft power in the sense of the attractiveness of their ideas or a real community of interests. The discussion shows that such an interpretation would have led to a misapprehension of the complex motivation, thinking and implicit understandings behind such decisions by foreign governments. Indeed, an awareness of the different understanding by the parties to an agreement or perceptions of American foreign policy might be a key element in enhancing the soft and ultimately hard power of the USA. Therefore, rather than seeing public diplomacy as a panacea to extend American soft power, American policymakers need to be better informed about the motivations of other countries in bilateral and multilateral negotiations, adjust their policies to accommodate the views of their partners (and occasionally their rivals and adversaries) and successfully narrativize the inevitable compromise as a triumph of American interests (and soft power) without undermining a potentially uneasy community of interests underpinning the eventual agreement.

Soft power and foreign students at American universities

In *The Power Play*, Nye examines another form of soft power: the creation of transnational elites through studying at American universities. While studying at Princeton, Peter Cutler befriends a Pakistani nuclear engineering student, Ali Aziz.[9] Given his open and engaging personality, Ali quickly becomes part of Peter's circle at Princeton. While enjoying his life in the USA and its material advantages, Ali feels the USA could never become his home and could not imagine marrying an American woman, objecting to their insistence on equality within a relationship. Despite remaining a Muslim, Ali made some concessions to American student life by drinking alcohol and inviting his friends to dorm parties. On one such occasion, Peter meets a young Chinese-American woman, Kate, who he later marries (Nye 2004b: 46–52, 144). Despite being well integrated into the student community at Princeton, Ali remains an enigma to his friends 'caught between his two worlds of Islam and science' (Nye 2004b: 144).

At the end of his studies at Princeton, Ali returns to Pakistan to take up a position within the country's nuclear programme. Ali and Peter continue to exchange birthday cards. When radical forces take over the government, pursuing a policy of selling its nuclear technology, Peter notices that the messages his friend sends have become less informative and more guarded. Unbeknown to Peter, Ali starts to provide American intelligence services with vital information on the Pakistani nuclear programme in order to prevent nuclear weapons from falling into the wrong hands. While Ali's motivations for spying for the USA remain unclear, a major consideration is his opposition to the new Pakistani government's dangerous policies facilitating nuclear proliferation. However, the narrative suggests that his actions may partly reflect his personal friendship with Peter, which in turn leads Peter to undermine his own government's attempt to destroy the nuclear weapons before they are transferred to Iran. Warned by Peter about the impending attack, rather than saving himself, Ali decides to remain at his post, fulfilling his patriotic duty, and dies in the attempt to prevent the destruction of the atomic bombs and nuclear laboratory of which he is in charge (Nye 2004b: 192–235).

As the plot of *The Power Game* suggests, Nye sees the experience of studying in the USA as potentially transformative for foreign students. Through their lived experience and intimate knowledge of American society, foreign students are likely to promote a better understanding of American politics, society and culture after their return to their countries of origin. To some extent, they will be able to generate a more favourable climate for American foreign policy aimed at promoting international understanding and cooperation. For example, Nye argues that the limited American student exchanges with the Soviet Union proved influential in de-escalating the Cold War and ultimately liberalizing the regime (Nye 2004c: 45–46). Along the same lines, Nye maintains that the USA benefited from the fact that many future leaders such as Anwar Sadat, Helmut Schmidt and Margaret Thatcher had spent some time studying in the USA (Nye 2004c: 108–9). Beyond creating a transnational elite familiar with life in other countries, historical studies of the student exchanges between West Germany and the USA document that former exchange students saw themselves as bridging the two cultures, overcoming preconceptions on both sides. Student exchanges between Japan and USA similarly helped to normalize the relations between two countries following World War II. In this process, American non-governmental organizations often took the lead in promoting better international understanding (Iriye 2002: 83–6). Therefore, Nye maintains that both international exchange programmes and the attractiveness of American higher education for overseas students, more generally, constitute a major asset in extending American soft power. This observation provides a strong argument for continuing to allow foreign students to live and study in the USA in a post-9/11 world. However, since 9/11 many prospective overseas students at American universities have either found it difficult to obtain student visas or have been deterred by the potential difficulties from applying to American universities. As some politicians acknowledge, this development might threaten not only the standing of American universities, but also the country's long-term competitiveness at a time when many American high-tech firms rely on recruiting foreign graduates in sciences and mathematics from American universities (Obama 2006: 139–41). Moreover, the tightened immigration rules have also undermined the ability of American universities to attract the world's leading scholars to teach at their campuses in the USA. Therefore, reversing this policy may be an effective step in creating goodwill for the USA worldwide and extending its soft power for the future. At the same time the question remains, how American policymakers might wield such soft power in pursuing a particular policy objective at a particular time.

If the continued openness of the USA to foreign students should be regarded as an investment in future soft power, it also constitutes a calculated gamble that the experience of studying in the USA will transform foreign students by inculcating in them a positive vision of American society, values and ideals. The extent of this transformation will ultimately depend on the experience of foreign students in the USA. For example, the open resentment and racism of ordinary Russians turned many foreign students on full studentships studying in the Soviet Union against communism (Caesar 2009). At the same time, governments of the student's home country may see them as potential agents of American power and therefore untrustworthy because of their Western education. Moreover, the absorption of American visions of equality and meritocracy, as well as a sense of belonging to a transnational elite, may make it difficult for American-educated students to reintegrate into their home countries after an extended period in the USA. Barack Obama's (2007) memoir *Dreams from My Father* provides anecdotal examples of this problem for foreign students in the case of both his own father in Kenya and his step-father in Indonesia. In *The Power Game*, Ali Aziz faces similar (justified) suspicions about his loyalties from the new rulers in Pakistan. At the same time, their strong personal friendship leads both Peter and Ali to question their respective governments' policies, raising questions as to where the loyalties of transnational elites lie (Nye 2004b: 197–9). The proliferation of international organizations, both intergovernmental and non-governmental, since 1945 has generated a new transnational elite of international civil servants, experts and activists committed to these institutions or issues. At the same time, an awareness of global interdependence has given rise to a global civil society (Iriye 2002). In examining the emergence of such transnational groupings, international historians have questioned the adequacy of national perspectives for the study of international relations (Clavin 2005).

Living across several cultures arguably changes the outlook of these transnational boundary-crossers, and becomes an integral part of their personal identities. Such transnational multicultural identities challenge the notion of a clearly defined monolithic national identity just as much as they do the idea of the modern Western multicultural society. Even within the context of some sort of national vision, such as the American dream, personal identities may be an amalgam of several cultural influences, thus defying stereotypes. While President Barack Obama's electoral success can be narrativized as a triumph of the American dream, such a reading obliterates his personal struggle to define himself as black American as part of this dream. From the perspective of the wider global community, it is tempting to see President Obama as personification of the increasingly transnational/international make-up of the world in the twenty-first century. Because of the incoming President's background, American foreign policymakers will find it easier to convince the global community that the new administration will play an active part in addressing the problems faced by all nations. Nevertheless, the new administration's public diplomacy will face several major challenges. Besides managing global expectations, the tremendous hopes of the global community could be easily dashed by a foreign policy disaster. For example, the incoming Kennedy administration found its international support quickly eroded by the Bay of Pigs fiasco (Schlesinger 2007: 120). Indeed, Melvyn Leffler (2007: 5–6) has recently observed that Cold War leaders found themselves constrained in their policies by having to listen to their allies and gain their support, suggesting that while having an important role in convincing the global community of the new administration's engagement with the world, public diplomacy will not succeed in extending American soft power if the administration does not consider the views of its allies.

While important to efforts extending American soft power, the close working relationship between American policymakers and their counterparts in its most important Western allies also carries with it certain risks. Since the 1940s, the contact between policymakers, officials and businessmen from the advanced Western economies, as well as representatives of non-governmental institutions has intensified through their regular meetings. Their familiarity has contributed to the increased transnational coalition-building among these elites. Through their constant discussions, officials of one country can form the policies of another. In the early Cold War, the close contacts between British and American diplomats in Moscow too contributed very similar assessments of Soviet regime as expansionary (Greenwood 1990). As Mark Lawrence has documented, British and French diplomats convinced their American counterparts in the late 1940s that the Vietnamese national independence struggle formed part of Soviet expansionism (Lawrence 2002). By exaggerating the threat emanating from strong national Communist movements, elites in both Italy and France hoped to persuade American policymakers of their country's urgent need for immediate American financial assistance in 1947 and 1948. Once Marshall aid started flowing, the governments of both countries used similar arguments to minimize American demands for domestic reforms.

Similar processes can be observed in the current war on terror. Advanced nations have used the terrorist threat to justify their military intervention against states that they claimed provided safe havens for terrorist networks. The shared perceptions of the threat may blind Western governments to the suffering of the local population and the inadequacy of its own response to the humanitarian crisis caused by their military interventions. At the same time, the relative invisibility of these victims in the Western media contributes to the outrage felt at the behaviour of the coalitions of 'advanced' countries in certain parts of the world. Such sentiments will contribute to the recruitment of further generations of terrorists. Moreover, the fact that 'what [the United States] stand[s] for just changed with the election of a new administration' (Schlesinger 2007: 107), will not necessarily persuade people living in countries suspected of harbouring terrorists, or posing a threat to Western countries that American foreign policy has changed fundamentally. Indeed, it may be just as hard to persuade domestic constituencies of the desirability of such a sea change as James Schlesinger, Jr found when he tried to overcome the United States Information Agency's opposition to the incoming Kennedy administration's changed position on Cuba.

Transnational coalition-building or lobbying by other governments co-produces American global power by turning to the USA for leadership. When in February 1947 the British government could no longer afford to support Greece and Turkey financially, President Truman appealed to Congress to aid these two countries in the name of defending freedom and their right to self-determination. While these objectives reflected wartime commitments laid down in the Atlantic Charter, Truman's speech to Congress marked the end of cooperation with the Soviet Union in attaining these goals.[10] Visiting Japan, South Korea and South-East Asia at the height of the Korean War, the Republican governor of New York, Thomas Dewey, noted that the American struggle for freedom and democracy meant little to peasants living in poverty in the Philippines, elsewhere in the third world, or in Greece or Turkey for that matter (Dewey 1952: 107–9). Undeterred by such reflections, the State Department published a public information leaflet on NATO depicting women doing their laundry in the ruins of Nuremberg as reflecting the determination of Western Europeans to defend their freedoms against the Soviet threat (United States Department of State 1952: 6).

Paradoxically, the citizens of Nuremberg saw themselves as victims of World War II including the allied bombing of the city (Gregor 2008: 25–36). At the same time, realizing its dependence on the USA, the West German government mounted a public diplomacy campaign by employing an American public relations firm to counteract what it saw as growing anti-German sentiments in the USA since the 1950s. By underlining West Germany's commitment to the West, these efforts affirmed the image of West Germans as a reliable ally in the Cold War in the mind of most Americans (Etheridge 2007). Such narrative constructions reinforced the perception of the USA as the vital country for resolving the world's problems.

At the same time, transnational elites tend to analyze the world through the prism of often American-dominated social science disciplines such as economics and IR. Having assumed the role of the world's predominant superpower, the American government enlisted the advice of scientists as well as social scientists to preserve the country's preponderance (Engerman 2007). In recent years, historians have studied the impact of social science thinking on American foreign policy. For example, modernization theory saw the USA as the model the third world should emulate, and came to influence American foreign policy toward the third world in the 1960s. Against the background of the Cold War struggle, the leading theorists would present modernization theory as an alternative to communism, despite its similarities to the Soviet model of development. Moreover, the shortcomings of modernization theory soon became apparent, undermining the theorists' claims of its universality and applicability for international development policy (Gilman 2003: 13–17). Nevertheless, the American academy began to dominate the production and, more importantly, the dissemination of new ideas. Even if ideas such as Keynesianism emanated from Europe, their acceptance by American economists ensured that such ideas were reexported to Europe influencing economic policymaking (Hirschman 1989). Another example is the adoption of the Meade-Stone double-entry national accounting system as the international standard in the late 1940s. Through the Marshall Plan, American economists and statisticians played a key role in the spread of this particular approach to national income accounting, originally pioneered in wartime Britain (Geiger 2002). At the same time, the centrality of the American academy in the process of the dissemination of ideas made it more insular. Despite efforts to encourage American students to spend part of their studies in Europe, a survey of international programmes of American universities in the late 1950s noted that many American scholars in disciplines such as economics, biology and psychology saw little value in reading the scholarly literature published in academic journals in other countries (Garraty and Adams 1959: 196). While the attractiveness of American universities has enhanced the soft power of the USA, Bruce Kuklick has questioned whether the increased influence of social science theory has improved American foreign policymaking and outcomes since the late 1940s (Kuklick 2006).

Such narrative constructions obscure the extent to which consumption of imported goods has shaped American society and culture. In turn, this dependence on such imports such as oil, cheap manufactured goods and food have constrained American foreign policy in the past and in the present. To regard the USA as the main driving force of globalization is to ignore the degree to which the USA itself is transformed by globalization and is itself globalized (Hoganson 2006).

The concept of soft power can be used to capture a myriad of facets of predominantly American power in the world. American soft power emerges from a complicated process of the constant renegotiation of America's place in the world. By directing our attention to American power, soft power reinforces the idea of American culture as universal, particularly in the USA, and at the same time strengthens notions that Washington or the National Security Council 'runs the world'. However, such notions are not just questioned by foreigners not persuaded or attracted by American soft power, but also by some of its allies and by many Americans outside the Washington Beltway. For their part, international historians have challenged these notions by exposing the limits of American hegemonic (soft) power, suggesting that in order to enhance American soft power effectively, American policymakers need to construct the USA as a constituent part of an interdependent world.

Soft power and the international historian

In contrast to IR scholars, international historians have generally not embraced Nye's concept of soft power.[11] The reason for this lack of enthusiasm may reflect the differences in the two disciplines, approaches to studying power. IR scholars theorize power with a view to influencing future foreign policy and predicting its impact. In their study of the past, international historians concentrate on analyzing the contingent nature of power, the importance of agents, the impact of ideas and the role of culture in constructing power materially and discursively. In line with this perspective, this chapter has treated soft power as a tool for enhancing the ability of American governments to govern the world. Using the discursive constructions of such power in the novel *The Power Game*, the analysis of this chapter has interrogated the concept, highlighting its contingency on historical circumstances and settings.

In order to understand American soft power better, we need to decentre America and interrogate those interactions with the outside world which transform American culture and power (Gienow-Hecht 2007). On the surface, *The Power Game* suggests that such interactions are minimal. While Peter Cutler is affected by his friendship with Ali Aziz, neither he nor the other American characters have lived or studied abroad or been influenced by the outside world in any major way. American values and culture are portrayed as emanating from the American landscape and as unalterable by foreign influences. Indeed, the world in *The Power Game* seems to pivot around the backroom politics of Washington. At the same time, these political struggles seem to inhabit a world of their own, out of touch with the 'other' American cultures such as the American academy and arts at the margins of the novel. In a telling aside, Kate, who has always abhorred the Washington power game, seeks refuge in France after she discovers

Peter's affair. At the same time, such discursive constructions are inimical to the pursuit of a foreign policy enhancing American soft power in an interdependent world.

Besides treating soft power as an argument for liberal internationalism, which can be instrumentalized as a technique/tool/governmental rationality for extending power, this chapter has analysed soft power as embodied in certain practices, systems, institutions, but also in persons and material goods. Therefore, governments will never be able to control all aspects of soft power or produce it at will. In embracing a foreign policy aimed at enhancing the country's soft power, American foreign policymakers will have to overcome notions of the centrality of the USA for the world and embrace international cooperation. Given the heavy investment in the discursive constructions of American power by policymakers, IR scholars and the media worldwide, such a major rethink will have to be spearheaded in part by those who champion such a foreign policy within the American academy, even if it proves a hard sell in the corridors of power, domestically as well as abroad.

Notes

1 I am grateful for the comments and suggestions of Ed Lock, Niamh Moore, Hilary Owen, Inderjeet Parmar and Natalie Zacek, as well as the members of the World Histories Research Group and audiences at the British International Studies Association (BISA), United States Foreign Policy Working Group Annual Conference held in Manchester, 20–21 September 2007; and the Symposium on Soft Power and US Foreign Policy held in Manchester, 22 May 2008. While their contributions have improved this chapter, the interpretation and all remaining errors remain my own.
2 As Nye (2004a: 218) recounts in a short autobiographical sketch on his career, one of his ambitions as a young graduate was to write a novel. His autobiographical sketch suggests that *The Power Game* allowed him to reflect on the differences between academia and public service as well as the morality of American foreign policy. It is noteworthy that Nye continues to refer to the novel in short biographical statements since its publication in 2004 (Nye 2008b: 94).
3 For the concept of sticky power, see Mead (2004).
4 For a survey of this literature, see Schröter (2005). Building on pioneering works (Locke 1989), economic and business historians have started to examine the actual implementation of these models into Western European business practices rather than studying the ideas and their reception in isolation. Many of these studies have been published in a number of collections of essays (Kipping and Bjarnar 1998; Zeitlin and Herrigel 2000; Barjot 2002; Barjot *et al.* 2002; Tiratsoo and Kipping 2002).
5 Michel Foucault developed the concept of liberal governmentality in relation to 20th century liberal democracies in his lectures to the Collège de France in 1978/9; see Foucault (2004); my use of the concept of liberal governmentality draws also heavily on Joyce (2003).
6 For a similar use of Foucault's concept of governmentality, see Engerman (2007).
7 There is a considerable literature on the tensions over the restriction on East–West trade during the Cold War (Adler-Karlsson 1968; Mai 1990; Jackson 2001; Dobson 2002; Eloranta and Ojala 2005; Enderle-Burcel *et al.* 2009).

8 After all, these British interests in the Middle East did not form part of the percentages agreement between Churchill and Stalin; see (Roberts 2007, 26)

9 In the novel, Nye refers to Ali Aziz primarily by his first name Ali reflecting the warm personal friendship between him and Peter Cutler. Therefore, I will follow Nye's practice and refer to both Peter Cutler and Ali Aziz by their first names as well as to other members of their circle of friends at Princeton in this section. In contrast to his use of first names when referring to his personal friends, Nye refers to the persons, Cutler encounters in his political dealings, by their surname.

10 During the World War II, most American policymakers saw such cooperation as vital for post war international cooperation and peace and stability (Leffler 2007). There was broad bipartisan support for this one world vision. See *Prefaces to Peace*, a symposium consisting of the following: *One World* (complete), Wendell L. Willkie; *The problems of lasting peace* (complete), by Herbert Hoover and Hugh Gibson; *The Price of Free World Victory*, by Henry A. Wallace (from the new book *The Century of the Common Man*); *Blue-print for Peace,* by Sumner Welles (from the new book *The World of the Four Freedoms*). 1943. New York: Doubleday, Doran.

11 Searches of digital archives of journals remain a rather crude method of measuring the prevalence of a concept in certain academic disciplines, but a quick search for the term 'soft power' in JSTOR in May 2008 revealed that the term occurred only in five articles published in the history journals included in JSTOR in contrast to 84 hits in politics journals.

Bibliography

Adler-Karlsson, G. (1968) *Western Economic Warfare, 1947–1967: A Case Study in Foreign Economic Policy*, Stockholm: Almqvist & Wiksell.

Arthur, J. (2004) Review of *The Power Game. Washingtonian.Com*, 4 December. Available at: http://www.washingtonian.com/bookreviews/43.html (accessed 8 May 2008).

Barjot, D. (ed.) (2002) *Catching Up with America: Productivity Missions and the Diffusion of American Economic and Technological Influence after the Second World War*, Paris: Presses de l'Université de Paris-Sarbonne.

Barjot, D., Lescent-Giles, I. and Ferrière le Vayer, M. d. (eds) (2002) *L'Américanisation en Europe au XXe siècle: économie, culture, politique*, Lille: Centre de recherche sur l'Histoire de l'Europe du Nord-Ouest, Université Charles de Gaulle.

Baylis, J. (1993) *The Diplomacy of Pragmatism: Britain and the Formation of NATO, 1942–1949*. Basingstoke: Macmillan.

Berghahn, V.R. (2001) *America and the Intellectual Cold Wars in Europe: Shepard Stone between Philanthropy, Academy, and Diplomacy*, Princeton, NJ: Princeton University Press.

——. (1986) *The Americanisation of West German industry 1945–1973*. Leamington Spa: Berg.

Caesar, B. (2009) *Black Students in Red Russia*. BBC Radio 4 documentary broadcast 14 January at 11 a.m.. BBC Radio 4. Available at: http://www.bbc.co.uk/programmes/b00gllnn. accessed: 1 February, 2009.

Clavin, P. (2005) 'Defining Transnationalism', *Contemporary European History*, 14(4): 21–39.

Cox, M. and Kennedy-Pipe, C. (2005) 'The Tragedy of American Diplomacy? Rethinking the Marshall Plan', *Journal of Cold War Studies*, 7(1): 97–134.

104   *Till Geiger*

Dewey, T.E. (1952) *Journey to the Far Pacific*, New York: Doubleday.

Dobson, A.P. (2002) *US Economic Statecraft for Survival, 1933–1991: Of Sanctions, Embargoes and Economic Warfare*, London: Routledge.

Eisenberg, C.W. (2004) 'The Myth of the Berlin Blockade and the Early Cold War', in E. Schrecker (ed.) *Cold War Triumphalism: The Misuse of American History after the Fall of Communism*, New York: New Press, pp. 174–200.

Eloranta, J. and Ojala, J. (eds) (2005) *East-West Trade and the Cold War*, Jyväskylä: University of Jyväskylä Press.

Enderle-Burcel, G., Franaszek, P., Stiefel, D. and Teichova, A. (eds) (2009) *Cold War and Neutrality: East–West Economic Relations in Europe*, Cracow: Jagellonian University Press.

Engerman, D.C. (2007) 'American Knowledge and Global Power', *Diplomatic History*, 31(4): 599–622.

Etheridge, B.C. (2007) '*Die antideusche Welle*: The Anti-German Wave, Public Diplomacy, and Intercultural Relations in Cold War America', in J.C.E. Gienow-Hecht (ed.) *Decentering America. Explorations in Culture and International History*, New York: Berghahn, pp. 73–106.

Fischer, J. (2006) *Die Rückkehr der Geschichte: die Welt nach dem 11. September und die Erneuerung des Westens*, München: Knaur Taschenbuch.

Foucault, M. (2004) *Naissance de la biopolitique: cours au Collège de France (1978–1979)*, Paris: Seuil/Gallimard.

Funigiello, P.J. (1988) *American-Soviet Trade in the Cold War*, Chapel Hill, NC: University of North Carolina Press.

Gaddis, J.L. (1972) *The United States and the Origins of the Cold War, 1941–1947*, New York: Columbia University Press.

Garraty, J.A. and Adams, W. (1959) *From Main Street to the Left Bank; Students and Scholars Abroad*, East Lansing, MI: Michigan State University Press.

Geiger, T. (1996) 'Embracing Good Neighbourliness: Multilateralism, *Pax Americana*, and European Integration, 1945–58', in T. Geiger and D. Kennedy (eds) *Regional Trade Blocs, Multilateralism, and the GATT: Complementary Paths to Free Trade?*, London: Pinter, pp. 56–78.

——. (2002) 'American Hegemony and the Adoption of National Income Statistics in Western Europe after 1945', in D. Barjot, I. Lescent-Giles and M. d. Ferrière le Vayer (eds) *L'Américanisation en Europe au XXe siècle: Économie, culture, politique*, vol. 1, Lille: Centre de recherche sur l'Histoire de l'Europe du Nord-Ouest, Université Charles de Gaulle, pp. 151–67.

——. (2004) *Britain and the Economic Problem of the Cold War: The Political Economy and the Economic Impact of the British Defence Effort, 1945–1955*, Aldershot: Ashgate.

——. (2008) The British warfare state and the challenge of Americanisation of western defence. *European Review of History* 15(4):345–70.

Geiger, T. and Toye, R. (2008). Britain, America and the Origins of the European Payments Union: A reassessment. Working Paper. Available at: http://hdl.handle.net/10036/31032. accessed: 15 March, 2009

Geiger, T. and Sebesta, L. (1996) 'National Defense Policies and the Failure of Military Integration in NATO: American Military Assistance and Western European Rearmament, 1949–54', in F.H. Heller and J.R. Gillingham (eds) *The United States and the Integration of Europe: Legacies for the Postwar Era*, New York: St. Martin's Press, pp. 253–79.

——. (1998) 'A Self-Defeating Policy: American Offshore Procurement and Integration of Western European Defence Production, 1952–56', *Journal of European Integration History*, 4(1): 55–73.

Gienow-Hecht, J.C.E. (2007) 'Introduction: Decentering American History', in J.C.E. Gienow-Hecht (eds) *Decentering America: Explorations in Culture and International History*, New York: Berghahn, pp. 1–20.

Gilman, N. (2003) *Mandarins of the Future: Modernization Theory in Cold War America*, Baltimore: Johns Hopkins University Press.

Goldstein, J. (1993) 'Creating the GATT Rules: Politics, Institutions, and American Policy', in J.G. Ruggie (ed.) *Multilateralism Matters: The Theory and Praxis of an Institutional Form*, New York: Columbia University Press, pp. 201–32.

Greenwood, S. (1990) 'Frank Roberts and the 'Other' Long Telegram: The View from the British Embassy in Moscow, March 1946', *Journal of Contemporary History*, 25(1): 103–22.

Gregor, N. (2008) *Haunted City: Nuremberg and the Nazi Past*, New Haven, CT: Yale University Press.

Hammerich, H.R. (2003) *Jeder für sich und Amerika gegen Alle?: Die Lastenteilung der NATO am Beispiel des Temporary Council Committee 1949 bis 1954*, München: Oldenbourg.

Hirschman, A.O. (1989) 'How the Keynesian Revolution Was Exported from the United States, and Other Comments', in P.A. Hall (ed.) *The Political Power of Economic Ideas: Keynesianism Across Nations*, Princeton, NJ: Princeton University Press, pp. 347–59.

Hogan, M.J. (1987) *The Marshall Plan: America, Britain, and the Reconstruction of Western Europe*, Cambridge: Cambridge University Press.

Hoganson, K. (2006) 'Stuff It: Domestic Consumption and the Americanization of the World Paradigm', *Diplomatic History*, 30(4): 571–94.

Ikenberry, G.J. (1992) A World Economy Restored: Expert Consensus and the Anglo-American Postwar Settlement', *International Organisation*, 46(1): 289–321.

Iriye, A. (2002) *Global Community: The Role of International Organizations in the Making of the Contemporary World*, Berkeley, CA: University of California Press.

Jackson, I. (2001) *The Economic Cold War: America, Britain and East-West trade, 1948–1963*, Basingstoke: Palgrave.

Joyce, P. (2003) *The Rule of Freedom: Liberalism and the Modern City*, London: Verso.

Kipping, M. and Bjarnar, O. (eds) (1998) *The Americanisation of European Business: The Marshall Plan and the Transfer of US Management Models*, London: Routledge.

Krige, J. (2006) *American Hegemony and the Postwar Reconstruction of Science in Europe*, Cambridge: MIT Press.

——. (2008) 'American Hegemony and the Postwar Reconstruction of Science in Europe'. Keynote address presented at. Dimensions of European armaments cooperation conference. Institute of Innovation Research, University of Manchester.

Kuklick, B. (2006) *Blind Oracles: Intellectuals and War from Kennan to Kissinger*, Princeton, NJ: Princeton University Press.

Lawrence, M.A. (2002) 'Transnational Coalition-Building and the Making of the Cold War in Indochina, 1947–49', *Diplomatic History*, 26(3): 453–80.

Leffler, M.P. (2007) *For the Soul of Mankind: The United States, the Soviet Union, and the Cold War*, New York: Hill and Wang.

Lehmann, A. (2000) *Der Marshall-Plan und das neue Deutschland: die Folgen amerikanischer Besatzungspolitik in den Westzonen*, Münster: Waxmann.

Locke, R.R. (1989) *Management and Higher Education since 1940: The Influence of America and Japan in West Germany, Great Britain and France*, Cambridge: Cambridge University Press.

Mai, G. (1990) 'Osthandel and Westintegration, 1947–57. Europa, die USA, die OEEC und die Entstehung einer hegemonialen Partnerschaft', in L. Herbst, W. Bührer and H. Sowade (eds) *Vom Marshallplan zur EWG: Die Eingliederung der Bundesrepublik Deutschland in die westliche Welt*, München: R. Oldenbourg, pp. 203–26.

Maier, C.S. (1992) 'Finance and Defense: Implications of Military Integration, 1950–52', in F.H. Heller and J.R. Gillingham (eds) *NATO: The Founding of the Atlantic Alliance and the integration of Europe*, London: Macmillan, pp. 335–51.

Matsuda, T. (2007) *Soft Power and its Perils: U.S. Cultural Policy in Early Postwar Japan and Permanent Dependency*, Washington: Woodrow Wilson Center Press.

Mead, W.R. (2004) 'America's STICKY Power', *Foreign Policy*, 141(March/April): 46–53.

Menon, R. (2007) *The End of Alliances*. New York: Oxford University Press.

Milward, A.S. (1984) *The Reconstruction of Western Europe, 1945–51*, London: Methuen.

——. (1992a) *The European Rescue of the Nation-State*. London: Routledge.

——. (1992b) 'NATO, OEEC, and the Integration of Europe', in F. Heller and J. Gillingham (eds) *NATO: The Founding of the Atlantic Alliance and the Integration of Europe*, New York: St. Martin's Press, pp. 241–52.

Newton, C.C.S. (1984) 'The Sterling Crisis of 1947 and the British Response to the Marshall Plan', *Economic History Review*, 37(3): 391–408.

Nuclear Suppliers Group (2005) 'The Nuclear Suppliers Group: Its Origins, Role and Activities', (INFCIRC/539/Rev.3) 30 May. Available at: http://www.nuclearsuppliersgroup.org/PDF/infcirc539r3.pdf (accessed: 5 May 2008).

Nye, J.S., Jr (1990a) *Bound to Lead: The Changing Nature of American Power*, New York: Basic Books.

——. (1990b) 'Soft Power', *Foreign Policy*, 80: 153–71.

——. (2002) *The Paradox of American Power: Why the World's Only Superpower Can't Go it Alone*, Oxford: Oxford University Press.

——. (2004a) 'Essay on career choices', in J.S. Nye, Jr (ed.) *Power in the Global Information Age*, London: Routledge, pp. 217–23.

——. (2004b) *The Power Game: A Washington Novel*, New York: Public Affairs.

——. (2004c) *Soft Power: The Means to Success in World Politics*, New York: Public Affairs.

——. (2008a) *The Powers to Lead*, Oxford: Oxford University Press.

——. (2008b) 'Public Diplomacy and Soft Power', *Annals of the American Academy of Political & Social Science*, 616: 94–109.

Obama, B. (2006) *The Audacity of Hope: Thoughts on Reclaiming the American Dream*, United States, New York: Crown Publishers.

——. (2007) *Dreams from My Father: A Story of Race and Inheritance*, Edinburgh: Canongate.

Pells, R.H. (1997) *Not Like Us: How Europeans Have Loved, Hated, and Transformed American Culture Since World War II*, New York, NY: Basic Books.

Ribuffo, L.P. (2004) 'Moral Judgements and the Cold War: Reflections on Reinhold Niebuhr, William Appleman Williams, and John Lewis Gaddis', in E. Schrecker (ed.) *Cold War Triumphalism: The Misuse of American History after the Fall of Communism*, New York: New Press, pp. 27–70.

Roberts, G. (2007) 'Stalin at the Thehran, Yalta, and Potsdam Conferences', *Journal of Cold War Studies*, 9(4): 6–40.

Ruggie, J.G. (1993) 'Multilateralism: The Anatomy of an Institution', in J.G. Ruggie (ed.) *Multilateralism Matters: The Theory and Praxis of an Institutional Form*, New York: Columbia University Press, pp. 3–47.

Schlesinger, A.M. (2007). *Journals, 1952–2000*. Ed. A. Schlesinger and S. Schlesinger. New York: Penguin Press.

Schröter, H.G. (2005) *Americanization of the European Cconomy: A Compact Survey of American Economic Influence in Europe since the 1880s*, Dordrecht: Springer.

Sewell, W.H., Jr (2005) *Logics of History: Social Theory and Social Transformation*, Chicago: University of Chicago Press.

Sjursen, H. (2004) 'On the Identity of NATO', *International Affairs*, 80(4): 687–703.

Soutphommasane, T. and Chau, S. (2005) 'Talking Power: Tim Soutphommasane and Shaun Chau interview Joseph Nye', *The Oxonian Review of Books*, 4(2). Available at: http://www.oxonianreview.org/issues/4–2/4–2–2.htm (accessed 8 May 2008).

Tiratsoo, N. and Kipping, M. (eds) (2002) *Americanization in 20th Century Europe: Business, Culture, Politics*, Lille: Centre de recherche sur l'Histoire de l'Europe du Nord-Ouest, Université Charles de Gaulle.

Trachtenberg, M. (2008) 'The United States and Eastern Europe in 1945: A Reassessment', *Journal of Cold War Studies*, 10(4): 94–132.

United States Department of State (1952) *North Atlantic Treaty Organization: Its Development and Significance*, Washington, DC: Washington.

Wilson, E.J., III (2008) 'Hard Power, Soft Power, Smart Power', *Annals of the American Academy of Political & Social Science*, 616: 110–24.

Zeitlin, J. (2000) 'Introduction', in J. Zeitlin and G. Herrigel (ed.) *Americanization and its Limits: Reworking US Technology and Management in Post-war Europe and Japan*, Oxford: Oxford University Press, pp. 1–50.

——. and G. Herrigel, (eds) (2000) *Americanization and its Limits: Reworking US Technology and Management in Post-war Europe and Japan*, Oxford: Oxford University Press.

6 Challenging elite anti-Americanism in the Cold War

American foundations, Kissinger's Harvard Seminar and the Salzburg seminar in American studies

Inderjeet Parmar

Philanthropic foundations are a significant force in the American political-ideological system. Their formation at the turn of the twentieth-century marked a key development in three ways. First, they were part of a set of east coast elite responses to rapid social transformations – industrialization and increasing concentration of corporate wealth, mass immigration and urbanization – that threatened to spiral out of control and lead the USA into a more collectivist direction. Philanthropy, as a source of intellectual and experts' mobilization – a technocratic response to change – aimed to manage and direct social change into 'safer' channels.[1]

Second, foundations' formation represented a key step in the gradual rise of US federal executive branch power because philanthropy – along with the rising universities, national church organizations and reform movements – aimed to root out the corruption and parochialism associated with party politics, electoral competition and Congress. Foundations acted as para-state organizations: their self-concept was state-oriented, seeing the problems of the state as their own, despite their 'private' voluntarist character. In Gramscian terms, foundations embodied 'state spirit' – a feeling among certain leading private figures and associations that they bear a grave responsibility to promote a historical process – state-building – through positive political and intellectual activity.[2] Seeing the USA in national, rather than local, terms, they sought to build federal institutional power upon a supportive national public opinion and undercut parochially oriented party organization and political representation.[3]

Third, Foundations' formation marked the rise of a global consciousness in the east coast elite and of the USA as a potentially great world power. Foundation leaders saw their role in addressing problems of world peace, tackling disease and underdevelopment, and spreading the benefits of the American dream to the world.[4] As the twentieth century progressed, the relationship between state foreign policymakers and philanthropy broadened and deepened, blurring the already vague distinction between private actors and public power. By the end of World

War II, the foundations were well ensconced at the heart of the foreign policy establishment, assisting America's rise to globalism by constructing university foreign affairs institutes, foreign policy think tanks, international studies and area studies programmes, graduate training courses for US Foreign Service officers, and enhancing the research and analysis capacity of the Department of State. Such efforts coalesced with the expansionist objectives of the American state with which the foundations were inextricably connected both ideologically and personally.[5]

Promoting Americanism and combatting anti-Americanism were among the foundations' key contributions to constructing post-war American hegemony. The foundations financed privately funded public diplomacy that sought to counter foreign elites' 'anti-Americanism'. This chapter briefly examines two influential initiatives to show how those programmes operated and to indicate their effects. But first, it is important, briefly, to examine the concepts of 'Americanism' and 'anti-Americanism' as they provided, at least, part of the underlying rationale of American post-war globalism.

Foundation leaders, as part of the east coast foreign policy establishment, saw the USA as a world power whose time had come, a power superior to all others – moral, advanced, anti-colonial, exceptional. The American system was, they believed, ready for export. Its scientific, industrial and military achievements were evidence of its superiority over all other systems, including inegalitarian Europe and communist Russia, not to mention the 'under-developed' post- or neo-colonial world. Only the USA – born out of an anti-colonial democratic revolutionary struggle – was fit to lead the world out of the mire of European imperial domination and to defend it against communist 'aggression'. In this regard, foundation leaders were squarely within the American exceptionalist tradition.[6]

Yet, the leaders of American philanthropy saw numerous threats to their globalist aspirations: European envy and resentment of American power and wealth, as well as ignorance or misunderstanding of the new superpower's society, culture and politics. Opposition to US foreign policy, therefore, was seen as based on emotion, ignorance and nostalgia. The solution for liberal internationalist Americans was cultural or public diplomacy specifically targeted at European elites to persuade them that the USA was a force for good in the world, defending freedom and fighting tyranny; that its culture was deep and not shallow, that its material wealth was not alone the obsession of its culture, that it had an abiding and serious interest in abstract problems and ideas – in art, music, and philosophy. In short, the aim was to show that US power was not the naked expression of a dangerously shallow society, a volatile political system prone to witch-hunts led by demagogues or a hollow political elite. They wanted to promote the image of a national leadership that was cultured, sophisticated, educated, serious, rational, sober, reflective and thoughtful. It was a leadership that could be trusted to use its power wisely in the interests of the world system, not purely in its own narrow national interests.

Foundations and post-war American hegemony

After 1945, foundation leaders developed a crisis mentality, mirroring that within the American state. With the developing perception of a 'communist threat', foundation leaders increasingly saw the world in stark terms: America's friends and foes, the forces of freedom versus the 'evil empire' or the 'slave state', as the infamous NSC-68 (National Security Council Paper 68) put it in April 1950.[7] They saw 'anti-Americanism' as a part of the communist threat or, at the very least, its fellow-traveller. Within the mindset of the national security state, criticism of American society or government was seen as 'anti-American'. The Carnegie, Rockefeller and Ford foundations lined up behind a programme of hegemonic expansion: promoting Americanism and combating anti-Americanism through public diplomacy were key dimensions of that project. This is an under-researched but fundamental aspect of the foundations' activities during this period, rich in lessons about the nature of the foundations themselves in a time of global transitions – the rise of US power, relative decline of Europe and the formation of post-colonial states – as well as about how American 'soft power' – trying to persuade other powers to back US foreign policies, as opposed to coercion – operated in a world of rising anti-Americanism.[8] The programmes contrast well with what critics argue is inadequate in public diplomacy today: the focus on 'selling' or 'rebranding' America, as indicated by the appointment of Madison Avenue advertising executive (and former CEO of the multi-billion dollar firm, Ogilvy and Mather), Charlotte Beers in 2001, rather than with engaging and debating with its European allies.[9]

Henry Kissinger's Harvard University international summer seminar

As Scott Lucas argues, Kissinger's Harvard Seminar illustrates the degree to which the USA's hegemonic project integrated culture, the academy and American foreign policy, tightening the integration of a state-private network to wage a war 'defending' the American way of life.[10] The advantage of such state-private networks was that official policy objectives – promoting American interests and pro-American ideas and elites – could be met, or at least advanced, especially in 'sensitive' areas or issues, by purportedly unofficial, non-governmental means.[11] American foundations – that claimed to be independent of the state, non-political and non-ideological – were ideal institutional mechanisms for the promotion of Americanism and combating anti-Americanism. The Seminar was originally formed by Harvard's William Y. Elliott, Central Intelligence Agency (CIA) consultant and Kissinger's doctoral supervisor, with initial funding (US$15,000) from the CIA in 1951.[12] From 1950, Kissinger became the linchpin of the Seminar, developing its ideological rationale and recruiting the participants. By 1953, Kissinger had obtained financial support from the Farfield Foundation, a conduit for CIA finances. In 1954, the Ford Foundation began its sponsorship of Kissinger's seminar, the beginning of a long relationship.[13] Public and private finances, therefore, were inextricably bound up in the origins of Kissinger's Seminar, fully exemplifying the state-private network concept.

The aim of the Seminar, Kissinger argued, was 'to create a spiritual link between the younger generation of Europe and American values' as Europeans were frustrated with the collapse of 'traditional values' and the rise of a seemingly unsympathetic USA, 'a bewildering spectacle of economic prosperity and seeming misunderstanding of European problems'.[14] This attitude opened the way for 'neutralism' and communism to win European support. The Seminar would 'assist in counteracting these tendencies, by giving inwardly alive, intelligent young Europeans an opportunity to study the deeper meaning of U.S. democracy'. The programme, however, would fail if it were merely one of 'dogmatic indoctrination'; therefore, it had to be focused around *persuading* Europeans that Americans were genuinely concerned with 'abstract problems' and not just 'material prosperity'. The programme was to be a forum for *'disagreement and criticism'*, with a view to *demonstrating* that 'self-reliance is a *possibility* despite the complexity of the present age and that the assumption of *personal responsibility* is more meaningful than unquestioning submission to an apparatus'. Just like communists, democrats needed to display 'the strength of their convictions' (emphasis added).[15]

Hence, this Seminar was no blunt-edged attempt at indoctrination: the deeper abstract and philosophical meaning of life in American democracy animated the programme by examining the concept of freedom, 'the striving for self-realization in art against the felt pressure of convention, the quest for a reconciliation of rationalism, personal responsibility and dogmatism in religion'. The Seminar aimed to produce no 'absolute solutions' to policy and social problems but to generate an *'elucidation of fundamental issues'*, making 'social problems … *challenges for normative concepts* …' (emphasis added).[16]

The role of the Ford foundation

Given the leadership of Ford in the early 1950s – men such as Paul Hoffman, John J. McCloy and Shepard Stone (all connected with the State Department or CIA) – the Foundation provided a perfect source for privately financing the Harvard Seminar.[17] Between 1954 and 1959, Ford awarded US$170,000 to the Harvard Seminar, bringing together leaders and potential leaders from across Europe and Asia, networking them with Americans and familiarizing them with American values and institutions. In all, Ford contributed millions of dollars to the efforts of Kissinger and others to improve transatlantic relations between 1954 and 1971.[18] For instance, the 1954 group of 40 – aged between 35–40 years (a group that often sought refuge in 'a narrow nationalism', according to Kissinger)[19] – participants included a German diplomat, a British Member of Parliament, a French journalist, a Korean lecturer and a Filipino lawyer, among others. Numbers were kept low enough to enable Seminar leaders 'to pay personal attention to each participant', the selection policy being based 'as much as possible on the personal recommendations of reliable individuals'. It was clear to Kissinger that the success of the programme depended 'to a large extent on its selection process'. The Seminar received around 700 European applications annually; final selection was based on recommendations by American and European elites – the contributors to Kissinger's journal, *Confluence*, Seminar alumni, 'Harvard faculty with European connections' and the recommendations of international societies such as the English-Speaking Union and various Institutes of World Affairs. Asians tended to be selected on the basis of recommendations by the US Information Service, Harvard alumni clubs and university recommendations.[20] In Japan, a group of 'private citizens' – headed by the president of the Harvard Club of Japan – made recommendations. All recommendations were assessed for short-listing by Kissinger, his assistant, and by a national of the applicant's country of origin, interviewed in Europe by a trusted representative (in France by Reverend Gerardus Beekman of the American Pro-Cathedral; in Germany and the Low Countries by Juergen Weichert, secretary of the West German parliament's Foreign Affairs Committee – a Harvard Seminar alumnus; in Italy, it was Gian Brioschi, head of the financial department at Olivetti whom Kissinger described as 'an outstanding "alumnus"' of the Seminar).[21] The final decision was made at Harvard, minimizing the chances of any dangerous elements.

It was argued that the Seminar members were 'prolific' writers and speakers upon return to their homes, spreading the Seminar's message far and wide. State Department and Institute of International Education representatives, who had observed the Seminar at close quarters, also endorsed its importance.[22] In 1956, Ford reported that the Seminar was yielding a number of positive effects on participants and for the USA in general. For example, the Seminar seemed to be an excellent forum in which to 'correct false impressions of the United States, notably among Asian visitors'; it attracted 'influential or potentially influential people' from strategic areas; its effects were felt beyond Harvard as 'responsible' press comments suggested that other US universities were influenced by the Seminar through the participation of faculty and dissemination of Seminar publications; and the Seminar 'helps to develop understanding and a sense of common purpose between Americans and influential foreigners and among the foreigners themselves ...' some of whom had set up Seminar alumni clubs and a regional seminar in India. Ford funded many of the alumni meetings and circulated Seminar literature to all Seminar alumni, helping to sustain the network.[23]

The Seminar was skilfully devised to provide a range of contacts with American life over a period of two months: seminars on politics, economics, philosophy, art, American democracy, and discussions on 'America's role in relation to other countries of the world'; evening lectures by outsiders and Harvard and other faculty, including a robust defence of the McCarthyite investigating committees by James Burnham; *foreigners' presentations on their own nations' problems*; visits to American business organizations, labour unions, newspapers, local families and baseball games. Weaved into a complex programme aimed at appreciating America's role in the world were numerous meetings devoted to such seemingly irrelevant topics as 'the nature of the poetic', French theatre, the German novel after World War II and the revival of religious art in France.[24] Yet, herein lay part of the strength of the Seminar, designed to illustrate the fabric and depth of American life, helping to achieve the Seminar's objective of overcoming 'national prejudices'.

Social occasions were explicitly arranged in order to 'encourage the establishment of personal friendships with Americans', thereby creating emotional bonds between elites.[25] The genuine *engagement* between the participants and Seminar leaders provided a sense of *ownership* among the visitors.[26] Kissinger outlined the detailed programme to the Ford Foundation, showing the way in which political scientist Earl Latham had led the discussion of the pluralistic character of the American political system and MIT economist Charles P. Kindleberger had examined economic conditions in the world system. In detailed discussions, issues such as communist China, neutrality and world communism, had been thoroughly aired and discussed. The social programme, Kissinger claimed, led to greater appreciation of American society than any formal lecture or reading courses. For Kissinger, the programme's most 'decisive' impact was the 'attitudes engendered in the minds' of participants in '*the crucible of informal conversations*' (emphasis added). It was noted, for example, that 'Seminar members found that an evening's conversation with an American couple and their friends resulted in a more profound appreciation of the American society than months of reading prior to coming here.'[27] Through the intensity and close contact over eight weeks, Seminar members discovered 'a wealth of channels toward general international understanding ...' In these ways, the Harvard Seminar, Kissinger concluded, 'provided them with a unique opportunity to assess the qualities of the nation which bears the heaviest burden of responsibility in the Western World. ... Each of them has carried away a deeper insight into what they had previously distrusted in America – an insight often resulting in elimination of their initial disturbance.' Working in the Widener Library at Harvard, participating in challenging discussions, and enjoying the performances of the Boston Symphony Orchestra, *dispelled participants initial ideas about the shallowness of American culture.*[28] In short, Kissinger declared the Seminar an unqualified success because it appeared to engender among elite Europeans and Asians empathy, understanding and appreciation of American society, its elite and its 'burden of responsibility' to the West.

More sinisterly, Seminar participants were under surveillance and reported on by faculty. For example, Professor Earl Latham reported in detail to Kissinger on the 1955 participants' personalities, attitudes and impact. Overall, though he felt that the group had been 'more pronouncedly leftish (sic). ...the voice of reason could be heard from time to time, speaking with a Chinese or a Korean accent'. Conversely, many of the Asians had doggedly attempted to hold to their 'neutralism', though with little success against an onslaught from the rest of the group. One participant – Burk – was suspected of Trotskyite tendencies; his 'outlook seems to be impenetrably rigid and narrow', Latham noted.[29]

According to the archival record, participants' evaluations of the Seminar were overwhelmingly positive. Kissinger passed on to the Ford Foundation excerpts from hundreds of letters of appreciation from participants as evidence of the

Seminar's effectiveness. Participants reported that the Seminar was 'exciting, informative, and remarkable for *candour*'; that the Seminar was 'forming an [international] elite which is so badly needed' in building world unity; that the knowledge and understanding gained would help to *challenge* any 'false accusation thrown against the American people'; that the Seminar exhibited little of the stereotypical American 'conformism'; that 'your method of recruiting [American] speakers who are *critical and who tell us the worst as well as the best is far more disarming and successful than any sort of traditional propaganda ...*'. Alain Clement, a journalist with *Le Monde* – a leading neutralist newspaper (i.e. supportive of concept of an independent Europe wedded to neither superpower) – returned a convert to American culture, Harvard and Henry Kissinger.[30] Kissinger thought that the Seminar, despite his own growing responsibilities (with the US State Department, National Security Council, US Arms Control and Disarmament Agency and the RAND Corporation), was so effective and important that he would continue to organize it.[31] Important alumni of the Seminar include such leaders as Japan's Yasuhiro Nakasone (1953), France's Giscard d'Estaing (1954), and Malaysia's Mahathir Mohammed (1968).[32] In form and content, the Harvard Seminar differed radically from the public diplomacy of the post-1989 and post-9/11 periods.[33] It provided to Seminar members 'a sense of actively participating rather than ...merely being recipients'.[34] The Seminar, however, was just one part of an impressive array of public diplomacy operations at the time.

Salzburg Seminar in American studies: 'the faint odour of cultural imperialism'[35]

The Salzburg Seminar in American Studies was, in effect, the overseas counterpart of the Harvard Seminar:[36] it was targeted at European men and women at the cusp of leadership positions in their own society – in law, politics, business, academia – and was run on the basis of *candid exchange, criticism and intellectual engagement*. It represented a kind of public diplomacy – as opposed to propagandistic advertising – that some today hope to restore, as the tide of anti-Americanism rises around the world.[37] It began in 1947 as a cooperative venture between the Geneva International Student Service and the Harvard Student Council to improve Europeans' understanding of American society. By the late 1960s, 6,500 fellows had attended courses at the Seminar's castle, Schloss Leopoldskron.[38]

The aim of the Seminar was simple: to improve transatlantic understanding (because even highly educated Europeans regarded the US in 'a distorted and negative light')[39] through '*dialogue* between people who count and who are going to count'. According to the president of Columbia University, the Seminar was designed to have its 'greatest effect upon men ...who must be counted upon by the public opinion-forming groups in their respective countries'.[40] It was further noted for its attempt to put forward the '*unvarnished facts* about the United States', and to explore transatlantic issues 'with *candour and in depth*'. If a 'true' picture were to be painted, 'it is not always flattering'. Great emphasis was placed on critical engagement among participants and American Seminar faculty, the flavour of which is captured by key terms recurring through every report on the Seminar: problems to 'hammer out' between faculty and participants, 'candour tempered by tolerance', 'seeking together', 'finding together', avoiding propaganda.[41] For Grayson Kirk, a keen Seminar supporter, the value of American resources expended on 'propaganda' was questionable.[42] It was the concept of a 'two-way avenue of learning' that motivated Seminar organizers, which was to bear fruit.[43] This was evidenced by a Czech Fellow's comment in 1967: '*Your propaganda is the best propaganda, because it is not propaganda at all.*'[44] On the basis of that 'non-propagandistic' propaganda, European elites were to spread their understanding far and wide through their organizations, newspapers, books and lectures.[45] As Salzburg officers argued in 1960, 'in Europe, more than in America, public opinion is molded by a relatively small number of people. They disseminate their *reorientated* [in light of their education at Salzburg] ideas on American life through their newspapers and periodicals, schools and universities, trade unions. ...'[46]

An analysis of Seminar Fellows by occupation (1951–9) reveals its success in recruiting emerging elites in its aim to 'educate' Europe's opinion leaders: of the 2,878 participants, there were 718 graduate students, 564 teachers/academics, 376 journalists, editors and writers, 343 government officials and civil servants, 260 lawyers and 60 union leaders. Fellows were drawn from a range of countries: the best represented were Germany (585), Italy (478) and France (411), all pivotal continental states.[47]

In their grant applications, Salzburg officers consistently differentiated their (American) ideas, methods and outlook from those of their European Fellows. Europeans were elitist in attitude, while the Americans were more egalitarian. Europeans were constantly impressed by American openness in contrast to their own reticence. For example, even the open-access character of the library facilities and resources at Salzburg (10,000 books, 100 periodicals, a wide range of newspapers, etc. ...) was reportedly 'a source of amazement to Europeans unused to such "open" procedures and is, again, an experience for them with a basic American characteristic.'[48]

The Ford Foundation began financial support for the Seminar in 1955, and covered 20 per cent of its financial costs for the next 20 years – total funding of almost US$1 million. The State Department and the Fulbright programme furnished much of the rest. The Fulbright programme was inaugurated in 1946 to increase mutual international understanding through exchange of scholars across the world. Ford believed that the Seminar was 'one of the most effective of all American Studies programmes', affording opportunities to further connect East and West European leaders, as attested by State Department officials.[49] The Seminar's board of directors included Harvard's Dean (and later national security adviser to the Kennedy and Johnson administrations, and Ford Foundation president) McGeorge Bundy, Emilio G. Collado of Standard Oil and MIT's Walt Rostow.[50]

In operation, the Seminar's schedule was intense. Run over four weeks (thrice a year), the Seminar featured morning lectures, afternoon small group work, and evening discussions and private reading in its well-stocked library. The 'seemingly informal' aspects of the programme, as organizers put it, were fundamental: 'The continual extra-curricular discussion among Fellows, faculty, and staff, all of whom live under the same roof throughout the session; the recreational activities in which everyone participates; in fact, the actual teaching method itself – the constant opportunity for questions during lectures and the close association with faculty which differs so radically from the European method, all give impressions in the understanding of America as a working democracy and, as such, are as important as the actual subject matters taught.'[51]

The specific effects are difficult to gauge. An internal Ford report surprised its own author as to the Salzburg Seminar's effectiveness over a period of two decades. Sociologist Daniel Bell lauded the Seminar as educating and bonding together European intellectuals, and launching the careers of several young scholars such as Ralf Dahrendorf (author, most famously, of *Class and Class Conflict in Industrial Society* in 1959, and director of the London School of Economics, 1974–84) and Michel Crozier (author of *The Bureaucratic Phenomenon* in 1964). He also indicated that Seminar alumni were now teaching at Columbia and Stanford universities. For Bell, Salzburg alumni were immediately distinguishable at the Congress for Cultural Freedom seminars he had directed during 1956–7.[52] Seminar president, Dexter Perkins, noted the formation of alumni clubs – 'Salzburg Circles' – that held reunions to 'discuss American society'. He also noted that alumni had a 'conception of the United States that is more sympathetic – or, at least, more objective …'. The Salzburg Seminar also inspired the formation of the European Association for American Studies after the former's 1954 conference of American Civilisation academics. The aim of EAAS was to 'continue the work begun by the Seminar-sponsored conference'.[53]

Conclusion

Taken together, Ford's American Studies programmes were a powerful means by which global elites' 'anti-American' prejudices and concerns were addressed through initiatives that *directly* touched thousands, probably tens of thousands of men and women. Indirectly, especially through the Congress for Cultural Freedom, Ford's public diplomacy struggle against 'anti-Americanism' affected millions of students, academics, journalists and the newspaper and magazine readers.[54] The Kissinger and Salzburg Seminars were integrated, coherent, focused, well-organized and profoundly engaging. They engaged their participants in total dialogue, disputation, argument and debate. They appeared to be authentic educational programmes designed for two-way exchange and learning – and were, thereby, not seen as condescending propaganda or, even, *any* kind of propaganda, or as the 'best' kind of propaganda. The programmes at Harvard and Salzburg created enduring nuclei of scholars and other opinion-formers, networked with American institutions and faculty, and with each other, functioning effectively long after the short Seminars were over. The message of the Seminars was not only in the spoken and written word; it was in the very texture of the whole experience: members *lived* Americanism when they criticized and debated race relations or foreign policy. Both Harvard's Kissinger and Salzburg's leaders recognized that the social aspects of the interactions made possible by the Seminars were as vital as the formal programme. As Herzog noted, 'The most lasting product of the Salzburg Seminar often is the by-product.'[55]

The Harvard and Salzburg Seminars were successful for one other reason: they were directed at elites whose national and world orientations were not *fundamentally* antagonistic to the aims of American power. After all, most Europeans were products of a colonial culture constructed over centuries. As post-colonial powers, their world-view transformed into a neo-colonial 'developmentalism' to redefine their relationship with the Third World. Their problems with the USA broadly sprang from resentment at their own nations' fall from global grace alongside America's ascendance as well as a fear of the consequences of American power in the nuclear age. That is, overall, despite their scepticism, they were not beyond persuasion by a sophisticated elite diplomacy set in prestigious Harvard Yard or an eighteenth-century castle to lend a patina of antiquity to the USA, and significant gravity to the proceedings. They were susceptible to the exercise of 'soft power' precisely because European elites had a vested interest in the world system the management of which had passed largely into American hands after World War II.

The Harvard and Salzburg programmes supplemented and supported, at the level of sub-state and private elite leadership, what states were trying to achieve in this period: alliance-formation as a way to greater western penetration of the Third World in a period of rising anti-colonial nationalism and global competition with communism. Indeed, the programmes were integrated into the objectives of the State Department, which worked with Harvard and Salzburg 'intimately but unofficially'.[56] Ford Foundation funding helped construct the infrastructure – the institutional settings, organizations, professional societies, conferences and seminars, alumni networks, publications – that enabled the formation and endurance of elite networks – that influenced the climate of intellectual and popular opinion – in an era of emerging American global leadership.[57] Ford – inextricably linked with the official makers of US foreign policy, major American corporations and prestigious universities – claimed to be acting non-politically, non-ideologically and independently of the state. Yet, its outlook as demonstrated by its own archival records, shows that Ford operated with a rather formal notion of 'independence' of the state, behind which lay a philosophy saturated with Gramsci's concept of state spiritedness. In practice, the Ford Foundation was a strategic part of an elite state-private network, a power elite, that united key elements of a Cold War coalition – an historic bloc – behind an imperial hegemonic project.

Notes

1 Robert F. Arnove, ed., *Philanthropy and Cultural Imperialism* (Boston: GK Hall, 1980).
2 Quintin Hoare and Geoffrey Nowell-Smith, eds, *Selections From the Prison Notebooks of Antonio Gramsci* (London: Lawrence and Wishart, 1971), pp. 146–7.

3 Eldon J. Eisenach, *The Lost Promise of Progressivism* (Lawrence, KS: University Press of Kansas, 1994); Inderjeet Parmar, *Think Tanks and Power in Foreign Policy: A Comparative Study of the Role and Influence of the Council on Foreign Relations and the Royal Institute of International Affairs, 1939–1945* (London: Palgrave, 2004).

4 Inderjeet Parmar, 'American Foundations and the Development of International Knowledge Networks', *Global Networks* 2(1) 2002, pp. 13–30.

5 Inderjeet Parmar, '"To Relate Knowledge and Action": the Impact of the Rockefeller Foundation on Foreign Policy Thinking during America's Rise to Globalism', *Minerva* 40(3) 2002, pp. 235–63; Parmar, 'The Carnegie Corporation and the Mobilisation of Opinion in the United States' Rise to Globalism, 1939–45', *Minerva* 37(4) 1999, pp. 355–78; Parmar, 'Engineering Consent: The Carnegie Endowment for International Peace and the Mobilization of American Public Opinion, 1939–45', *Review of International Studies* 26(1) 2000, pp. 35–48.

6 Seymour Martin Lipset, *American Exceptionalism. A Double-Edged Sword* (New York: WW Norton and Co., 1996).

7 Melvin P. Leffler, *A Preponderance of Power* (Stanford, CA: Stanford University Press, 1992); Kathleen D. McCarthy, 'From Cold War to Cultural Development: The international cultural activities of the Ford Foundation, 1950–80', *Daedalus* (Winter 1987), pp. 93–117.

8 'Soft power lies in the ability to attract and persuade rather than coerce. It means that others want what the United States wants, and there is less need to use carrots and sticks ... Soft power arises from the attractiveness of a country's culture, political ideals, and policies. When U.S. policies appear legitimate in the eyes of others, American soft power is enhanced'; Joseph S. Nye, 'US Power and Strategy after Iraq'. Available at: http://www.ksg.harvard.edu/news/opeds/2003/nye_usiraq_foraffairs_070103.htm.

9 Jeffrey Gedmin and Craig Kennedy, 'Selling America, Short', *The National Interest*, Winter 2003; Richard T. Arndt, *The First Resort of Kings* (Washington, DC: Potomac Books, 2005).

10 Scott Lucas, 'A Document from the Harvard International Summer School', in JCE Gienow-Hecht and F. Schumacher, eds., *Culture and International History* (New York: Berghahn Books, 2003), p. 258.

11 Inderjeet Parmar, 'Conceptualising the State-Private Network in American Foreign Policy', in Helen Laville and Hugh Wilford, eds, *The US Government, Citizen Groups, and the Cold War: The State-Private Network* (London: Frank Cass, 2005); see also, Liam Kennedy and Scott Lucas, 'Enduring Freedom: Public Diplomacy and U.S. Foreign Policy', *American Quarterly* 57(2) 2005, pp. 309–33.

12 George Kennan endorsed the Seminar plan as having 'a worthy, dignified and useful purpose' when he forwarded it to the Ford Foundation for support; Memorandum, John B. Howard to Joseph M. McDaniel, Jr, 'Harvard Summer School Foreign Students Project', 24 May 1951; PA 55–59, reel 0942.

13 Lucas, p. 259. Kissinger was Director of the Seminar, 1951–71.

14 Kissinger was involved in recent similar activities in behalf of the German Marshall Fund's transatlantic understanding programmes; *Annual Report*, 2003, pp. 1–6.

15 Henry Kissinger, 'Report of the Sub-committee on Academic Programs' (undated, October/November, 1950), in Lucas, pp. 261–2.

16 Lucas, p. 263.

17 In one letter concerning grant applications to Ford, Kissinger offered to provide supporting references from Allen W. Dulles (CIA Director) and C.D. Jackson, head of the Congress for Cultural Freedom initiative; Kissinger to Don K. Price

(FF associate director), December 10, 1953; PA53–159, reel 1118; Ford Foundation Archives (FFA), New York; see also, Volker R. Berghahn, *America and the Intellectual Cold Wars in Europe. Shepard Stone Between Philanthropy, Academy, and Diplomacy* (Princeton, NJ: Princeton University Press, 2001).

18 Ford Foundation annual reports; see also, Ford Foundation, *American Studies Abroad*; report 004642, April 1969; in total, FF granted Kissinger over US$390,000; FFA.

19 'Docket Excerpt. Executive Committee meeting September 27, 1956: International Programs: International Affairs: Harvard University International Seminar'; PA 55–59; reel 0492.

20 'Docket excerpt, Executive Committee Mtg. September 27, 1956: International Programs: International Affairs. Harvard University International Seminar'; Grant file PA 55–59; reel 0492; FFA.

21 'Docket excerpt, Executive Committee Mtg. September 27, 1956: International Programs: International Affairs. Harvard University International Seminar'; Grant file PA 55–59; reel 0492; FFA.

22 'Excerpt from Docket: International Affairs: Harvard International Seminar', 29–30 October 1954; Grant file, PA 55–59; reel 0492; Ford Foundation Archives (FFA), New York.

23 'Docket excerpt, Executive Committee Mtg. 27 September 1956: International Programs: International Affairs. Harvard University International Seminar'; Grant file PA 55–59; reel 0492; FFA.

24 'Docket excerpt, Executive Committee Mtg. 27 September 1956: International Programs: International Affairs. Harvard University International Seminar'; Grant file PA 55–59; reel 0492; FFA.

25 'Docket Excerpt. ... 27 September 1956'; Grant File PA 55–59; reel 0492; FFA.

26 Inter-Office Memorandum, Bernard L. Gladieux to Joseph M. McDaniel, 'Harvard International Seminar (-A351 Revised)', 13 August 1952); PA55–59, reel 0492; FFA.

27 'Docket excerpt, Executive Committee Mtg. 27 September 1956.

28 Henry Kissinger, report on 1955 programme; PA 55–59; reel 0492; FFA.

29 Letter, Latham to Kissinger, 25 August 1955; PA55–59, reel 0492; FFA.

30 'Extracts of letters from past participants,' attached to a letter, Kissinger to Harold Swearer (FF), 4 November 1968; PA69–134, reel 2248; FFA.

31 Letter, Kissinger to Harold Swearer (FF), 4 November 1968; PA69–134, reel 2248; FFA.

32 Walter Isaacson, *Kissinger* (London: Simon and Schuster, 1992), p. 71.

33 Gedmin and Kennedy.

34 Inter-Office Memorandum, 'Harvard International Seminar', Bernard L. Gladieux to Joseph McDaniel, 13 August 1952; PA 55–59, reel 0942.

35 Inter-office memorandum, Richard C. Sheldon to W. McNeill Lowry, 'American Studies,' 5 March 1968, p. 2; PA69–134, reel 2248.

36 Indeed, this was precisely how Kissinger and Elliott contextualised their own efforts; letter, Elliott to Don K. Price (Ford Foundation), 13 February 1954; PA55–59, reel 0942.

37 Gedmin and Kennedy.

38 David E. Bell and McNeill Lowry, Grant Allocation to Salzburg Seminar in American Studies, Inc., 20 January 1970; p. 3; PA55–216; reel 2081; FFA.

39 Dexter Perkins, 'A Proposal to Strengthen the Salzburg Seminar in American Studies', March 1960; PA55–216, reel 2081; FFA. The Fellows were selected by 'responsible' men in Europe and officers of the US Information Service; many alumni subsequently

went on to take up Commonwealth Fund study scholarships in the USA, becoming networked in a tightly organized set of US east coast establishment organizations.

40 Letter, Grayson Kirk to Dexter Perkins (President, Salzburg Seminar), 8 March 1960; PA55–216, reel 2081.

41 All quotes are from: Paul M. Herzog (President, Salzburg Seminar), 'Application to the Ford Foundation for a Grant for the Period 1970–75', October 1969; PA55–216, reel 2081; FFA.

42 Letter, Grayson Kirk to Dexter Perkins (President, Salzburg Seminar), 8 March 1960; PA55–216, reel 2081.

43 Perkins, 'A Proposal to Strengthen the Salzburg Seminar in American Studies', March 1960; PA55–216, reel 2081; FFA.

44 Cited by Herzog, 'Application to the Ford. …'; PA55–216, reel 2081.

45 Bell and Lowry, Grant Allocation to Salzburg Seminar, 20 January 1970; PA55–216, reel 2081.

46 Perkins, 'A Proposal to Strengthen the Salzburg Seminar in American Studies', March 1960; PA55–216, reel 2081; FFA.

47 Perkins, 'A Proposal to Strengthen the Salzburg Seminar in American Studies', Exhibit IV; March 1960; PA55–216, reel 2081; FFA.

48 Perkins, 'A Proposal to Strengthen the Salzburg Seminar in American Studies', March 1960; PA55–216, reel 2081; FFA.

49 Bell and Lowry.

50 Perkins, 'A Proposal to Strengthen the Salzburg Seminar in American Studies …', Exhibit XIV; March 1960; PA55–216, reel 2081; FFA.

51 Perkins, 'A Proposal to Strengthen the Salzburg Seminar in American Studies', March 1960; PA55–216, reel 2081; FFA.

52 Letter, Daniel Bell to Dexter Perkins, 1 March 1960; PA55–216, reel 2081.

53 Perkins, 'A Proposal to Strengthen the Salzburg Seminar in American Studies. …', March 1960; PA55–216, reel 2081; FFA.

54 Ford Foundation, *American Studies Abroad*, April 1969; report 004642; FFA.

55 Paul M. Herzog, 'Application to the Ford Foundation …', October 1969; PA55–216, reel 2081.

56 Letter, Elliott to Price, 13 February 1954; PA55–59, reel 0942. Ben Whitaker argues with conviction that American foundations rarely, if ever, considered a course of action without first consulting the State Department, providing further succour to the state-private network concept; *The Foundations: An Anatomy of Philanthropy and Society* (London: Eyre Methuen, 1974).

57 Inderjeet Parmar, 'Institutes of International Affairs: Their Roles in Foreign Policy-making, Opinion Mobilization and Unofficial Diplomacy', in D. Stone and A. Denham, eds, *Think Tank Traditions* (Manchester: Manchester University Press, 2004), pp. 19–34; Parmar, 'American Foundations and the Development of International Knowledge Networks', *Global Networks* 2(1) 2002, pp. 13–30. See also, Lewis Coser, *Men of Ideas* (New York: The Free Press, 1965).

7 Technological leadership and American soft power

John Krige

'We're an empire now, and when we act, we create our own reality. And while you're studying that reality – judiciously as you will – we'll act again, creating other new realities, which you can study too [...]. We're history's actors ... and you, all of you, will be left to just study what we do.'[1] Thus spoke an aide to President Bush in an exchange with Ron Susskind, a former senior reporter for the *Wall Street Journal,* in summer 2002. Thus did he invert the negative valency surrounding imperialism, so transforming it from an outdated form of European oppression into a desirable mode of American governance. Thus did he presume that the social is infinitely plastic and malleable, ignoring local variation and the sedimented layers of history that will resist the creation and recreation of new, imposed realities by an imperial actor. And thus did he write off a judicious analysis of the exercise of contemporary American power, dismissing empirically grounded research as irrelevant to the imagined futures of policymakers at the metropolitan centre of the imperial project.

If we were to take President Bush's man in the White House at face value, we could not but conclude that, as scholars and intellectuals, we are necessarily condemned to the margins of power, irrelevant irritants to the grand historical project of remaking the world in America's image. Yet, as our anonymous speaker doubtless knows, empire has always had its critics who have given voice to those whom it oppressed, and its proponents who have served to enhance its respectability, and to legitimate its exploitative agenda. The claim that the USA is an empire is usually associated with left-wing historians such as William Appleman Williams and Walter LaFeber who, writing in the 1950s and 1960s, used it as a critical lens through which to view, first, America's internal westward expansion in the name of Manifest Destiny, and then the urge to global expansion to conquer markets and to export the ideals of liberal democracy. Now, however, the tables are turned. In the shadow of the attacks on the World Trade Center and the Pentagon, unashamed talk of empire has, as the conservative *Washington Post* put it in 2002, suddenly become 'hot intellectual property within Washington's beltway'. Max Boot, a senior fellow for national security studies at the Council on Foreign Relations confidently asserts that 'Afghanistan and other troubled lands today cry out for the sort of enlightened foreign administration once provided by self-confident Englishmen in jodhpurs and pith helmets'.[2] In 2003, as Sadam

Hussein's statue was toppled from its pedestal by American troops, the historian Niall Ferguson enthused that if 'America has embarked on a new age of empire, it may turn out to be the most evanescent empire in all history', proudly going on to write 'Let me come clean. I am a fully paid-up member of the neoimperialist gang'.[3]

Empire talk taps into what Walter Hixson calls the Myth of America, a pervasive conception of national identity which expresses itself most palpably in the exercise of American foreign policy. As he has recently written, that policy 'flows from cultural hegemony affirming "America" as a manly, racially superior, and providentially destined "beacon of liberty", a country which possesses a special right to exert power in the world. Hegemonic national identity drives a continuous militant foreign policy, including the regular resort to war'.[4] Scientific and technological leadership have become essential inputs to the projection of American power abroad, and to the construction of this identity. As Michael Adas has put it, 'America's emergence as a global power has been consistently driven by a sense of can-do confidence, a faith in scientific and technical solutions, and a missionary certitude that the United States was destined to serve as a model for the rest of humanity.'[5]

Joseph Nye shares the view that the USA has, perhaps not the right, but at least the resources and the responsibility to maintain world order. As he put it in his seminal article in *Foreign Policy* in 1990, 'if the most powerful country fails to lead, the consequences for international stability could be disastrous'.[6] At the same time he will have no truck with neoimperialist ambitions underpinned by massive military force: he would doubtless agree with Eric Hobsbawm that, as a response to its eroding global position, the unchecked exercise of politico-military force by the USA will 'promote not global order but disorder, not global peace but conflict, not the advance of civilization but of barbarism'.[7] For Nye, military force and economic incentives are not the only or indeed necessarily the best instruments for one country to get others to do what it wants. These traditional levers of influence, he argues, are no longer as effective in a globalized interdependent world, a world in which power is diffuse, in which multinational corporations and NGO's can bypass and sometimes usurp the ability of nation states to affect outcomes, and in which even weak states can have a major impact on the behavior of great powers (e.g. by not controlling the international traffic in drugs produced domestically or the outbreak at home of epidemics like SARS). Hence Nye's emphasis on the need to complement the use of traditional, hard forms of power with what he calls soft power, a form of power enshrined in the attraction that American culture, science and technology, ideology and institutions have for others. As he put it:

> Soft co-optive power is just as important as hard command power. If a state can make its power seem legitimate in the eyes of others, it will encounter less resistance to its wishes. If its culture and ideology are attractive, others will more willingly follow. If it can establish international norms consistent with its society, it is less likely to have to change. If it can support institutions that make other states wish to channel or limit their activities in ways that the

dominant state prefers, it may be spared the costly exercise of coercive hard power.[8]

Science and technology have a privileged place in this repertoire of instruments of soft power. A 2002 Pew Global Attitudes Project, cited by Nye, reveals that from Europe to the Americas, from Africa to South East Asia, and in seven countries with majority Muslim populations, American scientific and technological advances were admired by almost 80 per cent of those questioned.[9] This was about 20 per cent more than those who were attracted by American cultural exports, like music, movies and television programmes and about 50 per cent more than those who favoured the spread of American ideas and customs abroad. Apparently, for many, the attraction of American scientific and technological pre-eminence overwhelms their dislike for other features of American life. As a result, where Adas sees domination, Nye sees opportunity. Where Adas sees technological advantage as a tool in the service of America's civilizing 'offenses',[10] Nye sees it as an instrument to persuade, rather than to prescribe, allegiance to American strategies. For him American science and technology can be instrumentalized to maintain leadership and to ensure international stability 'in a world of growing interdependence'.

There is an ongoing political struggle within the USA, which is both a struggle over national self-representation and identity and over foreign policy. Claims to empire, like the one with which I began this chapter, are to be situated in an agonistic field in which warring factions agree on the ends – a stable world order under American leadership – but disagree on the means to achieve it, and on how most effectively to secure the legitimacy of the American transformative project. Indeed a case could be made for aligning the social actors who celebrate empire, and those who advocate the use of soft power, along the two faces of liberal internationalism, one seeking democratization through liberal imperialism, the other seeking to spread democracy through promoting self-determination.[11] They first celebrate the potential for regime change and the construction of democracy through confrontation. Others, like Nye, who seek to secure legitimacy through co-option are sensitive to the expressed aspirations of local elites and stress that cultural resources, like American scientific and technological pre-eminence, can serve as instruments to consolidate modernization and self-determination – perhaps complemented by the eventual use of hard power, operationalized through military coercion or economic incentive.

At the heart of these diverse normative discourses lies the recognition that America acts in an asymmetric field of force concentrated at one node in that diffuse system of power known generically as globalization, and that it has a suite of instruments at its disposal to get others to do what it wants. This current ferment, intellectual and political, over the nature and limits of US power should not distract us from the fact that soft forms of power have long been the subject of intellectual analysis – Gramsci and Foucault immediately spring to mind –[12] and that the asymmetric situation that US policymakers celebrate today has prevailed for much of the twentieth century, and most obviously since World War II. Indeed the knowledge/power nexus that was crucial to the American transformative project was part of a more general attempt by the USA after World War II to put in place what Charles Bright and Michael Geyer call an American (corporate) regime of world order. In their view the main coordinates of this regime were the containment of communism – as a means of fostering the industrial recovery of the West –, and the resubordination and ordering of the suppliers of primary materials – to feed that economic boom. This hegemonic regime moved 'beyond the extension of power *over* others toward a direct and sustained organization *of* others, simultaneously, and in many parts of the world'. Knowledge played a central role in this process. American scientific, technical and intellectual leadership, and the massive investment in education after the war that made that possible were 'as important as its economic and military power in making world order cohere and, more important, in developing and organizing the consent of subordinate participants'.[13] Contrary to what Adas has suggested, the pursuit of American leadership, not to say dominance, in an increasingly interdependent world has not been a top-down project of command and obedience, but an interactive process that is made and remade by cultivating consent and by trying to manage opposition and resistance. Science and technology played an increasingly important role in that process after World War II, and even more so with what Daniel Bell called the coming of post-industrial society in the 1970s and the emergence of the knowledge economy.[14]

Nye freely admits that states have used various forms of soft power for centuries: he simply believes that, in a world of diffused power, force has become less acceptable, and economic incentives less effective, as instruments of influence. Legitimizing leadership demands the intelligent use of a cocktail of soft and hard power (what he calls smart power) adapted to the specifics of each situation. This chapter explores one such situation: the mobilization of American scientific and technological pre-eminence as an instrument of power in the two decades after World War II. At that time, precisely to distinguish itself from the colonial powers, the USA sought to eschew military intervention in the developing countries (and indeed Western Europe) in a battle for hearts and minds against a Soviet Union that scored one spectacular technological triumph after the other. This historically antecedent case study draws on Nye in seeing science and technology as instruments used – as he has put it – to 'support institutions that make other states want to channel or limit their activities in ways the dominant state prefers […]'. Its emphasis is on such techno-scientific institutions as platforms around which to promote the economic and political integration of Western Europe. However, it goes beyond Nye in exploring in detail the hazards and pitfalls of the exercise of soft power, the resistance and the opposition it encountered both in the USA and abroad and its ultimate failure to achieve the policy objectives so assiduously laboured over in the State Department and other key Washington agencies.

To keep my project manageable I will concentrate on nuclear power and rocketry.[15] The USA had a commanding lead over continental Europe in the 1950s and 1960s in both these sensitive and strategically important domains, a technological gap which the Europeans hoped to overcome with American help.

Key actors in the State Department, along with the Atomic Energy Commission (AEC) and the National Aeronautics and Space Administration (NASA), were willing to help narrow, if not close that gap. However, they aimed to do so in ways deliberately intended to accelerate European integration, and at the same time to divert limited European scientific and technological resources down channels that did not threaten American leadership on the continent. More precisely, this is a story about the efforts made to enrol science and technology as tools of European integration through promoting supranational institutions that would evolve *at the expense of* national programmes in strategic domains like the nuclear and space. At least, that was the imagined future that drove the American national security state apparatus, a future that was contested and reshaped by the stamina of national technological and political cultures, and by the economic realities of utopian projects like the pursuit of commercially viable nuclear power.

Atoms for peace and Euratom

On 8 December 1953 President Dwight D. Eisenhower addressed the General Assembly of the United Nations in New York. He said that he feared that the two superpowers were 'doomed malevolently to eye each other indefinitely across a trembling world' unless ways were found to use the atom to promote peace, not war. To this end Eisenhower suggested that the leading nuclear powers set up an international atomic energy agency (IAEA) under the auspices of the UN. Joint contributions to the agency from their stockpile of fissionable materials would be made available to those who wanted to exploit the atom for peaceful purposes, for example in the areas of agriculture and medicine. Above all, the President said, fissionable material would be available 'to provide abundant electrical energy in the power-starved areas of the world'. In this way, Eisenhower concluded, 'the contributing powers would be dedicating some of their strength to serve the needs rather than the fears of mankind'. The proposal was greeted with rapturous applause.[16]

Atoms for Peace was a polyvalent initiative with implications on many levels.[17] I will mention only a few. First, it promoted nuclear proliferation under a regime of safeguards and inspections, implemented by the IAEA, that was intended to ensure that fissionable material was only used for civilian purposes. As such it would serve to maintain the monopoly of nuclear weapons in the hands of those that already had them. Second, it was supposed to drain resources from the Soviet weapons programme: in planning Eisenhower's speech, his aides suggested that the amount of fissionable material to be donated to the atomic bank should be X, where, and I quote, 'X could be fixed at a figure which we could handle from our stockpile, but which it would be difficult for the Soviets to match'.[18] Finally the promise of markets in the 'power-starved areas of the world' was intended to encourage an immensely reluctant private sector to invest in a civilian nuclear power programme. In 1952, reactor technology was still classified by the Navy which was developing a reactor for its submarine fleet. Energy was also extraordinarily cheap, thanks to the abundant supply of fossil fuels. Eisenhower's December speech triggered a massive declassification effort that included special arrangements for engineers from the American power industry. This was complemented by a decision by the AEC to build a full scale demonstration reactor at Shippingport in Pennsylvania on which firms like General Electric and Westinghouse could cut their teeth in the civil nuclear power field.[19] *U.S. News and World Report* was ecstatic: 'An international race for supremacy has started', it wrote. 'Britain, with one atomic-powered project, is in the race. Russia is probably starting. Now the U.S. is jumping in.'[20]

The hope that nuclear power would produce 'energy too cheap to meter', in the words of AEC Chairman Lewis Strauss, was aggressively promoted at the spectacular Atoms for Peace meeting that was orchestrated by the USA and held at the United Nations building in Geneva in August 1955.[21] Homi J. Bhabha, Secretary to the Government of India, Department of Atomic Energy, emphasized the revolutionary potential of the atom in his presidential address. 'For the full industrialization of the under-developed areas, for the continuation of our civilization and its further development, atomic energy is not merely an aid; it is an absolute necessity', said Bhabha.[22] To stimulate the utopian fantasies of 1,400 delegates from 73 countries, as well as of the general public, the USA installed a swimming pool reactor in the grounds of the UN, appropriately domesticated in a wooden structure reminiscent of a Swiss chalet. Privileged access to the reactor was granted to official participants from national delegations seven hours a day, six days of the week. During their visit they could actually bring the reactor up to power by gradually removing its control rods. In parallel the AEC began arranging bilateral nation-to-nation agreements in which the USA offered to supply slightly enriched uranium for research or power reactors to friendly nations: by 1961 about 40 of these agreements had been signed.

The euphoria surrounding the peaceful atom was shared in Europe.[23] In June 1955 the foreign ministers of the six member states of the European Coal and Steel Community (France, Germany, Italy and the Benelux countries) met in Messina, Italy. The mood was gloomy: the momentum towards European integration had been slowed in August 1954 by the French Parliament, which rejected proposals for a European Defence Community (EDC) that included the rearmament of Germany. At Messina the Six decided that, notwithstanding this setback, it was worth pursuing their efforts at horizontal economic integration in a common market, and at 'vertical' integration in certain key sectors, including atomic energy. Strange as it may seem with hindsight, they believed that an integrated atomic energy programme, with its promise of cheap power to fuel the economic take-off of the continent, would be relatively easy to achieve. Progress with Euratom, as it was called, would inspire those who were dragging their feet in the far more complex negotiations over the construction of a European common market.

The *relance* in Messina and the success of the Geneva Atoms for Peace conference created a window of opportunity for the State Department. Washington strongly favoured European integration, arguing that it would 'remove the burden of Europe from the back of the United States, draw France and Germany together, and constitute a unified pool of power to balance the USSR'. Only a united Europe would have the 'organic strength and unity of purpose' to achieve the 'double containment' of Soviet aggression and German nationalism and militarism, binding Bonn, and 'eventually a united Germany, organically into the Western and Atlantic community'. If Euratom could accelerate this process it was worthy of support. More, as one officer emphasized in November 1955,

> I think it would be most regrettable if, for whatever reason, atomic energy was not used in the U.S. as a lever to obtain a further major step forward in the integration of Western Europe. As I see the problem, in its simplest terms, all the U.S. has is roughly a three year head-start over and above, of course, our tremendous overall engineering knowledge, personnel depth, etc ... I have long felt that it was within the power of the U.S. to force almost any reasonable institutional form that it desired in this field but only if we act courageously and soon.[24]

Thus, in the words of the official historians of the AEC, Euratom 'became a cornerstone of Eisenhower's grand design for a United States of Europe'.[25]

The State Department, and the promoters of Euratom in Europe led by Jean Monnet (dubbed the patron saint of European integration), faced an uphill struggle. German industry was highly suspicious of the scheme seeing it as a French led 'socialist' attempt to cripple their development of nuclear power reactors. The French military feared that it would impede their ability to develop their own nuclear deterrent. Though both countries sought to take advantage of American technological support, many felt it would be preferable to do so through bilateral agreements on a nation-to-nation basis with the AEC rather than through a supranational organization like Euratom. Lewis Strauss was more than willing to cooperate. He thought that Euratom had little hope of success, and preferred relying on the safeguards built into bilateral agreements to contain the illicit diversion of American nuclear material.

In the face of this opposition, two basic technological 'levers' were used by the State Department to secure allegiance to Euratom-in-the making. First, its officers put immense pressure on Strauss and the AEC to delay bilateral agreements with any of the Six until the Euratom Treaty had been signed in March 1957. The State Department reasoned that as long as European governments believed that they could develop their nuclear power capability by acquiring nuclear materials and technology on a nation-to-nation basis with the USA, they would be reluctant to dilute their sovereignty in a supranational organization. By persuading the AEC to route requests for nuclear material and know-how through Euratom, the State Department hoped to 'force' the support of recalcitrant scientists, statesmen and industrialists in Europe for the supranational institution.

This policy of technological denial was complemented by a number of financial and political incentives to states that agreed to join Euratom. Self-inspection was one of the most important concessions the State Department was willing to make. In a normal bilateral agreement with the AEC, the USA could demand full access to the foreign nuclear facility and its records to ensure that no fissile material of

American origin was being diverted from peaceful to military ends, or passed on to third parties. This condition would be relaxed for Euratom, and packaged along with other advantages to encourage governments to commit to the supranational organization. As the State Department stressed repeatedly, 'The United States Government could make available substantially greater resources and adopt an attitude of substantially greater liberality toward a real integrated community possessing effective common responsibility and authority than would be possible for countries separately.'[26]

The tenacity with which the State Department pursued this agenda against all odds was, as I have suggested, inspired by the view that Euratom was at the cutting edge of European integration, and by the willingness of key actors in Europe, men like Monnet and Belgian Foreign Minister Paul-Henri Spaak, to persist with the scheme. But deeper forces were at work as well. The State Department also saw Euratom as helping curb the development of nuclear weapons, above all in France. The USA was able to accommodate its foreign policy to an independent British deterrent; the special relationship secured the guarantees Washington needed that London would not behave 'irresponsibly'. By contrast, France's determination to build its own nuclear programme and the associated delivery systems was perceived as an unacceptable threat to the regime of order that Washington sought in Europe; everything had to be done to discourage it. As Robert Schaetzel, the senior officer responsible for the Euratom file in the State Department put it:

'The fundamental point is that the French are motivated by a desire to recover status in the world which, they feel, either rightly or wrongly, is a function of nuclear weapons capability. In this situation our basic strategy is not to hit the French directly, but to envelop them' [in a joint supranational project like Euratom that] 'should make increasingly difficult the disengagement of the scientists and technical people from one country to work on separate, national military projects', [and that] 'would tax to the utmost the industrial and technical resources of the Six nations.'[27]

In sum, the State Department through Euratom wanted both to add another keystone to post-war European integration, and to divert limited European resources into civilian projects that would not pose a challenge to American hegemony in the region.

Notwithstanding its early optimism, by the summer of 1957 the State Department's scheme was in the doldrums. With the Euratom treaty signed in March that year, the floodgates were opened to bilateral agreements: State could no longer keep the AEC and its European suppliants in check. What is more, the hope for counterweight, namely the offer of American nuclear technology and know-how under more advantageous terms through Euratom, had lost much of its attraction. Fifty European industrialists were taken on a grand tour of the American program in July 1957. They were impressed by the vast financial and technological scale of the effort, and the close collaboration between government and industry. But they concluded that reactor development in the USA was behind that in Britain, and still in an early, experimental stage: indeed no less than eight different reactor designs were being explored in the USA and none was anywhere near commercialization. The much-vaunted 'three-year' lead had turned into a lag.

> our problem [wrote Schaetzel] is that we are late – I would guess by about two years, [and that] U.S. bargaining power does not have the effectiveness it once had – or the force some Americans think it contains.[28]

America's presumed lead in civil nuclear power was a myth, shattered on the rock of cheap fossil fuels and classified programmes which restricted access to essential scientific and technological knowledge. As the technological lead dissolved, so too did the political leverage.

The Sputnik shock in October provided the State Department with a new opportunity to define atomic collaboration as crucial to American foreign policy and national security, and to successfully promote what was now called a Joint Program which took account of these scientific and technological realities. As Douglas Dillon, the Under Secretary of State explained to Congress,

> Voices in Europe have questioned whether the historic position of the United States in the field of science, engineering and general industrial development, is not being overtaken by the Soviet Union. Atomic energy, [he went on,] is rightfully considered a bellwether of scientific and industrial accomplishment. Rapid progress on a joint [U.S. – Euratom program] ... will do much to dispel this questioning attitude, and furthermore, will lay the foundation of the kind of meaningful scientific cooperation which is indispensable to the survival of the West.[29]

The Joint Program had two components. One was a collaborative R&D venture with European and American firms intended to improve the performance and reduce the costs of reactors. The other was a power demonstration programme, in which several large American reactors using enriched fuel, offered at a heavily subsidized price to member states, would be built under Euratom's auspices. Here was a scheme that gave Europeans access to American technology and know-how, and vice versa. It was also an avenue through which USA power companies could gain a foothold in the European market, thanks to government subsidies. London was predictably incensed, arguing that the USA was violating the very policies it had been criticizing others for in GATT. It also remarked that the French had just cancelled an agreement to buy a reactor from the UK, citing the more favourable terms the Americans were offering through Euratom. Washington was unyielding; the British objections were dismissed out of hand on the grounds that 'programs of this sweep, purpose and effect appear to the United States to be quite different from the export subsidies we both seek to avoid in normal commercial dealings'.[30] Indeed by the late 1960s the USA had captured about 80 per cent of the world market for nuclear power.

The Joint Program never lived up to its promise. It was crippled by the reduced costs of operating conventional fuel stations, by concerns in the USA about subsidizing the European nuclear industry, and by fears that American enriched uranium might be diverted into national weapons programmes. This does not mean that the hegemonic enterprise failed. It simply shows that the State Department's repeated attempts to build a stable regime around the peaceful atom did not flower because the technology was not yet mature, and the potentially destabilizing effects of technological leakage through the porous barrier between the civil and the military weighed more heavily in the balance. There were conflicting strategies available for maintaining order without coercion, and in the event the path preferred by the State Department proved too risky for the national security state to tolerate, especially in the face of France's determination to acquire an independent nuclear deterrent.

The civilian satellite launcher and ELDO

The situation in France also dominated American policy in the 1960s regarding the development of a civilian satellite launcher in Europe. Here the crisis was precipitated in spring 1966, when the British government announced that it intended withdrawing from ELDO, the European Launcher Development Organization. So as not to belabour the argument, let me briefly explain the origins of the crisis and the US reactions to it and, in particular, how the State Department and NASA hoped to exploit American technological leadership to defuse the issue.

ELDO was born in the early 1960s of the need by the British government to find a new role for its Blue Streak missile.[31] The liquid-fuelled rocket was rendered obsolete by the long time required to prepare it for launch and by the cost, which spiralled to new heights as the expenditures on reinforced concrete silos were factored into the budget. Hence the idea to recycle Blue Streak, stripped of its military characteristics, as the first stage of a multistage satellite launcher, built together with partners in continental Europe. Lengthy negotiations ensued before Blue Streak was given a new lease of life. The French would build the second stage atop the British rocket, the Germans would build the third stage, and the Italians would build a test satellite. The rocket would be launched from Woomera in South Australia.

ELDO was born of political expediency; from the outset it was criticized for the lack of any formal mechanism to ensure stage integration and overall project management. Indeed the three main partners went to great lengths to retain clean interfaces between the separate stages. They wanted to limit technology transfer between firms in different countries, and to protect competitive advantage and national security in rocket and missile technology. By 1966, as many had predicted, ELDO faced the first of many crises that led to its eventual demise in 1972. Development costs had increased from the initial estimate of about US$200 million to over US$400 million, and no end to the upward spiral was in sight. Blue Streak had been successfully commissioned, while the French and German stages were still under development. What is more, in January 1963, French President de Gaulle had vetoed Britain's application to join the Common Market. For Britain, who was paying almost 39 percent of the ELDO budget, the original technological, industrial and political rationale for launching the organization had evaporated. In February 1966, her Minister circulated an aide-memoire to his partners in the ELDO member states announcing that the UK intended to withdraw from the programme.

Britain's moves sent shockwaves through her European partners. The USA was also deeply distressed. The Chief Scientific Adviser, Sir Solly Zuckerman was invited over to Washington in May and asked to reconsider Britain's position. He was given three main reasons why the USA wanted to keep ELDO afloat.

First, the Johnson administration feared that the collapse of ELDO would strike a major blow to the gradual movement toward European unity on the continent that was in a very brittle state at the time. The French, for whom integration had come to mean 'subordination', had precipitated a crisis in both the European Economic Community and in NATO. For the USA, by contrast, to quote Under Secretary George Ball, 'integration was the most realistic means of achieving European political unity with all that implies for our relations with Eastern Europe and the Soviet Union ... [It] is the precondition for a Europe able to carry its proper share of responsibility for our common defense'.[32] ELDO was not central to European integration. However, its collapse would provide additional encouragement for those who were increasingly hostile to supranational ventures in the Europe.

Saving a European launcher was also justified on the grounds that it would help close the so-called 'technological gap' that had opened between the two sides of the Atlantic. Beginning in summer 1965, there were increasingly strident complaints in France, and to some extent Germany, that American business was invading Europe and dominating key sectors of European industry.[33] This gap, as one senior NASA official put it, could 'only lead to political and economic strains and to weakness'.[34] A White House task force that was set up to look into the matter concluded that while 'the Technological Gap [was] mainly a political and psychological problem', it did have 'some basis in actual disparities'. These included 'the demonstrated American superiority in sophisticated electronics, military technology and space systems'.[35] While Britain was thinking of pulling out of space collaboration in Europe, the USA was looking to expand technological collaboration in space with continental Europe as a way of closing the technological gap.

There was a one-third, even more fundamental reason given for supporting the development of a launcher in the ELDO framework. It was to divert scarce European resources away from national military programmes into supranational civilian ones. In the words of NASA Administrator James Webb, international collaboration in space would be 'a means whereby foreign nations might be increasingly involved in space technology and diverted from the technology of nuclear weapons delivery'.[36] As one key interagency document prepared in spring 1966 explained, multilateral programmes should be encouraged since

> [i]n such a framework rocket programs tend to be more open, serve peaceful uses and are subject to international control and absorb manpower and

financial resources that might otherwise be diverted to purely national programs. National rocket programs tend to concentrate on militarily significant solid and storable liquid fueled systems, are less open and less responsive to international controls. Any break up of ELDO might lead to strengthening national programs tending in the latter direction.[37]

As with Euratom so with ELDO. In both cases Washington strongly supported collaborative organizations as a means of solidifying European integration and to contain national military ambitions. In both a package of technological incentives was defined to encourage European partners to remain committed to the supranational framework. In ELDO's case that package included help with the development of a complex cryogenic third stage of the ELDO rocket. Cryogenic rocket fuels (typically a mixture of liquid oxygen and a kerosene derivative) were bulky and not easily storable, and so particularly unsuited to military programmes. The US hoped to retard missile development by diverting scarce resources away from solid or storable liquid fuels to civilian-only cryogenic fuels.

As with Euratom, so with ELDO. It was French ambitions that were of greatest concern to the USA. On 26 November 1965, France had become the third space power by launching its own satellite with its own launcher, Diamant, in Algeria. Diamant was derived from the French missile programme and used solid fuel and storable liquid fuel in its several stages. France's nuclear capability was thus substantially enhanced: it had successfully tested its first atomic bomb in 1960, now it was on the way to developing a lethal delivery system to go with it. In May 1966 Washington told Sir Solly Zuckerman in no uncertain terms why Britain should not withdraw from ELDO. 'The US is concerned that, if ELDO were to be dissolved, France might devote more of its resources to a national, military-related program or that it might establish undesirable bilateral relationships for the construction of satellite launch vehicles' probably with the Soviet Union.[38] Zuckerman and the British caved in, but the French did not. Between 1967 and 1971 a fleet of Mirage bombers carrying the A-bomb became operational, two nuclear submarine missile launchers were completed, and surface-to-surface strategic ballistic missiles were implanted in the French Alps.[39] To cap it all, in 1973 Paris also took the lead in equipping Europe with its own successful civilian satellite launcher, Ariane, so breaking America's monopoly on access to space in the free world.

What have we learnt from these two short case studies? A scientific and technologically strong, integrated Europe were essential to America's plans for stabilizing the post-war situation under Washington's leadership. It was necessary to meet the Soviet threat, to hold German nationalistic and military ambitions in check, and to secure a market for American high technology. America's scientific and technological leadership, and the knowledge and managerial skills that were embodied in it were key instruments of soft power deployed to consolidate this regime of order. They were selectively mobilized with a view to strengthening Europe without undermining American leadership. Above all they were used to promote supranational civilian organizations like Euratom and ELDO as a means of diverting resources from national military programs. This grand design was repeatedly and successfully challenged by the French, to the frustration, and anger of successive American administrations. But then, as Prime Minister Couve de Mourville remarked in 1962, France 'will not blindly follow American policy. The whole problem is there.' It is a problem that interventionist policies, hard or soft, will always have to face.

Conclusion

It is widely accepted that the first two or three decades after the war were marked by an asymmetry in economic and military power between the two sides of the Atlantic. However, there was also a significant structural asymmetry in scientific and technological capability between America and Europe. By virtue of that asymmetry, the USA could not only hope to make over European systems of production, patterns of consumption, ideological agendas and forms of culture, but it could also try to use its scientific and technological leadership as an instrument of soft power to organize consensus around its transformative agenda. The national pursuit of American scientific and technological achievement, so exhaustively studied by historians of American science and technology, cannot be understood apart from seeing it also (as did many actors at the time) as intrinsic to the global pursuit of American leadership: performance at home and leadership abroad were two sides of the same coin. American scientific, technological and managerial advantage, as measured by the capacity to dominate the research frontier, to produce more sophisticated technological products, and to organize complex techno-scientific systems, provided the USA with knowledge-based instruments to reshape Europe, a Europe whose elites were convinced, as were their American counterparts, that a strong scientific and technological base was essential to the health, security and, ultimately, the autonomy of the modern state.

This article has explored the exercise of soft power through institution-building around a technological core in two strategic domains. But it has done more. It has gone beyond Nye to expose the limits of co-option as a strategy to ensure the construction of a regime of world order under American leadership. Those limits are a consequence of the necessarily fractured nature of any social formation whose trajectory a dominant state seeks to determine. They express the presence of multiple and conflicting definitions of the future, and of the domestic struggles for power that national elites, working alongside their American counterparts, necessarily have to deal with in implementing Washington's agenda.

By foregrounding soft power as a way of legitimizing the exercise of American leadership abroad, Nye has also legitimized the arguments of policymakers at home who are sensitive to the disastrous effects that the recent exercise of hard, command power has had on America's standing in the world and its subsequent loss of influence in the global arena. Nye's aim has been to refocus the terms of the debate in Washington on how best to secure America's historic mission as the promoter and defender of democracy. My aim, by contrast, has been to unravel the mechanisms and limits of the exercise of soft power. I have moved beyond the affirmation of the importance of soft power and its mobilization in a domestic struggle to define the contours of American foreign policy. Instead, I have sought to analyze its practices and, in so doing, to give voice both to those who have sought to wield it, and to who have been co-opted into, but who have also resisted, its implementation. In doing so my hope, to quote Cooper, is that by '[t]hinking about the varied ways in which power has been exercised, constrained, and contested [this chapter] may help to open the political imagination and focus the mind on the stakes and the consequences of political action', – both the imaginations of those like Nye, who seek to make American 'leadership' less 'costly' and more legitimate, *and* the imaginations of those 'others' who are enrolled, whether they like it or not, in the American-led regime of world order.[40]

Notes

1 Ron Susskind, 'Without a Doubt', *New York Times Magazine*, 17 October, 2004. Available at: www.cs.umass.edu/~immerman/play/opinion05/WithoutADoubt.html (accessed on 26 October 2006).
2 Max Boot, 'The Case for American Empire', *The Weekly Standard* 7(6), 15 October 2001.
3 Niall Ferguson, 'The Empire Slinks Back', *New York Times Magazine,* 27 April 2003. See also Niall Ferguson, *Empire: The Rise and Demise of the British World Order and the Lessons for Global Power* (New York: Basic Books, 2004).
4 Walter L. Hixson, *The Myth of American Diplomacy. National Identity and U.S. Foreign Policy* (New Haven, CT: Yale University Press, 2008), pp. 1–2.
5 Michael Adas, *Dominance by Design. Technological Imperatives and America's Civilizing Mission* (Cambridge: Belknap Press, 2006), p. 8.
6 Joseph S. Nye Jr., 'Soft Power,' *Foreign Policy,* 80 (Fall 1990), pp. 153–72.
7 Eric Hobsbawm, *On Empire. America, War, and Global Supremacy* (New York: Pantheon Books, 2008), pp. 90–1.
8 Nye, 'Soft Power', op. cit.
9 Joseph S. Nye, Jr. *Soft Power. The Means to Success in World Politics* (New York: Public Affairs, 2004), pp. 69–72.
10 Adas, *Dominance,* op. cit., p. 12.
11 This distinction is emphasized by Anne-Marie Slaughter, 'Wilsonianism in the Twenty-First Century', in G. John Ikenberry, Thomas J. Knock, Anne-Marie Slaughter and Tony Smith (eds), *The Crisis of American Foreign Policy. Wilsonianism in the Twenty-first Century* (Princeton, NJ: Princeton University Press, 2009), pp. 89–117.
12 For a useful survey, see Mark Haugaard and Howard H. Lentner, *Hegemony and Power. Consensus and Coercion in Contemporary Politics* (New York: Lexington Books, 2006).
13 Charles Bright and Michael Geyer, 'Regimes of World Order: Global Integration and the Production of Difference in Twentieth-Century World History', in Jerry H. Bentley, Renate Bridenthal and Anand A. Yang (eds), *Interactions. Transregional Perspectives on World History* (Honolulu: University of Hawai'i Press, 2005), pp. 202–38 at p. 228.
14 Daniel Bell, *The Coming of Post-Industrial Society. A Venture in Social Forecasting* (New York: Basic Books, 1973). See also Manuel Castells, *The Rise of the Network Society* (Malden, MA: Blackwells, 2000) and Manuel Castells, *The Power of Identity* (Malden, MA: Blackwells, 2004).

15 The case studies that follow are based on extensive research at the National Archives and Records Administration at College Park, MD (NARA), the Lyndon Baines Johnson Presidential Library located at the University of Texas in Austin, TX (LBJ Library), and the National Aeronautics and Space Administration (NASA) Historical Records Collection, NASA Headquarters, Washington DC.

16 For a more comprehensive account, including references, see John Krige, 'Atoms for Peace, Scientific Internationalism and Scientific Intelligence', in John Krige and Kai-Henrik Barth (eds) *Global Power Knowledge. Science, Technology and International Affairs,* Osiris Vol. 21 (Chicago, IL: University of Chicago Press, 2006), pp. 161–81.

17 Joseph F. Pilat, Robert E. Pendley and Charles K. Ebinger (eds), *Atoms for Peace. An Analysis After Thirty Years* (Boulder, CO: Westview Press, 1985) provides a range of insights from social actors who were directly involved with the programme. For the propaganda dimension see Kenneth Osgood, *Total Cold War. Eisenhower's Secret Propaganda Battle at Home and Abroad* (Lawrence, KS: University Press of Kansas, 2006), chapter 5.

18 Martin J. Medhurst, 'Atoms for Peace and Nuclear Hegemony: the Rhetorical Structure of a Cold War Campaign', *Armed Forces and Society,* 23(4) (Summer 1997), pp. 571–93.

19 This is covered extensively in the official history, Richard G. Hewlett and Jack M. Holl, *Atoms for Peace and War 1953–1961: Eisenhower and the Atomic Energy Commission* (Berkeley, CA: University of California Press, 1989).

20 Ibid., p. 195.

21 'It is not too much to expect that our children will enjoy in their homes electrical energy too cheap to meter, will know of great periodic regional famines in the world only as matters of history, will travel effortlessly over the seas and under them and through the air with a minimum of danger and at great speeds, and will experience a lifespan far longer than ours as disease yields and man comes to understand what causes him to age'. Lewis L. Strauss, Speech to the National Association of Science Writers, New York City, 16 September 1954, from http://www.atomicinsights.com/AI_03-09-05.html. Walter Marshall made the same claims in Britain: http://news.bbc.co.uk/1/hi/world/europe/792209.stm, accessed on 3 December, 2006.

22 For Bhabha and this paragraph, see John Krige, 'Techno-utopian Dreams, Techno-political Realities. The Education of Desire for the Peaceful Atom', in Michael Gordin, Gyan Prakash and Helen Tilley (eds), *Utopia/Dystopia: Historical Conditions of Possibility* (Princeton, NJ: Princeton University Press, forthcoming).

23 A detailed account with extensive references is provided in John Krige, 'The Peaceful Atom as Political Weapon: Euratom and American Foreign Policy in the Late 1950s', *Historical Studies in the Natural Sciences* 38(1) (2008), 5–44. See also John Krige, *American Hegemony and the Postwar Reconstruction of Science in Europe* (Cambridge, MA: MIT Press, 2006).

24 Extract from letter, Vultee to Van Dyke, 9 November 1955, circulated by Barnett, 28 November 1955, NARA, RG59, Box 363, Folder 19.8 Regional Program Euratom General, November–December 1955.

25 Hewlett and Holl, op. cit., p. 324.

26 Telegram to Belgian Minister, 15 May 1956, NARA, RG59, Box 363, Folder 19.8 Regional Program Euratom General May–September, 1956, Part 1 of 2.

27 Schaetzel to Isenbergh, 26 March 1957, NARA, RG59, Box 364, Folder Regional Programs Euratom General March–April 1957, Part 1 of 2.

28 Schaetzel to Butterworth, 26 July 1957, NARA, RG59, Box 362, Folder 19.8s Euratom Visits 2. Fifty European Industrialists, 1957.

29 'Opening Statement Before Joint Committee on Atomic Energy by Mr Dillon with Respect to the US-Euratom Joint Program', 30 June 1958, NARA, RG59, Box 360, Folder 19.8r Joint Program Part 1 of 2.

30 Draft memo referring to UK, 25 November 1958, and memo, 14 January 1959, both in NARA, RG59, Box 357, Folder 19.8m.

31 For the full story see John Krige, 'The Launch of ELDO,' in John Krige and Arturo Russo, *A History of the European Space Agency, 1958–1987. Vol. 1. The Story of ELDO and ESRO, 1958–1973* (Noordwijk, Netherlands: ESA SP-1235, 2000), Chapter 3. For more detail on the specific events discussed here see John Krige, 'Technology, Foreign Policy, and International Cooperation in Space', in Steven J. Dick and Roger D. Launius (eds), *Critical Issues in the History of Spaceflight* (Washington, DC: NASA-SP 2006-4702, 2006), pp. 239–60. For the military origins of Blue Streak see Stephen R. Twigge, *The Early Development of Guided Weapons in the United Kingdom* (Chur: Harwood Academic Publishers, 1993).

32 Department of State to Amembassy Bonn, 1209, outgoing telegram, 18 November, 1965, signed [George] Ball, LBJ Library, National Security File, Country File, Europe and USSR, Germany, Folder Germany Erhard Visit [12/65], 12/19–21/65, Box 192.

33 The *locus classicus* of the argument is Jean-Jaques Servan-Schreiber, *The American Challenge* (New York: Atheneum Press, 1968) (translated from the French: *Le défi americain*).

34 Arnold Frutkin, quoted in *Space Business Daily,* 25:35 (18 April 1966), p. 286.

35 National Security Advisory Memorandum (NSAM) 357, 'The Technological Gap,' November 1967, available online at http://www.lbjlib.utexas.edu/johnson/archives.hom/NSAMs/nsam357.gif (accessed on 9 March 2005).

36 James Webb to Robert McNamara, 28 April, 1966, NASA Historical Reference Collection, Record No. 14459, International Cooperation, International Cooperation and Foreign Countries, Folder Miscellaneous Correspondence from CODE I-International Relations, 1958–67.

37 T.H.E. Nesbitt, 'Meeting No. 1, Committee on Expanded International Cooperation in Space Activities. Subject: Cooperation Involving Launchers and Launching Technology, 17 May 1966, LBJ Library, National Security Files, Johnson File, Folder Cooperation in Space – Working Group on Expanded International Cooperation in Space, ELDO #1 [2 of 2], Box 14.

38 Position Paper, 'US Cooperation with ELDO', 21 July, 1966, National Security Files, Charles Johnson File, ibid.

39 Pierre Messmer, 'De Gaulle's Defense Policy and the United States from 1958–69', in Robert O. Paxton and Nicholas Wahl (eds), *De Gaulle and the United States. A Centennial Reappraisal* (Oxford: Berg, 1994), pp. 351–7.

40 Frederick Cooper, 'Empire Multiplied: A Review Essay', *Comparative Studies in Society and History,* 46(2) (April 2004), pp. 247–72, at p. 272.

8 The military use of soft power – information campaigns

The challenge of application, their audiences and effects

Angus Taverner

Introduction

Over the past two decades, military campaigns have increasingly focused on winning what many have come to describe as the 'information high ground'. As the USA and UK have become further involved in Counter-Insurgency Operations in Afghanistan, in Iraq and in the struggle against Islamist terrorism, the British and American governments, and especially, the US Department of Defense (DOD) and the UK Ministry of Defence (MOD), have attempted to develop and implement Information Campaigns as a central plank of their 'strategic approach'. Increasingly, these campaigns have been designed, or 'shaped', to address all aspects of so-called 'soft' engagement with an opponent, an adversary or a designated target population. Moreover, they have acknowledged that target audience perceptions have a significant impact on the likelihood of achieving desired outcomes.

Traditionally, 'audience perception' has not been considered as a factor at the core of the military strategic planning process, although it would be fair to suggest that every successful military commander has always understood that battle is as much psychological as it is physical. However, latterly, on battlefields increasingly dominated by the agile use of the electromagnetic spectrum this has come to be described as the effects based approach that emphasizes a focus on the mind of an adversary. As Professor Richard Holmes commented during a lecture at the UK's Army Headquarters in 1998: 'A battle is not lost, until the losing side believes that it has lost. This is a mental process rather than a physical one' (Seminar, Chairman's opening lecture 1998: 8). In this regard, it is important to understand the primary drivers that affect the thinking of the enemy and then to use means to influence those drivers. Accordingly, an effects based approach emphasizes the need to influence an adversary to follow courses of action that are of a commander's choosing rather than his own. As one of the outcomes of this transformation in military doctrine, the information dimension has assumed an increasingly high profile to support strategic and operational plans. That said, it may also be argued that it is still too frequently left to the Media and Public Affairs staff to determine how best to manage the communication of policy and to react to events as they unfold. And while the process has attempted to maintain some focus on the impact of 'soft effects', shifting audience perceptions is still rarely been considered to be a key determinant of strategic success.

While most politicians and policymakers in Whitehall and Washington today understand the vital importance of communication and the need to convey key messages to various audiences, it is argued that this continues to be one of the most difficult challenges to deliver in terms of consistency and applicability. Indeed, one of the frustrations for military Information Campaign planners is the fact that too often theatre focused activity is diverted by domestic and political considerations with the resulting portrayal of events for a 'home audience', ending up sending the 'wrong message' to the 'theatre audience'. As an example, the US's widely trailed theme of 2003 that it intended to 'Shock and Awe' Iraq and the Iraqis, while also sending a robust message to the wider Middle East, simply ended up communicating a message of invasion and defeat – not of liberation and optimism.

This article examines how the well-intentioned communication of 'soft power' in the military sphere frequently ends up as miscommunication to the very audience it is intended to influence. It also argues that the military's desire to shape and define the 'information landscape' may be raising unrealizable expectation that under appreciates the importance and impact of soft power during military operations and campaigns.

Perception, the media and the military

Unless engaged in a war of national survival, military operations are usually intended to influence a particular leadership, audience or group in support of government policy. For example, target audience receptiveness to the UK's intent is invariably a function of how they perceive the UK's objectives and the actions that are being taken to achieve those objectives. Considerable academic and commercial research has been dedicated to the subject of perception. As Lord Bell, the Chairman of Chime Communications and Margaret Thatcher's former advisor has put it: 'Perceptions are real. If you're playing to win they have to be favourable. Your ability to persuade people to listen to you, understand what you are saying, and support you, will determine whether you win or lose' (Chime Communications website 2004: 2). Arguably, people's view of their world is shaped through a series of external filters rather than through direct experience. Accordingly, shaping target audience perceptions is central to determining attitudes, and how people may be expected to behave and react.

Achieving these shifts is reflected in Clausewitzian theory that links policy and military action, and brings them into the information age. The Napoleonic era military theorist is attributed with the recognition of war as the pursuit of policy by other means – linking military means with political outcomes. Of pertinence is his observation that: 'all military action is intertwined psychological forces and effects' (Von Clausewitz 1976: 20). The so-called effects based approach emphasizes a focus on the mind of an adversary, its supporters and, particularly, the principal protagonists. To this end, from a government's perspective, it is essential to understand the primary drivers that affect the thinking of an adversary and then try to influence those drivers. The effects based approach is about influencing military adversaries or insurgents to follow courses of action that are of the government's choosing rather than its opponents. Increasingly, this is using a full spectrum of strategic public relations techniques that are collectively termed: 'the information campaign'. As Professor Robin Brown (2003: 4) has put it:

> As politics and society change so does the nature of war. In the twenty-first century, politics is conducted via the mass media so that, for example, the 'war on terrorism'[1] is a war that is also waged through the media. The way in which the mass media represent the conflict is part of the conflict. Media coverage has effects not simply on 'the audience', understood as a set of passive bystanders, but on those actually and potentially involved in the conflict. Shaping the perceptions of opponents, supporters and neutral groups influences whether they will become involved and how they will participate. Mobilizing, informing and persuading are integral to the conduct of war. The result is that attempting to shape the representation of the conflict becomes more important for the belligerents even as it becomes harder to do.

The effects based approach therefore has to deal, not only with maximizing friendly force dominance of the information spectrum – what the US military has termed: 'full spectrum dominance'-but it must also counter an adversary's ability to do the same. As Bruce Berkowitz (2003: 3) has observed: 'In Information Age wars, victory will usually go to the side having more influence over technology and better access to the world's electronic infrastructure.'

In the UK, many journalists have criticized the apparently increasing trend for the government to try to shape the way in which the public interprets events. What has become known colloquially as 'spin' has, in the eyes of many (Kurtz, 1998; Jones, 1999; Cohen, 2003; Pitcher, 2003; Wheen, 2004) diminished the authority of government itself. However, as Susan Carruthers has noted, in the context of the media's coverage of recent military campaigns, this is largely due to the experience of trying to control directly the adversaries' access to the media. In her 2000 study, 'The Media at War', she dedicated a full chapter to the UK government's, ultimately unsuccessful, experience of trying to limit Sinn Fein/IRA's access to the media by banning broadcasts of any interviews with known activists. As she concluded: 'Governmental attempts to curb the media have generally been more successful in doing just that than in eliminating or reducing terrorism. Drawing on empirical case studies, it is hard to sustain the thesis that denial of "oxygen" does indeed stifle publicity-dependent terrorists' (Carruthers 2000: 5). The same may be said for the wider conduct of war in the twenty-first century.

So it seems to be generally accepted that, what was once regarded as a relatively straight forward relationship between military opponents and watching journalists, policed on the basis of self-regulation as far as the media was concerned, has, increasingly, become a three-way relationship with governments becoming more and more engaged, not only in trying to control access to the media, but also attempting to impose its own narrative of events through the media. The government approach that seeks to wield soft power by dominating the media 'high ground' through Information Campaigns has, of course, also been condemned as 'spin'. This appears to have left publics with a cynical eye and a general suspicion of both the media and government intentions, particularly in mounting recent military campaigns. Arguably, and with direct access through the Internet, as well as the gateways of a, seemingly ever-proliferating, range of media outlets, this has also left the way open for sophisticated adversaries to engage public emotions and fears, build reputations and communicate complex ideas more readily than has ever been previously possible. Accordingly, soft power is not only a tool of the West but is also fast becoming the weapon of the West's adversaries as well and therefore the need to combat soft power, particularly as wielded by asymmetric insurgents, is also becoming a challenge that governments must confront.

The psychological dimension

Turning now to how information operations might be planned, it immediately becomes clear that a deeper and more nuanced understanding of an adversary is now required. It is no longer sufficient to limit intelligence effort to determining the physical component of an enemy's capability arrayed against you. Instead, it becomes as important, if not more so, to understand the 'moral dimension' of an opponent and to determine how he may best be influenced both directly and indirectly.

This reinforces the growing emphasis on information operations that are designed to influence an enemy to change their behaviour and force them to bend to one's will. At the strategic level, this emphasizes the need for strategic intelligence not only to estimate numbers of tanks, ships and aeroplanes, the disposition of those forces and enemy courses of action given geography and climatic conditions – it also demands a concentration on understanding what makes an enemy tick.

Resistant to the accepted norms of international relations (IR) and diplomacy, many of the regimes or organizations, which the West has recently tried to coerce by military force, have been autocratic by nature, with power vested largely in a single, all powerful individual. This explains the political tendency to personalize regimes so that figures such as: Slobodan Milosevic, Osama bin Laden and Saddam Hussein have been characterized as the adversary rather than the societies or movements over which they exerted power and control. It is also why, information campaigns have recently focused on efforts to draw a distinction between a leadership and the people: 'Our fight is with Saddam's regime not you, the people of Iraq' or '… we are here to liberate you from Saddam's oppression', being typical psychological operations messages used during the opening stages of the 2003 Iraq operation.

In order to achieve psychological effects at both strategic and tactical levels, intelligence effort therefore needs to focus on gathering, what is sometimes called, 'soft intelligence' – how people think, who they listen to, what interests them, what attracts and disgusts them, and who are the key decision takers. This type of intelligence requires access to both signals intelligence (electronic eaves dropping) and human intelligence primarily from in-place sources.

Where accurate intelligence can be gleaned successfully, psychological profiling can then be used to develop an understanding of the moral vulnerabilities of both the leadership and the general population. This is not a straightforward science and requires focus, sustained effort and constant evaluation. This makes it expensive both in terms of cost and time. Accordingly, if it is to be used to best effect, strategically gathered material must be capable of being disseminated to lower operational and tactical levels. In the UK and the USA, this has often proved problematic with the strategic, non-military, agencies often reluctant to share material with their military counterparts for fear of compromising sources. If the psychological approach is to be optimized, protocols have to be agreed between all government departments involved, as well as coalition partners, which allow intelligence material, particularly human and signal sourced product, to be disseminated to relevant military planners so that they can derive maximum advantage. Furthermore, psychological material should ideally be 'pushed' forward rather than simply waiting for it to be 'pulled' only in response to specified requirements.

Information campaigning

While intelligence work underpins the broadest understanding of an adversary, and particularly the influences that affect his decision making at all levels, the next step is determining how to exert that influence to best effect – the ways. Over the past decade, Western military doctrine in particular has emphasized the growing importance of Information Operations.[2] This has been broadened not only to include the psychological dimension but also exerting influence using what is coyly described as 'kinetic attack'. Military doctrine has evolved concepts that entwine the psychological with the physical – or kinetic – on the basis that weapon effects will always have a pronounced psychological impact on those at the receiving end – what the military describes as shattering an enemy's will or what Field Marshall Bill Slim (1956: 15) more prosaically set out as: 'There's only one principle of war and that's this. Hit the other fellow as quick as you can and as hard as you can, where is hurts him most, when he ain't looking'.

Dealing with the media in this context adds a fresh layer of complexity. It is broadly understood that, as the armed forces of a democratic state, the UK should always be open and honest in their dealings with the press. However, UK Media Operations doctrine (Joint Warfare Publication 3–45, published by the UK Joint Doctrine and Concepts Centre 2002) also has to be acknowledged that the media is a powerful influence which acts on friendly and hostile forces alike. As the UK MOD's 2001 *Future Strategic Context for Defence* noted: 'Effective communication strategies to promote wider understanding of the rationale behind the conduct of the operations will be vital if we are to avoid constraints which compromise our ability to achieve military objectives' (UK MOD 2001: 19). But a way has to be found to harmonize psychological operations efforts with dealings with the media and this has led to UK policy planners developing the concept of information campaigning – a pan-government, ideally pan-coalition, activity aimed at emphasizing the rectitude of military action and, as likely as not, highlighting the wrongness of the opposing position. It also enables effects to be planned across the board in a properly coherent and coordinated manner.

In terms of effects, the media now has a profound influence on how operations can be conducted. Any perceived notions of gentler times in the past when British correspondents stood 'shoulder to shoulder' with their British comrades in arms have been swept away over the past 20 years. As Susan Carruthers (2000: 5) puts it: 'The military in many twentieth-century wars have come to recognize potentially positive applications of media power in wartime. Mass media – too influential to be left to their own devices – have thus been harnessed to military purposes in the pursuit of victory.' It was probably chimera in any event, and closer examination of the relationship between the media and the military through history shows that it has often been strained at best and, on occasions, positively poisonous. None of this gainsays the immediacy and impact of modern media practice, particularly its ability to turn a low-level tactical event into a matter of strategic importance. This 'vulnerability' or susceptibility to media influence has also been recognized as a powerful force in conducting operations against the West by 'asymmetric' forces. The images of a dead US serviceman being dragged through the streets of Mogadishu in 1993 are largely credited with the Clinton administration's decision to halt the USA's then involvement in trying to stabilize Somalia. It is also suggested that al-Qaeda fully understood this dimension in planning the attacks on New York and Washington in September 2001.

If intelligence leads, information campaign planning now sits at the heart of any effects based approach, primarily focusing on four interdependent audiences. First, it needs to take account of the adversary audience and within that, the key individuals and agencies that influence and shape the thinking of the enemy's leadership. This is often most difficult with strongly autocratic regimes without a free media or any clearly identifiable third-party opinion leaders. Exercising influence over the leadership of Milosevic, for example, required access to his inner circle of trusted confidantes – business advisors, the military leadership and, of course, his family. In the case of Milosevic, his wife Mila was recognised as having a profound influence on his thinking and decision making. Her vulnerability was identified as her extensive web of business interests. Accordingly, financial pressure on Milosevic supporters and diplomatic pressure on natural allies, principally the Russians, are now largely credited with the successful conclusion of the 1999 NATO intervention in Kosovo. Not, perhaps, what NATO planners had originally intended but arguably effective nonetheless.

The second, broader audience to be considered is in the region surrounding an enemy state. Again, the intent is to isolate an enemy state or dissident element within it – not just physically, and probably economically, but also philosophically so that the development of 'pariah status' compels either supportive or neutral neighbours to distance themselves from the target adversary and to form a coalition that induces change through the psychological pressure of international isolation. Arguably, it is the very difficulty of finding a similar lever with which to attack al-Qaeda's core leadership that has made it such an intractable foe. It is also worth noting the increasing attempts by the West to exert influence over Iran in order to coerce it into suspending its nuclear programme, that have failed to date (2008) largely because Iran has continued to sustain relations with a number supportive regimes, particularly among the Non-Aligned Movement (NAM) which has partially given the lie to Western efforts to portray Iran as a rogue regime. Anti-Western it may be but devoid of support it is not.

The third audience to be considered and 'targeted' is the wider sphere of worldwide, international opinion. Once successfully engaged, not only does this further isolate the target state but it also underpins the development of coalitions of the willing and subsequent coalition action that may result. If a formal alliance such as NATO is involved or a UN deployment is to be undertaken, the widest international support provides the key to ensuring unity of purpose and prevents the target regime from using propaganda or other counter-information operations techniques to divide international opinion.

In considering an Information Campaign, the final critical audience is the domestic public opinion of the nation. The British public is heavily sensitized to the manner in which the media reports events and, probably more importantly, whether it condones military action or not. The military is beginning to accept that the media is the prism through which the wider public, both at home and abroad, forms its opinions about strategic security and national defence. In the UK today, it is estimated that less than 7 per cent of the population has any direct experience (either personally or through immediate family) of life in uniform. Unlike health or transport, or law and order, individuals therefore have little personal basis on which to form a view. Accordingly, as with IR, public perceptions of defence, and therefore of military operations, are largely shaped by long-term perceptions and the manner in which events are reported in the media. Public support, which is so influenced by media reporting, therefore becomes crucial to military success. Reflecting on his experience as the Commander of British forces in the Gulf in 1991, General Sir Peter De La Billiere (1991: 6) observed: '… if I could win reporters on to my side they would do a lot for the forces … and if I put over a consistent message, that message would start to filter into the hearts and minds of people in the United Kingdom. Further, that message would permeate through to every level of British society, because if one influenced the people of Britain, one began to influence politicians as well – and support across the whole political spectrum was essential for the kind of major overseas operation we were mounting.'

With information becoming more and more accessible through web-based technology, data processing which allows information to be ever more precisely targeted, and the reach and quality of modern communication systems, the control of information has enabled both states and non-state actors to manipulate the electro-magnetic spectrum to their advantage. However, for the more sophisticated insurgent, it also offers the capability to disrupt and to dominate in a manner out of all scale with its actual force size and capability – what the military calls 'asymmetry'. Therefore, the effects based approach has to deal, not only with maximizing friendly force dominance of the information spectrum – what the USA has called: 'full spectrum dominance' – but it must also counter the adversary's ability to do the same.

Terrorism as manifested in today's Islamist insurgent strategy seems to be trying to do something similar. As Andrew Sinclair (2003: 14) has suggested in his 'Anatomy of Terror', individuals and organizations have been using the tactics of terror as a means of achieving goals since before the birth of Christ. As a methodology, it does not seek to destroy physically an enemy's ability to fight. Nor is it bound by generally agreed international conventions that dictate how and when wars may be fought. Terrorism succeeds, or may succeed, because it challenges governments and authorities to respond while, at the same time, seeking to appeal to a range of sympathetic or concerned audiences.

Terrorism is the tactic of the underdog and success lies not in destructive acts themselves but in the way that these attacks may change the perceptions, attitudes and behaviour of wider publics. The key link between the act and wider perception is most likely to be publicity. Arguably, therefore, terrorism and insurgent war-fighting are less about the physical damage caused by violence, appalling though this may be for individuals caught up in the aftermath, but about the effect these attacks will have on the much larger numbers of people, across a range of target audiences, who will bear witness to these attacks, primarily through the prism of the media.

It seems undeniable that most insurgents understand that the widest media coverage is essential to the success of their activities. As Schmid and De Graaf (1982: 13) put it in the opening of their discussion of this relationship: 'violence is mainly perpetrated for its effects on others [rather] than the immediate victims.' David Peletz and Alex Schmid (1992) have subsequently suggested that a variety of audiences: terrorists, governments, the press, the general public and victims, all try to manipulate the media in the face of insurgent activities. As recently as October 2005, Harvard Professor Joseph Nye (2005: 12) was writing in the *Financial Times*: 'The current struggle [with al-Qaeda] is not only about whose army wins but also whose story wins ... Terrorism is about theatre and a competition for audience.' Similarly, the *Glasgow Herald* in an editorial leader (2005: 18) noted Ayman al-Zawahiri, the al-Qaeda deputy, allegedly telling his subordinates: '[al-Qaeda is involved in] a media battle in a race for the hearts and minds of our Ummah (the world-wide Muslim community).'

Moreover, recent international insurgency provides a number of examples of how 'received perception', rather than judgement, based solely on direct experience determines popular behaviour. This leaves people vulnerable to asymmetric manipulation of their own perceptions of events – electing not to fly post-9/11, people more fearful for their personal security because of media coverage of terrorist attacks, and people laying in emergency supplies because of a perceived increase in the threat to their well-being. The reality people experience in their daily lives in most cases does not change – their trains run normally, coffee is still available in their favourite café, their children go to school and colleagues appear at work each day – however, their exposure to media coverage that highlights how other people are behaving, sometimes on opposite sides of the world, prompts them to behave differently – and feel concerned – even when this is clearly irrational when viewed objectively.

It is suggested that this phenomenon is largely related to the increasing reach and breadth of the media (not just news but brand-led marketing, entertainment, the world wide web and advertising) and a growing tendency to be guided by received opinion. And this seems to be as much the case in less sophisticated societies as it is in the 'developed world' – albeit that the media that makes an impact in developing countries may not be television reporting but local radio, the mobile telephone, word on the street, rumour or simply gossip.

The reasons for this continue to be widely debated in terms of mass communications theory but it is generally agreed that people today see a worldwide view – no longer constrained to their immediate community or locality or even state. A tsunami occurs in the Indian Ocean and a worldwide reaction is evoked resulting in billions of dollars of aid. It has become a commonplace to talk about the 'global village' – but conversely individuals do not feel that they have an influential voice in this village – they have to trust the mass views of the wider world to which they are connected and therefore feel a part of. Increasingly, this is as true for a Tuareg tribesman as it is for a banker on Wall Street and reflects the fact that soft power influences us all. However, shaping and targeting this influence is, it is argued, altogether more challenging and seems to have led some in the military to doubt that information campaigns can deliver on their promise.

Audiences and soft power

Current military campaigns in both Iraq and Afghanistan, together with continuing US and European efforts to shape perceptions within the Arab Middle East, offer many examples, both large and small, to bolster the proposition that 'soft power' is difficult to apply in a precise and timely manner to achieve a set of desired outcomes, and particularly in the face of unexpected 'events'. Moreover, it seems to be particularly difficult to persuade audiences from widely divergent cultural backgrounds to develop a consistency of view that supports an over-riding desired campaign outcome.

In this context it is interesting to consider the current British campaign in Afghanistan (2008) in the context of the original set of information campaign messages that were developed before the UK's forces deployed south into Helmand province in 2005. These included:

- This is an Afghan-led process.
- Life in Afghanistan has improved since the removal of the Taliban.
- Afghanistan's future is best served by supporting, and working with, the Government of Afghanistan (GOA).
- Continued participation in the democratic process is critical.

- The UK and the wider International Community are committed to the region for the long term.
- Opium production is not in the interests of Afghanistan.
- Economic development depends on peace and stability.

Three years on, it is easy to deride these themes that were planned to support the British-led campaign in southern Afghanistan which the then British Secretary of State for Defence, John Reid, famously told the House of Commons would last three years, 'ideally without a shot being fired'. The way these general themes are used in an information campaign are evident in a subsequent BBC Radio 4 *Today Programme* interview (BBC 2006: 1) between the presenter, Edward Stourton, and John Reid, who was visiting Kandahar Airbase at the time:

ES: In practical terms, what does that mean for what British troops in Helmand Province will do?

JR: We will give assistance, intelligence, protection to the Afghan Government and their anti-narcotics' force as they lead the fight to undermine the corruption and the trade in narcotics which fuels that corruption in Helmand Province. So we're here, as I said, to protect the development of good Government in the local area by the democratically elected Government of President Karzai but also to help them build their security forces and their economy ...

ES: Yeah. So just to, just ...

JR: ... and the economy can only be built on legitimate grounds if the illegitimate economy which President Karzai wants to attack, that's the opium trade, is undermined. So they will be leading on it politically.

In the fighting that has followed and in the resurgence of the Taliban, arguably these fine intentions have been lost – not only on the Afghan audience but also in the UK. An editorial in the *Independent on Sunday* newspaper on 2 March 2008, prompted by the revelation that Prince Harry had been serving with his regiment in Helmand, illustrates this point:

'... as Leo Docherty writes in our report today, the images of Prince Harry in Helmand 'seem dangerously close to propaganda'. If you had read the newspapers on Friday, you would have learnt little of the problems of poppy eradication or of why support for the Taliban – the unseen enemy – might be increasing.

So now is in fact a good time to ask, again, is this a just war? What are we hoping to achieve? How, therefore, do we define success? Our view is that it was a just war, but that its conduct over the past six years has seriously weakened its legitimacy. The overthrow of the Taliban in 2001 was overwhelmingly supported by the nations of the world and by the people of Afghanistan. It was accomplished quickly and with relatively little bloodshed. The election of Hamid Karzai as president in 2004 concluded the first – and an uplifting – part of the story of a nation rescued from theocratic tyranny by a world community acting from the highest motives. But that was also, looking back, the easy part.

Since then, two problems have come to dominate: that of fostering economic progress in one of the poorest countries in the world, whose farmers are dependent on the opium trade; and that of resisting the resurgence of fundamentalist Islamic nationalism. Both have proved harder than expected, and neither has been handled well.

The example illustrates the essential point that it is easy to develop communication themes and messages but it is significantly harder to press these home in the face of events particularly over time. Looking again at the original campaign themes listed previously, it may be argued that the important messages about Afghan primacy and the need to overcome Afghanistan's economic dependence on opium farming, appear to have become obscured by the renewed threat from the Taliban and the clear failure of the UK government's 'alternative livelihoods' agenda.

The Western military has embraced the concept of soft power as a means of pursuing what once again are being termed 'hearts and minds' operations. Today there is much talk in military circles of 'non-kinetic operations', 'information campaigns', 'influence operations', 'media operations', 'information operations' and 'achieving joint effects'. This trend perhaps reflects a broader shift in doctrinal thinking that recognizes that the application of military force must increasingly be used in concert with other levers of power, particularly the political and the economic. General Sir Rupert Smith (2005: 16), widely regarded as one of Britain's finest post-World War II commanders, suggests in his recent book, *The Utility of War*, that there has to be recognition that militaries around the world are increasingly engaged in what he describes as 'war amongst the people'. He lists six attributes that mark this shift of which the first two are apposite to a discussion of the military use of soft power:

- The ends for which we fight are changing from the hard absolute objectives of interstate industrial warfare to more malleable objectives to do with the individual and societies that are not states.
- We fight among people, a fact amplified literally and figuratively by the central role of the media: we fight in every living room in the world as well as on the streets and fields of a conflict zone.

These broad truths have been taken up by doctrine centres on both sides of the Atlantic and are the substance of much debate at military staff colleges. However, this whole approach with its implied acknowledgement of public relations, marketing and advertising techniques has fostered a belief that soft power can somehow be deployed and employed in a military theatre of operation in a similar fashion to a few brigades of armour and infantry. As has been suggested above, this is patently difficult to achieve and particularly so above the local tactical level. This is well-illustrated by some remarks by Mahamed Baharoon, an Arab analyst working for the Dubai-based think tank, DCRMC, (pers. comm., 2006) on the Arab reaction to President Bush's announcement of the US 'surge strategy' for Iraq in January 2006:

> The surge strategy adopted by President Bush in Iraq has faced much criticism in the Arab media. Many believe that it lacks the evidence of clear political will on the part of the US and that the additional numbers of forces being committed will be insufficient to meet the requirements of the task at hand. In a similar vein, others see the plan as merely President Bush's final attempt to save American face rather than Iraqi lives. Even the most sympathetic media reports, notably in Kuwait, have been sceptical as writers have asked why Arab governments should support a plan that is widely disputed by the American people. A number of commentators have also compared President Bush to an addicted gambler who is always trying to make one last bet, finally betting everything he owns.

It is important to note here that much of the Arab media criticism which followed President Bush's rejection of the Baker-Hamilton report of 2006, and the announcement of a 'surge' in force levels, appears to have been directly influenced by criticism in the US media. As an example of this, the *Washington Post* commentator David Ignatius (2007: 9) had observed:

> Regardless of whether there is a troop surge it is important to note General Petraeus's insistence that: 'The Host Nation Doing Something Tolerably Is Normally Better than Us Doing It Well.' In making this point, Petraeus cites the godfather of counterinsurgency warriors, General Creighton Abrams, who said when he was US commander in Vietnam in 1971: 'We can't run this thing. ... They've got to run it.' It's Petraeus's luck, good or bad, that he has a chance to see whether these precepts of counterinsurgency warfare can still work in Iraq, despite all the mistakes made over the past three years. His chances will be slim if President Bush and the Democratic Congress can't agree on a bipartisan plan for Iraq.

Examples of Western media comment reinforcing the criticism of Arab commentators have become frequent, particularly in the context of the present Iraq campaign and western engagement in the Middle East more generally. Indeed, it may be argued that as long as the Western media pillories the US-led coalition for its failures in Iraq and the manner in which the USA has pursued its War on Terror – Guantanamo et al – strategic information campaigns that seek to influence target audiences in the Middle East seem doomed to almost certain failure. In short, the narrative only takes you so far and ultimately events and outcomes will determine whether military intervention is seen to be successful or otherwise.

Again in the USA, much was made of the perceived failures of President Bush's high profile Under-Secretary of State for Public Diplomacy, Karen Hughes, when she resigned from her post in October 2007. As one career public diplomacy specialist concluded: 'Not even Hughes, whose message magic helped carry Bush to state and national electoral victories, could turn the Iraqi sow's ear into a silk purse as the US image plummeted right along with the president's popularity, which now hovers around 30 percent' (Farmer 2007: 7). Similarly, a *Los Angeles Times* editorial (2007: 10) suggested that: 'Hughes inability to solve anti-Americanism was less a reflection on her talents than on the impossibility of her job … Public diplomacy is people-driven, but people do not do diplomacy. Governments do.'

Conclusion

The current military enthusiasm for thinking of information campaigns as a form of collateral-free 'weapon system' suggests a misunderstanding of the essence of 'soft power', except perhaps at the lowest tactical levels. In 2001, the British made much of their success in Sierra Leone but this was a limited tactical operation where the UK was able to seize the 'information high ground' and hold it. Moreover, the operation took place in the pre-Iraq/Afghanistan era when the British press in particular remained well-disposed not only toward British military intervention but more broadly toward the Blair government's belief in intervening in failing states to support humanitarian objectives.

Military campaigns and operations by their very nature have carefully defined parameters in terms of: time, space, resources, objectives and, perhaps most importantly, constraints. Accordingly, the military is well schooled in applying military force to achieve a given objective and to having control over many of the variable factors, with the obvious exception of the reaction of the adversary. Soft power, it may be argued, does not sit comfortably with this type of militaristic approach. As Professor Nye (2004: 11) defines it: 'Soft power is not merely the same as influence. After all, influence can also rest on the hard power of threats or payments. And soft power is more than just persuasion or the ability to move people by argument, though that is an important part of it. It is also the ability to attract, and attraction often leads to acquiescence. Simply put, in behavioural terms, soft power is attractive power.'

For the military, this has become a doctrinal truism but, in a world increasingly defined by the availability of information and the perceptions that flow from media and non-media interpretation, the military has to understand that 'soft power' is more challenging to wield in terms of the application of military force – particularly if what that force is doing is not seen as 'attractive'. Moreover, if General Rupert Smith's concept of 'war amongst the people' is accepted as the defining descriptor of warfare at the beginning of the twenty-first century, then the military probably has to recalibrate its thinking about how to shape the attitudes and perceptions of both its adversary and the people among whom it is campaigning. Military planners cannot and should not expect information campaigns to deliver results either to a fixed timetable or to a firm plan. The best that they can probably ever hope for is to create and sustain a supportive information environment that encourages popular support and engenders goodwill and positive identification with the aims and objectives of a given operation.

It is also vitally important that military planners understand that the 'information environment' has few boundaries and therefore this requires unity of effort by all. If the other levers of soft power: diplomatic, political, economic and cultural; are not pulling in the same direction, then it is hard, if not impossible, for the military to set about creating favourable conditions on its own. Equally, the military has to make greater efforts to avoid inflicting damage on its own reputation, such as the events that led to the Abu Ghraib scandals for the USA in 2004 or the death of Baha Musa in British military custody in 2003. The evidence suggests that these swiftly erode the efforts of government directed public diplomacy, as well as the military's own efforts to create favourable impressions.

This, in turn, begs questions of how much resource and effort should be directed to supporting military information campaign efforts. In the Middle East, there has been widespread criticism of US efforts to set up its own broadcast outlets to communicate coalition-friendly messages. A survey of viewing and listening habits across the Middle East in October 2005 found that just 6 per cent of Arabs tuned in to news broadcasts by Al Hurra, the US-funded Arabic station. This contrasted with the 65 per cent who watched Al Jazeera (Telhami 2005: 17). Many would argue that the money spent funding Al Hurra would have been better spent trying to influence the popular Arab news stations of Al Jazeera and Al Arabiya to a more positive perception of the invasion of Iraq and its aftermath.

In what may appear to be a very negative assessment of the success of information activities in the Iraq campaign, there are some positive points to note. The high turn out for the Iraqi elections in 2004 should be partially attributed to, what was at the time, a veiled advertising campaign conducted by the commercial firm Bell Pottinger. This informed Iraqis of the electoral process and urged them to use their votes. The claimed 63 per cent turn out, in the face of the mounting threat of violence, was deemed a considerable success and was partly attributed to Bell Pottinger information campaign.

As an exercise in the application of soft power, military information campaigns have become a central part of every strategic planning process. However, there remains a tendency to flirt with information and communication planning; commanders sometimes still seeing it as an after-thought. This is because strategists have learned not to expect swift and measurable outcomes from these campaigns. Popular opinions may swing around in a dramatic manner but perceptions and attitudes are enduring features of any community and it takes a sustained effort on all sides to shift these to a point where a desired end-state is reached with the confidence that it will endure.

Notes

1 The 'Global War on Terrorism' is a US term. From 2005, the UK government has preferred to term it 'Global Counter-Terrorism'.

2 Joint Warfare Publication 3–80 defines Information Operations as: 'Co-ordinated actions undertaken to influence an adversary or potential adversary in support of political and military objectives by undermining his will, cohesion and decision-making ability, through affecting his information, information based processes and systems while protecting one's own decision makers and decision-making processes.'

Bibliography

Bell, T. (2004) *Chime Communications Chairman's Home Page* (online). London. Available from: http://www.chime.plc.uk/ (accessed July 08, 2004).

Berkowitz, B. (2003) *The New Face of Warfare*, New York: Simon & Schuster.

Brown, R. (2003) 'Political Communications, Information Operations and Public Diplomacy in the War on Terrorism', in D.K. Thussu and D. Freedman (eds) *War and the Media*, London: SAGE Publications, ch. 6.

Carruthers, S.L. (2000) *The Media at War*, London: Macmillan Press.

De La Billiere, P. (1992) *Storm Command*, London: Harper Collins.

Farmer, G. (2007) 'PR Advisor Hughes Bails Out on Her Pal Bush', *Nevada Appeal*, 11 November.

Holmes, R. (1998) 'Facilitator's Introductory Remarks', HQ Land Command Seminar, Warminster.

Ignatius, D. (2007) 'Lessons for One Last Try', *Washington Post*, 10 January.

Los Angeles Times (2007) 'Linking Public Diplomacy to Policy', *Los Angeles Times*, 3 November.

Nye, J., Jr (2004) *Soft Power*, New York: Perseus.

—— (2005) 'How to Counter Terrorism's Online Generation', *Financial Times*, 13 October, p. 19.

Schmid, A.P. and De Graaf, J.F.A. (1982) *Violence as Communication: Insurgent Terrorism and the Western News Media,* Newbury Park, CA: SAGE Publications.

Sinclair, A. (2003) *Anatomy of Terror*, London: Pan MacMillan.

Slim, W. (1956) *Defeat into Victory*, London: Cassell.

Smith, R. (2005) *The Utility of Force*, London: Penguin Allen Lane.

Telhami, S. (2005) *Poll of Arab Attitudes Towards Political and Social Issues, Foreign Policy and Media*. Baltimore, US: University of Maryland and Zogby International.

The Herald (2005) 'Could Amman Bomb Attacks Turn Muslim Minds Again to al Qaeda?', *The Herald*, 12 November, p. 18.

UK MOD (2001) *The Future Strategic Context for Defence*, London: The Stationery Office.

Von Clausewitz, K. (1976) *On War*, M. Howard and P. Paret (eds and trans). Princeton, NJ: Princeton University Press.

9 Public diplomacy and the information war on terror

Philip M. Taylor

Since 9/11, it has been frequently asserted that the West is losing the propaganda war against Islamic extremism. Of course, the Western democracies do not label what they do as 'propaganda'. That historically pejorative label is reserved for 'enemy information activities' such as al-Qaeda websites, bin Laden videotapes and – often unfairly[1] – Al Jazeera news reports. Instead, the West prefers a variety of euphemisms to describe its own information campaigns, from public diplomacy in the diplomatic sphere to information operations on the battlefields of Afghanistan and Iraq. Since 2006, the phrase 'strategic communications' has emerged as the preferred overarching phrase for official democratic state 'influence activities' (replacing the dreadful 'perception management', which preceded it). But, whatever it is called, there is widespread agreement that both al-Qaeda and the Western democracies are engaged in an information war that needs to be defined in a much broader sense than that outlined in narrow military doctrines. Washington and London have now relabelled 'The Global War on Terror' as 'The Long War' – which is what the terrorists have been fighting all along. They thought that President Bush was right to initially label it as a 'crusade' because, for them, that is precisely what it is. For al-Qaeda, Iraq and Afghanistan are merely the latest battles in a thousand year crusade being waged by the infidels against Islam.

To get into this mindset is one of the greatest challenges for the West's information warriors. It is part of Sun Tzu's dictum that you should 'know your enemy' *as well as* knowing oneself:

> Knowing the other and knowing oneself,
> In one hundred battles no danger
> Not knowing the other and knowing oneself,
> One victory for one loss.
> Not knowing the other and not knowing oneself,
> In every battle certain defeat.

I think it would be fair to suggest that this is one of the greatest failures of Western propaganda campaigns since 9/11. It is astonishing to reflect in poll after poll on how levels of anti-Americanism have increased since *Le Monde's* famous headline the day after the terrorist attacks on New York and Washington that 'we are all Americans'. The 'war' fought since then is now longer than World War II – and with no end yet in sight. In the Muslim world in particular, even in moderate Islamic countries, some polls have revealed that many people think the American President is a greater threat to world peace than bin Laden, or that the West is in reality engaged in a 'clash of civilizations' or even a minority view that the collapse of the Twin Towers was a controlled explosion engineered by the CIA working alongside Mossad which is why '4000 Jews failed to turn up to work that day'. With the election of President Obama, we shall see whether such conspiracy theories were directed more at the policies of the Bush administration than at the value system which the people of the USA have represented on the world stage. Or will it become a personalized struggle between Obama and Osama?

It is too easy – and a big mistake – to dismiss such nonsense or, for that matter, the myriad of conspiracy theories and rumours that thrive in places like Iraq and Afghanistan, as the irrelevant ranting of a few mad mullahs. While it should be remembered that many of the conspiracy theories originate from within the USA itself, al-Qaeda has proved particularly adept at propaganda resonating with their target audiences throughout the Islamic world. They are opportunistic – exploiting Abu Ghraib and Guantanamo with some skill and even claiming that Hurricane Katrina was 'God's revenge against the city of homosexuals'. However, unlike in the West, there is also an acute strategic vision amongst the terrorist leadership of what the end-state will look like. Their videotapes, websites, CDs and DVDs target their audiences with a resonance and empathy that is often lacking in Western information campaigns directed towards the Islamic world. Of course, they do not have to play by the same rules and they frequently deploy misinformation and disinformation. Their websites have proliferated enormously since 2001 and al-Qaeda has its own video production unit known as As Sahab ('Clouds') which uploads its products on YouTube.

To give a flavour of one their video-productions, here are some quotes from the narration of the film, *Will of the Martyr,* praising one particular suicide bomber (which they call 'martyrdom operations'):

> This Ummah has become subject to the Jews and Christians and has been enslaved by the United Nations Security Council which was created for the security of the *kufr* and its allies. This kufr has put into place a set of international laws against Allah's Shariah. This kufr has contaminated our educational systems with apostasy and heresy. It has trapped our economics in the chains of usury. It has undertaken its program of limiting our population and killed our offspring under the banner of family planning and consequently our sisters and daughters have become barren. And by sheltering under the labels of information technology and culture, it has unleashed a storm of decadence and immorality that has ruined the ethics and character of the young generation and resulted in the death of shame in Muslim societies.

And under this very same global structure of kafir, both the theoretical and hands-on training of the thinkers and politicians of the Muslim world started on a basis of atheism, in order to make them capable of upholding Western ideologies and values under a cloak of democracy. With the help of secret conspiracies and clandestine revolutions, these international Tawagheel imposed upon this Ummah of Tawheed, factions and rulers who, instead of prostrating themselves to the Lord of the Ancient House, the Kaaba, prostrate themselves to the Lord of the White House. These apostate leaderships in turn imposed laws of kufr, which are in open contradiction to our divine Shariah and explicitly ridicule Islamic traditions and our religious rights ... By using these evil crusader rulers, the pharaoh of our age, America, proceed to personally conquer our lands by establishing military bases throughout the Islamic world. And so today the entire Muslim nation is subject to the tyranny and oppression of this Crusader disbelief. ... To avenge these atrocities of the kuffaar, there rose from the gate of Islam, Sindh, a brilliant star by the name of Hafiz Usman' [the suicide bomber].

The video opens with computer generated graphics of a car reversing into an American military patrol and then exploding. It is skilfully edited with images, *inter alia,* of Israeli troops and their Palestinian 'victims' shouting 'we are all bin Laden' and it is overlaid with music and passages from the Koran. It then goes on to weave a political-religious vision of the Western evils it is fighting against, including family planning and USAID campaigns to assist, or rather corrupt, Islamic values. And this is but one example from a range of 'documentaries', news releases and videotaped speeches and even feature films, which al-Qaeda releases on the Internet. Depending on the target audience, As Sahab netcasts CNN-style news bulletins, mimics State Department press releases, and subtitles its statements according to their target audiences. All in all, it is a much more impressive information campaign than anything yet seen by Western governments.

   The degree to which al-Qaeda propaganda is centrally coordinated is the subject of considerable debate. But there does appear to be some centralized direction. For example, on 6 July 2006 (the day before the first anniversary of the 7/7 bombings in London) As-Sahab released a video entitled 'Will of the Knights of the London Raid (Part 2)', which contained the last will and testament of 7/7 London bomber Shehzad Tanweer. Twelve days later, Muhammed Gulzar – later placed on trial for the Heathrow bombing plot – arrived in Britain under a false name. Nine days after Gulzar's arrival, and two weeks before the Heathrow bombers were arrested, As-Sahab released a video on 27 July featuring al-Zawahiri. The backdrop featured three large photographs: one of Mohammed Atef (al-Qaeda's senior military chief who was killed in Afghanistan in late 2001), one of 9/11 operational commander Mohammed Atta and one of the burning World Trade Center towers.

   In this last video, al-Zawahiri discussed a lecture Atef gave in 2000 to al-Qaeda trainees about Palestine. He recalled that Atta – who was among the trainees – asked: 'What is the way to defeat the attack on Palestine?' Al-Zawahiri supplied his own answer in the video, saying that the nation which produced the 19 'martyrs who shook America' is 'capable of producing double that number. As two Strafor analysts have recently written:

> It could be a coincidence that a large plot involving aircraft – nearly twice as many as were hijacked on 9/11 – was thwarted only two weeks after this video surfaced. But we are not big believers in coincidence – nor do we believe there are obvious (or even hidden) messages in every al-Qaeda message. However, to our minds the 27 July tape was a clear message meant to be viewed in retrospect – that al-Qaeda was behind the Heathrow airline plot.
>
> (Burton and Stewart, 2008)

Al-Qaeda's patterns of operations were again repeated when police seized pre-recorded videotapes by several of the Heathrow bombers in Gulzar's flat. To the terrorists, these 'martyrdom videos' uploaded to the Internet are the digital equivalents in cyberspace of Western-style cenotaphs or war memorials to their 'glorious dead'.

A recent report by Radio Free Europe/Radio Liberty identified two organizations other than As-Sahab which regularly received videotapes from various armed groups for posting to the Internet. These were Fajr and the Global Islamic Media Group. The report stated that these:

> same media entities that 'brand' jihadist media also create virtual links between the various armed groups that fall into the general category of al-Qaeda and affiliated movements. ... Jihadist media are attempting to mimic a 'traditional' structure in order to boost credibility and facilitate message control. While conventional wisdom holds that jihadist media have been quick to exploit technological innovations to advance their cause, they are moving toward a more structured approach based on consistent branding and quasi-official media entities. Their reasons for doing so appear to be a desire to boost the credibility of their products and ensure message control.
>
> (Kimmage 2008: 1)

In February 2006, in a speech to the Council on Foreign Relations, Donald Rumsfeld conceded that:

> Our enemies have skilfully adapted to fighting wars in today's media age, but for the most part we, our country, our government, has not adapted. Consider that the violent extremists have established media relations committees – these are terrorists and they have media relations committees that meet and talk about strategy, not with bullets but with words. They've proven to be highly successful at manipulating the opinion elites of the world. They plan and design their headline-grabbing attacks using every means of communication to intimidate and break the collective will of free people.
>
> (Rumsfeld 2006)

When, however, some observers suggest that the West is losing the information/ propaganda war, it is usually because of the levels of anti-Americanism prompted by the latest opinion polls rather than by any sustained analysis of terrorist cyber-propaganda skills. However, 'for the post-Iraq (post-2003) generation especially, Internet chat rooms are now supplementing and replacing mosques, community centres and coffee shops as venues for recruitment. In short, cyberspace is now the battlefield, and the "war" is one of ideas' (HSPI, 2006) that said, al-Qaeda has not yet achieved its strategic goals which are essentially twofold: the establishment of an Islamic Caliphate under Shariah law and the destruction of the US economy. Conversely, the 2003 invasion of Iraq prompted bin Laden to reconfigure his Caliphate's capital city to Baghdad – thus creating a 9/11-Iraq connection when none had existed before. And the damage caused to the American and world economy by the sub-prime credit crisis from 2007 onwards may well result in another Western self-fulfilling prophecy.

Too often do Western responses, especially with regard to incursions on civil liberties, play into al-Qaeda's hands. But the real difference between terrorist propaganda and the Western approach to information and psychological operations, public diplomacy and public affairs (the three 'pillars' of strategic communications) lies in the emphasis given to a long-term approach to achieving their retrospective vision of a Caliphate free from 'non believers'.

Terrorism and the information age are synonymous. Terrorists would be relegated to the status of anarchists or even common criminals without the information society. By labelling the Western response to 9/11 as a Global *War* on Terror or now The Long *War*, it empowered those criminals with the status of 'warriors'. Terrorists also know that their activity is 10 per cent violence and 90 per cent publicity, whereas the US response in Afghanistan and Iraq is 90 per cent violence and 10 per cent strategic communications. But inverting those figures would still not solve the problem.

Part of the predicament is structural. Western democracies still govern with essentially the same governmental structures as they had during the Cold War, plus a few add-ons like the Department of Homeland Security. The same is true of Western militaries which are best suited to waging war rather than fighting an information war, minus the existence of a central information department such as the United States Information Agency which was folded into the State Department in 1999. In such an environment, influence activities are too often relegated to a support function of kinetic activity. To the terrorists, information is much more than a force multiplier; it is *the main weapon*.

Another part of the problem is cultural. As non-Muslims, Western secular governments have little hope of engaging in debates within the Islamic world about such things as the meaning of jihad or whether terrorists are martyrs or criminals. As 'non-believers', Western words merely fall on deaf ears. This is a real problem for public diplomacy initiatives like the 'shared values' campaign and is exacerbated by the strand of the Bush Doctrine that plans to spread Western-style democracy to places like Iraq and beyond. In other words, the West needs to explain more carefully what its values are rather than telling 'others' to be more like 'us'. This is the role for soft power, although it needs to be recognized that Western films and television programmes that are successfully exported to Islamic countries contain values (like drug abuse, crime, divorce, infidelity and promiscuity) that are *ostensibly* anathema to the teachings of Mohammed.

If the 'Long War' is anything, it is indeed a war of ideas or the much vaunted struggle for 'hearts and minds'. Information warfare must embrace both rational (minds) and emotional (hearts) 'human factors' if it is to succeed. So who is winning? Guantanamo Bay and Abu Ghraib have certainly not helped America's cause. These are, however, but two examples of propaganda 'own goals' over the past six years. False stories in Western media outlets – such as the *Newsweek* report that a Koran had been flushed down the toilet at Gitmo or the faked pictures of British soldiers mistreating Iraqi prisoners in the *Mirror* – certainly undermine Anglo-American assertions about being a 'force for good in the world'. But they are a price to pay for attaching the spread of democracy to the Bush Doctrine as the justification for 'why we fight'.

That phrase was, of course, the title of a series of seven World War II 'indoctrination films' made by Frank Capra for the US Office of War Information between 1941 and 1946. The rhetoric of World War II is ever present in our twenty-first century conflict, whether it be an 'axis of evil' or attacks on 'appeasers' who suggest that there might be another way to win a long information war against the ideas – and conditions – that generate extremist violent actions. Part of this dissent suggests that military actions in places like Iraq have made the world a more dangerous place than it was before 2003, with the hawks pointing to 9/11 itself as evidence of terrorist intentions. But 9/11 did not come out of the blue. And despite the views of those American neo-conservatives who suggested that Iraq and 9/11 were connected, it was in fact American policy decisions to implement 'regime change' after the attacks on New York and Washington that created a self-fulfilling prophecy.

In one less spurious sense, 9/11 and Iraq were indeed connected but not in the way 70 per cent of Americans at one point believed them to be. The terrorist attacks can in fact be traced back to Operation Desert Storm and the arrival of infidel troops (men and women) into the holy land of Mecca. While some people who asked why the coalition did not 'finish the job' after Iraqi forces were driven out of Kuwait in 1991, it became bin Laden's obsession to see the expulsion of these *kafir* invaders and the deposition of the corrupt Saudi sheiks who had allowed this desecration. The first attempt to down the World Trade Center was in 1993. Bin Laden publicly declared his war (jihad) on the USA in 1996 with the words 'the occupying American enemy is the principle and the main cause of the situation. Therefore efforts should be concentrated on destroying, fighting, and killing the enemy until, by the Grace of Allah, it is completely defeated.' So it was not so much a question of believing whether Saddam Hussein was behind the 2001 attacks but understanding that one of the root causes of 9/11 was the USA not engaging in 'regime change' in 1991 while keeping its troops in the region. In his 1998 fatwah against the West and Israel, 'to kill the Americans and their allies – civilians and military – is an individual duty for every Muslim who can do it in any country in which it is possible to do it, in order to liberate the al-Aqsa Mosque and the holy mosque [Mecca] from their grip, and in order for their armies to move out of all the lands of Islam, defeated and unable to threaten any Muslim'.

Another little known aspect of Desert Storm blowback from 1991 was also to affect subsequent events in 2003. Operation Desert Storm was halted once Iraqi forces had been physically expelled from Kuwait. There was no UN mandate to do anything else at that time. However, covert radio broadcasts from coalition sources – allegedly the CIA – encouraged uprisings against the Saddam regime among the Shias to the south and the Kurds to the north of Iraq. When those uprisings were brutally crushed by Saddam's forces, no help was forthcoming from the coalition. This left a deep sense of betrayal and suspicion amongst the Shias especially. At least the plight of the Kurds had appeared on CNN and a resultant humanitarian mission (Operation Provide Comfort) was despatched to alleviate the suffering. Accordingly, when coalition forces invaded southern Iraq in 2003, without a UN mandate to implement regime change but full of statements about the liberation of Iraqi citizens from Saddam's tyranny, the locals failed to greet them as liberators showered with flower petals. The British forces quickly realized the problem. One of their psychological operations leaflets attempted to reassure them that 'this time we won't abandon you'.

Iraq in 2003 and the subsequent insurgency have greatly muddied the waters of Western information warfare. Bin Laden seized the opportunity and declared Baghdad as the centre of the new Caliphate. Foreign fighters flooded into the country under the banner of al-Qaeda in Iraq. The Global War on Terror now had a new battlefront, although emboldened Taliban fighters were to also to renew their conflict in Afghanistan following their expulsion from Kabul in late 2001. As Robert Pape wrote in *Dying to Win: The Logic of Suicide Terrorism*:

> Since 1990, the United States has stationed tens of thousands of ground troops on the Arabian Peninsula, and that is the main mobilization appeal of Osama bin Laden and al-Qaeda. People who make the argument that it is a good thing to have them attacking us over there are missing that suicide terrorism is not a supply-limited phenomenon where there are just a few hundred around the world willing to do it because they are religious fanatics. It is a demand-driven phenomenon. That is, it is driven by the presence of foreign forces on the territory that the terrorists view as their homeland. The operation in Iraq has stimulated suicide terrorism and has given suicide terrorism a new lease on life.

So, as the Long War enters its eighth year, let us return to the title of this chapter. I think implicit in the question of my chapter is the answer: No. If we take the word 'information' out of the title for a moment, we need to ask whether the war on terror can be won, and we begin to see that the problem arises from the phrase 'war on terror' – just like other 'wars' declared on drugs, the war on want, cancer or anything else. We know when the war began – on 9/11 – and the first words of the US fight-back aboard Flight 93 – 'Let's role'. But how will it end?

Indeed, what we must now call 'The Long War' needs a definition of Victory and an understanding of what that victory would look like. The extermination of the 'bad guys'? Unconditional Surrender? A negotiated peace? How do you do that when Western governments openly pronounce that they do not negotiate with terrorists (unless, as we subsequently discovered, they are in Northern Ireland)? War on an idea or a concept, or whatever terrorism is in the minds of its perpetrators, requires both a clearly understood end-state and a Grand Strategy. We have neither. Until they are in place we may as well call it the Forever War or the Eternal War.

To win a war against an idea, we need to put the word 'information' back into the title. It should have primacy over the word 'war' itself – although it would be better to drop the word altogether. The word 'war' merely empowers terrorists with the status of 'warriors'. As Rupert Smith (2005: 1) noted in his book, *The Utility of Force*:

> War no longer exists … war as cognitively known to most non-combatants, war as battle in a field between men and machinery, war as a massive deciding event in a dispute in international affairs; such war no longer exists.

He (2005: 284–5) went on to point out:

> … we fight and operate amongst the people in a wider sense: through the media … Whoever coined the phrase 'the theatre of operations' was very prescient. We are conducting operations now as though we are on stage, in an amphitheatre or Roman arena. There are two or more sets of players – both with a producer, the commander, each of whom has his own idea of the script. On the ground, in the actual theatre, they are all on the stage and mixed up with people trying to get to their seats, the stage hands, the ticket collectors and the ice-cream vendors. At the same time they are being viewed by a partially and factional audience, comfortably seated, its attention focused on that part of the auditorium where it is noisiest, watching the events by peering down the drinking straws of their soft-drink packs – for that is the extent of the vision of a camera.

As President Bush has stated, it is a 'new kind of war'. Iraq, in contrast, has become a classic counterinsurgency challenge. But what about the wider conflict? Terrorism used to be about killing civilians. A war on terrorism sees terrorists in armed militias attacking soldiers. It is a new kind of terrorism but propaganda, as well as 'propaganda of the deed', remain central to its conduct. Western information warriors are not talking about a clash, as in a clash of civilizations, but they are talking about a sustained information campaign that needs to be waged against their adversaries who argue that this is precisely what is going on. And for that there needs to be a Grand Strategy as well.

There used to be one in a previous global ideological conflict, first outlined in George Kennan's famous Long Telegram back in 1946. In that document – which was also read by Stalin – Kennan wrote that 'All Soviet propaganda beyond Soviet security sphere is basically negative and destructive. It should therefore be relatively easy to combat it by any intelligent and really constructive program.' What has been tried since 9/11, however, has been Radio Sawa and Al Hurra television, *Hi* magazine, the Lincoln Group, the failed Offices of Global Communications and of Strategic Influence. These were all tactical fixes for operational problems without any real strategic understanding of what is required for a long information *confrontation*. That is why they are either not working or have been closed down. True, it took time for the previous ideological warfare machinery to be constructed, with the United States Information Agency (USIA) only being formed in 1953. Yet this Cold War machinery for waging strategic information warfare was virtually dismantled within a decade of the collapse of the Soviet Union. Recreating the USIA today in the form of a Centre for Global Engagement[2] may be part of the solution that is required, but the global information environment is today infinitely more complex than it was during the Cold War, with many new info-players like Al Jazeera or on the Internet. The Smith-Mundt Act would have to go, and that might prove unacceptable to American citizens. But in a world in which the line between the national and the international can no longer be drawn on the shores of the Atlantic and Pacific oceans, not just in cyberspace but also in a global 24/7 news mediasphere, a successful information campaign needs to recognize that it is no longer about 'winning' but *competing*.

Western governments historically were able to monopolize or dominate global news flows and the consequent global views flows which that dominance enabled. They can no longer do that in an age of regional news players like Al Jazeera or the new Iranian Press television that are streamed on the Internet, or indeed in an the age of the so-called 'citizen journalist'. For all the military talk about taking 'command and control' of the battle space, when the battle space is the global mediasphere in which an individual with a cell-phone camera can access a global audience on the worldwide web, 'full spectrum dominance' is nigh impossible.

So what can be done? Many argue that what is needed is a renewed emphasis on soft power. But in trying to make Western democracies more attractive so that others want to be like them, the democracies and their free media – which still arouse global popularity – unleash images and perceptions that damage that attractiveness. In the Muslim world, audiences for Hollywood movies receive constant reinforcements of how Western values are decadent, violent, promiscuous, corrupt, drug- and divorce-ridden. Whereas Western governments see democracy, individualism and free market liberal capitalism as the tenets of their value system – that was what won the Cold War after all – Islamic extremists use Western media products as symbols of their own moral authority, not that of the West. That said, a recent study of British Muslims cautiously revealed that they were largely resistant to propaganda messages contained in Jihadist videos (Baines *et al.*, 2006). More alarmingly, 'some Western Muslims are self-radicalizing through a process of small-group socialization fed by images from the Western media which Islamist propaganda confirms and reinforces rather than initiates; meanwhile, a large number evince understanding and even sympathy for terrorist protagonists as victims, resorting to desperate measures out of frustration; and there is a growing belief in the fundamental Islamist proposition that there is a real war against Islam' (wordpress.com 2008). Whether this is also true of places like Pakistan or elsewhere in less developed countries where old-fashioned modems take hours to download large text or moving image files remains to be seen. But finding this sort of thing out is one of the main issues for any strategic communications strategy before the broadband revolution reaches those places.

Nor are Muslims the only target audiences in cyberspace. In June 2007 the Global Islamic Media Front (GIMF) announced a media campaign designed to counter Arab and Western messages against the Islamic State in Iraq (ISI) and to stop the increasing Sunni military campaign against the ISI. In a message entitled 'The Battar Media Raid: How to Participate? How to Help? What Is My Role?' methods were described on how to infiltrate non-Islamic forums for the purpose of disseminating pro-ISI propaganda:

> What we expect from you brothers and sisters is for the [Islamist] forum to be like beehives during the raid ... [where] one person takes part in distributing [information] ... another generates links ... one person writes an article ... while another writes a poem ... People must feel and notice that the forums have changed radically during this blessed raid ... beloved, the raid is dependent on you ... The raid demands of you many things ... such as expertise, especially in the following areas: seeking religious knowledge, montage, translation into any language, uploading material onto various types of websites, web design, graphic design, journal and publication design, and hacking and security. If you have expertise in any of these [fields], contact the GIMF representative on any of the forums. If, however, you do not possess this expertise ... there are other things you can [do]: for example, posting matters related to the raid in most [jihad] forums ... posting [material] in non-jihad forums, posting in non-Islamic forums such as music forums, youth forums, sports forums, and others.
>
> (MEMRI, 2007)

I have not been able to find any Western strategic communications equivalent of this type of activity.

There have undoubtedly been some serious mistakes which will make the Long War longer and the strategic communications campaign more difficult. The initial response – perhaps understandably – to 9/11 was hard power. But, following immediate worldwide sympathy for the USA, the story since then has been one disaster after another – and has resulted in a considerable drop in trust not only of and among the USA's closest allies but also of their elected heads of government. But when you are 'at war' – as distinct from being in a counter-terrorist campaign – your warriors are in the driving seat and they deploy information warfare strategies in accordance with their military doctrines.

It is really only in the last 18 months that we have seen this primacy shift back to thinking about how soft power and public diplomacy may be better suited to winning the struggle for hearts and minds at the strategic level. But, as I said, the task of soft power and public diplomacy is even harder now than it was before the hard-power response in Afghanistan and Iraq. On the Internet, the early rhetoric becomes not something one can express regret about but rather 'facts' providing 'proof' of some neoconservative plan to dominate the world's oil and impose democracy on the Middle East.

Part of the problem lies with what politics in the West has become. Everything is short-term, epitomized by Harold Wilson's famous dictum that a 'week is a long time in politics'. Western politicians think about the future in terms of the next election – even over issues like climate change. And the way we do politics reflects the way we do information. True, democracies are their own worst enemies in this regard, especially if counter or anti-terrorist legislation undermines civil liberties and cherished freedoms which are such a central part of their value systems. As the Very Reverend Nathan Baxter, then Dean of the National Cathedral in Washington, DC, who had led the nation in a National Day of Prayer and Remembrance on 14 September 2001, warned: 'we must not become the evil we deplore'. He might have added that 'we' must not do things which play into the hands of the enemies of democracies.

There is no need to rehearse here the mistakes that have undermined Western credibility or why those mistakes were made. But it does need saying that strategic communications, to be effective, must be credible. It is the single most important word in the lexicon of successful influence activities. In the struggle for moral authority, credibility is everything. It is not like virginity; it can be got back. Although this will take time, Western information warriors need to understand in the meantime the dangers which, for example, short-termist politics – or even black propaganda campaigns such as that tried in 1991 – can have upon the long-term credibility of a value system that others really do want to emulate. It is not just a matter of talking the talk; actions always speak louder than words. As Richard Holloran (2007: 2) has pointed out: 'Successful strategic communication assumes a defensible policy, a respectable identity, a core value. In commercial marketing, the product for sale must be well-made and desirable. The strategic communication stratagem hasn't been built that can pull a poor policy decision out of trouble.'

The West is certainly facing a formidable enemy in terms of the propaganda it conducts. Its response has been cumbersome and, it has to be said, misdirected. However, the propaganda war is not yet lost. What the West can do in positive, non-warlike actions can have a genuine impact. But a temporary success seems to be followed by yet another informational disaster. Nor can the struggle for hearts and minds be waged solely by the military.

So how long will it take to win? In Islamic thought, a genuine grievance against a member of the Umma requires seven generations to avenge. A historian defines a generation as 25 years. So there you have it. If the West is to start winning today, making no more mistakes, it needs a Grand Strategy for the next 175 years.

But what is really required is a switch in thinking. A counter-terrorist campaign might not take quite so long. Provided it is engaged effectively by visually literate information warriors (not the text-based analysts of the past) using the second generation of Internet technologies (Web 2.0) terrorist propaganda can be confronted, provided it is recognized that information is *the* primary tool, not some support weapon. Otherwise, many more 'bad guys' will no doubt be killed, causing family members to join the quest for vengeance, thereby prolonging the war still further.

Perhaps it is finally time to stop thinking about the conflict in terms of it being a war at all. Even 'information war' seems unduly bellicose. This is not appeasement = surrender. That much misunderstood policy was originally about negotiating away legitimate grievances in order to avoid war. It was Hitler's determination to go to war regardless, together with Britain's refusal to negotiate over illegitimate claims to incorporate non-Germans in Poland into the Third Reich, which prompted Neville Chamberlain's declaration of war on Germany. However, appeasement became a word associated with cowardice in light of these events. It became part of a propaganda war. It still is and its misuse today reflects the remarkable level of historical ignorance among many Western politicians. Anyone with an understanding of the denazification of Germany after World War II would have cautioned against the wholesale de-Bathification of Iraq after 'Mission Accomplished' was proclaimed in April 2003, and all problems this has caused in Iraq since then. Today, politics is more image than substance. Francis Fukuyama was wrong to write about the 'end of history'. He should have called his book 'the end of ideology'. Since the end of the Cold War, politics has become a matter of governing rather than leadership while policy has become a matter of 'what sells best' rather than what is best for the nation in the long-term. It is a remarkable contrast with the ideology of bin Laden and his followers.

Public diplomacy, if conducted seriously, has the potential to build bridges and rebuild trust. This is because it is essentially a long-term process that is both mutual and reciprocal in its attempts to forge international understanding. It needs to reconsider the validity of the 'to know us is to love us' philosophy that underpins the concept of soft power because familiarity – as the 9/11 hijackers proved – can breed contempt. Nevertheless, thinking this way internationally cannot avoid thinking about actions at home because, in the era of global media and the Internet, what happens domestically can jeopardize public diplomacy's success abroad. Time will tell whether the election of President Barack Obama will bridge this particular problem, although the extraordinary reception worldwide of news of his success suggests a real opportunity. So it is not just a matter of Knowing the Enemy. A good deal of research has now been done on al-Qaeda propaganda and the Grand Strategy it supports. The problem lies closer to home. Indeed, since 9/11 when 'we' were all Americans, it is the USA that has become the enemy in the minds of many people around the world. In the information war being waged in the Islamic world, the USA and the West have become 'the enemy' rather than their self-proclaimed desire to be seen as a 'force for good in the world'. While Sun Tzu was right to warn that 'not knowing the other and not knowing oneself, in every battle certain defeat', when oneself has become the enemy there is a need to engage in deep contemplation not just on how others see 'us' but what kind of people 'we' really are, or have become.

Notes

1 Although Al Jazeera frequently airs news reports from an Arab perspective that are not normally seen on Western television stations, it is this perspective that annoys many people not used to having their hegemonic messages challenged. Al Jazeera sees itself in the public service broadcasting tradition of the BBC (where many of its staff was trained) whereby if you broadcast one point of view it needs to be balanced by the opposing point of view.
2 As recommended by the Defence Science Board Task Force on Strategic Communication in January 2008.

Bibliography

Baines, P., O'Shaughnessy, N.J., Moloney, K., Richards, B., Butler, S. and Gill, M. (2006) 'Muslim Voices: The British Muslim Response to Islamic Video Polemic – an exploratory study', Research Paper no. 3/06, Cranfield School of Management. Available at: http://kingsofwar.files.wordpress.com/2008/02/baines-rp-3-06.pdf

Defence Science Board Task Force on Strategic Communication (January 2008). http://www.acq.osd.mil/dsb/reports/2004-9-Strategic_Communication.pdf

Burton, F. and Stewart, S. (2008) 'The Heathrow Plot Trial: Retrospection and Implications', 9 April. Available at: http://www.strafor.com, (accessed 19 August, 2009).

Halloran, R. (2007) 'Strategic Communication', *Parameters, US Army War College Quarterly*, Vol. XXXVII(3), pp. 1–6.

Homeland Security Policy Institute (HSPI) and Critical Incident Analysis Group (CIAG) (2006) 'Task Force on Internet-Facilitated Radicalization, A Special Report by The George Washington University Homeland Security Policy Institute.'

Kimmage, D. (2008) 'The Al-Qaeda Media Nexus: The Virtual Network Behind the Global Message, An RFE/RL Special Report'. Available at: http://docs.rferl.org/en-US/AQ_Media_Nexus.pdf (accessed 30 August, 2009).

MEMRI (2007) 'Global Islamic Media Front Instructs Islamists to Infiltrate Popular Non-Islamic Forums to Spread Pro-Islamic State Propaganda', MEMRI Special Dispatches Series 1621 (14 June). Available at: http://memri.org/bin/articles.cgi?Page=archives&Area=sd&ID=SP162107, (accessed 25 August, 2009).

Rumsfeld, D. (2006) 'New Realities in the Media Age', speech delivered at the Council on Foreign Relations, 17 February, New York. Available at: http://www.cfr.org/publication/9900/ (accessed 25 August, 2009).

Smith, R. (2005) *The Utility of Force: The Art of War in the Modern World*, London: Allen Lane.

10 Soft power in an era of US decline

Giles Scott-Smith

> Soft power is not just a matter of ephemeral popularity; it is a means of obtaining outcomes the United States wants. … And when U.S. policies lose their legitimacy in the eyes of others, distrust grows, reducing U.S. leverage in international affairs.
>
> (Nye 2004b)

> Power in a global age, more than ever, will include a soft dimension of attraction as well as the hard dimensions of coercion and inducement. The ability to combine hard and soft power effectively is 'smart power.' The United States managed to deploy smart power throughout much of the cold war. It has been less successful in melding hard and soft power in the period since 9/11.
>
> (Nye 2008b: 107–8)

> Just six years into the 21st century, one can say this is not shaping up to be anything like an American century. Rather, the US seems much more likely to be faced with a very different kind of future: how to manage its own imperial decline. And, as a footnote, one might add that this is a task for which pragmatists are rather better suited than ideologues.
>
> (Jacques 2006)

> Diminishing US economic and military influence only underscores a third trend: the wilting of America's 'soft power'. … In a fast-transforming economic climate, a new president will be faced with a difficult balancing act: exercise flexibility while coming to terms with weakness, compensating for strengths lost during the past eight years while giving up ground in pragmatic ways. If that doesn't happen, then hard questions will linger, even after the last credit swops have been unwound, about America's capacity to project influence in the world.
>
> (Huq 2008)

It is somewhat ironic to write about US soft power in a period when everything related to US power seems to be collapsing. If soft power and public diplomacy rely on anything, they rely above all on credibility, and it is this commodity that has largely deserted the USA over the past eight years, first politically, and now economically/financially. Under President Bush a vast difference opened up between how a large part of America saw itself and how a large part of the rest of the world saw America. President Obama has already started to bridge this gap, but success won't be easy because it will require a fundamental reassessment of US national interest along with a recognition that exceptionalism can no longer be claimed. Following 9/11 there have been countless reports analyzing precisely the problems are with US public diplomacy, and what resources and approaches can be utilized in order to revive it and, in so doing, repair America's image around the world.[1] The underlying trend of these reports, however, was that the relative power and legitimacy of the USA remained the same, it was simply a matter of rearranging the governmental or state-private apparatus, coupled with an increased injection of funding. Joseph Nye's recent *The Powers to Lead* may have a point in arguing that a US-led liberal world order is a better outcome in general than any possible alternative, but in doing so it nevertheless perpetuates the image of a USA able to decide on which course to take, taking for granted that whatever it may be will be in the interests of all concerned (Nye 2008a). Aligned with this is a creeping militarization of diplomacy and public diplomacy that reflects the increasingly dominant position of the Pentagon in US foreign affairs over the last eight years. Inevitably the focus of the military has been on how to utilize information programmes in support of strategic objectives, but the result has been a further undermining of the State Department's role and a hollowing out of US diplomatic credibility and capability. What this militarization and urge for unabashed supremacy misses, however, is that it is doomed to failure in the current political and economic circumstances. The challenges, in an era of declining US soft power, are going to be as much domestic as global as the USA adjusts to its changing status within political and financial hierarchies of power. The popularity and political nouns of President Obama has already achieved some success to redress this situation, but charisma can only go so far when faced with major structural difficulties. The main point of this chapter is that the deficiencies exposed during the Bush years will continue to plague US efforts to regenerate its soft power potential in the years to come.

In a decade when hard power has largely set the tone for the US foreign policy approach, soft power has become the passion of analysts and academics alike. Underlying this 'movement' is a renewed liberal wish for a peaceful paradigm in international relations (IR) that eschews the use of force, but there is also an understanding that competition between state entities is now as much about imagery and values as it is about power in the traditional sense 'of getting others to do what you want'. The genealogy of the term 'soft power' stretches back several decades, but it is Joseph Nye who has given us a relatively clear interpretation: 'the ability to shape the preferences of others ... [which] tends to be associated with intangible assets such as an attractive personality, culture, political values and institutions, and policies that are seen as legitimate or having moral authority'. This is thus a form of 'co-optive' rather than command power (Nye 2004a: 5–7).[2]

From the broad starting-point of soft power, public diplomacy can achieve more specific goals. If soft power emanates from a nation's culture, political values and foreign policies, then 'public diplomacy is an instrument that governments use to mobilize [soft power] resources to communicate with and attract the publics of other countries, rather than merely their governments' (Nye 2008b: 95) Creating a favourable international environment with this instrument, a nation can more easily claim legitimacy as it seeks to 'shape international rules that are consistent with its interests and values' and so achieve its foreign policy objectives (Nye 2004a: 10). At the same time, not all foreign relations are reduced to the indirect machinations of public diplomacy, since hard power is still required to enforce the national interest if necessary. Credibility is as important with the threat or actual use of force as it is with persuading others to accept your viewpoint as being in their general interest. Hence the recent articulation, by Nye and influential colleagues, of 'smart power' as a combination of the two (Commission 2007).

The logic of this combination is both appealing and compelling. Any emphasis on the ability to achieve goals without resort to the use of force or coercion and in the general interest is a welcome shift in the post-9/11, post-Iraq world. The challenges to implementing this model are formidable, however. The rise in importance of public opinion for foreign policy formation, closely connected to the transformation ('democratization') of communications and media, has led to a wider diffusion of power with states no longer able to act as the sole direction-finder. Diplomacy, often unwillingly, is made more transparent, and non-state actors can assume pivotal roles in undermining, strengthening or even setting the dominant discourse on world events. The outcome of this has been a realization that the state has to realign itself as one player among many competing for airtime. The credibility of the 'official' voice is no longer taken for granted, and importance is placed on 'branding' to reinforce credibility. This challenges one of the fundamental precepts of realist thinking in IR, namely that the state, even in the context of complex interdependence, remains the prime actor for decision making and agenda-setting.

The responses to this situation have been mixed, but the path of the USA has revealed an inability to accept this new global contested environment. In particular, the determination of the US military to apply psychological warfare practices and strategic thinking to the information field has overshadowed all attempts to upgrade public diplomacy in the post-9/11 period. The focus during the Bush administrations was on short-term, rapid-reaction information management instead of long-term alliance-building, and this was how each successive Under Secretary of State for Public Diplomacy and Public Affairs was judged (see Khalaf 2008). Above all, the trend since 2000 has been dominated by a nationalist perspective, highlighting the merits of the USA, at the expense of a transnational perspective finding common ground with others across a range of policies. This perspective was driven by national security concerns as an addendum to the War on Terror, resulting only in the fall-out of declining legitimacy and credibility of the US position. In the midst of the credit crisis in September 2008, President Bush addressed the UN General Assembly for the eighth time and to the general disbelief of those present he focused yet again on the issues of terrorism and terrorist regimes.

Another factor, the continuing endurance of the US-inspired normative order in the post-Cold War era, is now also under scrutiny. The post-World War II security framework centred upon NATO has come under increasing criticism from Russia. In July 2008 a set of propositions were floated by the Russian ambassador to NATO, Dmitri Rogozin, as part of a developing Russian concept to restructure the Eurasian security architecture, reduce the importance of NATO and the Organization for Security and Cooperation in Europe and involve other powers such as China and India.[3] Yet although the USA with its post-9/11 unilateralism has set the standard in rejecting Cold War security structures, ending the Anti-Ballistic Missile Treaty and agreeing to a nuclear deal with India in defiance of the Non-Proliferation Treaty, there is little willingness to allow other powers to do the same.

The Bretton Woods institutions were created for a post-World War II world framed around US leadership. During the 1990s criticism of the dismal failure of the 'Washington Consensus' in reducing global poverty was escalated, fuelled by the International Monetary Fund's disastrous reactions to the Asian crisis, the World Bank's dismal environmental record, and the World Trade Organization's inability to resolve deadlock between the global North and South. As a result, in the twenty-first century all three institutions have suffered from a serious decline in legitimacy and credibility.[4] On 18 April 2008 British Prime Minister Gordon Brown spoke of 'reframing the international architecture' to accommodate the rise of new economic powers, and the credit crisis has given a further boost to critics of deregulated neoliberalism such as Angela Merkel (BBC 2008). The IMF's hope to gain more supervisory power out of this crisis situation (as it has tried to do during previous crisis situations) is almost certainly going to meet with indifference from many nations around the world.

This situation has been exacerbated by the steep rise in energy prices, redistributing wealth and economic power. The emerging 'axis of oil', made up of 'a loose and shifting coalition of energy-exporting and -importing states, anchored by Russia and China', is potentially a serious counterweight to US global influence, a process given extra impetus by the decline of the US dollar and the inexorable rise of US trade and budget deficits (Leverett 2008). Up till now this has been no more than an act of 'soft balancing', but there are clear signs of greater assertiveness, best exemplified by the Shanghai Development Corporation's efforts for economic, political and security cooperation in central Asia and Hugo Chavez's oil-fuelled counter-hegemonic strategy in Latin America and beyond (de Haas and van der Putten 2007; Mahbubani 2008).

There has been little evidence, outside of a consistently militant rhetoric, of the USA accommodating itself to this changing global environment. The ideology of the George W. Bush years was driven by the militarized vision of 'full spectrum dominance' and the insistence that there should be no challenger to the undisputed global reach of US power. The assumption of US leadership in the world and that without it there is far less chance of achieving progress in the general interest was not the exclusive preserve of the Bush administration, however. In the words of Madeleine Albright, Secretary of State under Bill Clinton, the USA is the 'indispensable nation'. Joseph Nye's continued insistence that the USA is pivotal for shaping the path that global governance will take is also indicative of this thinking (Nye 2008a), as is Arquilla and Ronfeldt's analysis of the global 'noosphere' (realm of ideas) that includes 'much that America stands for: openness, freedom, democracy, the rule of law, humane behaviour, respect for human rights, a preference for peaceful conflict resolution'. The 'complex organizational and technological bases' required in this evolving realm are held by the USA, which remains the only country 'who can pull this off' (Arquilla and Ronfeldt 2007). This is despite the fact that the War on Terror was used as justification for a series of transgressions of international law (for instance rendition, Guantanamo, use of torture), a trend that has further undermined the very normative order that the USA itself claims to uphold.

Successful public diplomacy is being able to merge the interests of others with those of your own. Nye (2008c: 64) is correct that the delivery of 'global public goods' is going to be a crucial feature in the politics of the twenty-first century. The challenge is how to shift US public diplomacy, and diplomacy in general, away from realpolitik and towards the realities of twenty-first century interdependence.

The militarization of public diplomacy

An influential report in 2003 noted that the increasing dominance of the Pentagon in US foreign policy was having major consequences for the conduct of public diplomacy:

> [T]he role the Defense Department plays in public diplomacy is neither broadly recognized nor well coordinated. ... While the State Department is considered the lead agency ... we are concerned that the Defense Department, with resources that dwarf those of all other agencies of government, is not fully integrated into the public diplomacy architecture.
>
> (Advisory Group 2003: 68)

The Pentagon's wish to control information and media affairs is based on its aim to secure 'strategic influence' and 'influence opinions, attitudes, and behaviour of foreign groups in ways that will promote US national objectives' (Gough 2003: 1). However, the methods to achieve this have crossed into explicit propaganda and psychological warfare operations. The determination to dominate the infosphere since the onset of the Afghan and Iraq campaigns has its roots in the First Gulf War (or Vietnam, for those with a longer historical perspective), its perfect gestation in Kosovo, and its ultimate expression in the targeting (both verbally and militarily) of Al Jazeera; the outcome is a severe case of 'mission creep' as the Pentagon's information operations, given legitimacy by the War on Terror, demonstrated no limits, either geographically or ethically.

Throughout the Iraq conflict the Defense Department has developed a series of initiatives to further its desire for information dominance. In October 2001 the Office of Strategic Influence (OSI) was created to conduct covert disinformation and deception operations, including planting false news items with disguised origins in the media abroad. When it was revealed that it was the intention to have these fabricated news reports picked up by American news media and distributed in the USA to bolster domestic support for US actions overseas, OSI was shut down but its operations were transferred to another unit, the Information Operations Task Force (IOTF) (Bamford 2005a). In October 2003, the Department issued the Information Operations Roadmap, which called for the formation of a strategic psychological operations unit and increased budgetary support for these activities. This was supported by the National Defense Strategy of March 2005, which included within the US military's dossier the intention to help 'change Muslim misperceptions of the United States and the West' and to project the message that the war on terror 'is not a war against Islam' (National Defense Strategy 2005). Alongside these in-house operations have been a plethora of contracts for private sector groups, the most notorious being the public relations firm the Rendon Group. The Group effectively ran an Information War Room in the Pentagon's IOTF; its principal target was the Qatar-based satellite channel Al-Jazeera, which the Pentagon considered its chief adversary in the War on Terror's information campaign (Bamford 2005b).

In November 2007 Robert Gates, the successor to Donald Rumsfeld as Secretary of Defense, spoke of the need 'to make the case for strengthening our capacity to use "soft" power and for better integrating it with "hard" power'. Declaring that the civilian tools of government must be upgraded, Gates continued, 'Public relations was invented in the United States, yet we are miserable at communicating to the rest of the world what we are about as a society and a culture, about freedom and democracy, about our policies and out goals.'[5] Yet, despite Gates' concerns, the Pentagon's public diplomacy role has been further extended. In late 2004 the Defense Science Board Task Force on Strategic Communication stated that 'public diplomacy, public affairs, psychological operations (PSYOP) and open military information operations must be coordinated and energized', and it recommended a more streamlined infrastructure linking the White House, the National Security Council and the Defense and State Departments.[6] The document emphasized strategic communication, which required

> a sophisticated method that maps perceptions and influence networks, identifies policy priorities, formulates objectives, focuses on 'doable tasks,' develops themes and messages, employs relevant channels, leverages new strategic and tactical dynamics, and monitors success. This approach will build on in-depth knowledge of other cultures and factors that motivate human behavior. It will adapt techniques of skillful political campaigning, even as it avoids slogans, quick fixes, and mind sets of winners and losers. It will search out credible messengers and create message authority. It will seek to persuade within news cycles, weeks, and months. It will engage in a respectful dialogue of ideas that begins with listening and assumes decades of sustained effort.[7]

The reference to 'a respectful dialogue of ideas' may be well-meant, but it remains an anomaly. The driving force behind the report's recommendations is control of the infosphere in support of realpolitik.

With the 'militarization' of US public diplomacy and the continuing 'spill-over' of Pentagon programmes into State Department territory, the question is how 'limited firewalls' can contribute to rebuilding credibility (Gregory 2005).[8] In December 2006, Gates created a new position, the Deputy Assistant Secretary of Defense for Support to Public Diplomacy. The first occupant of the post, Michael Doran, spoke in late 2007 of acting as 'a transmission belt between the Department of State and Defense'. Crucially, he noted the 'current governmental structure [that] was not meant to resolve the problems of the global Information Age – the mismatch between authorities for public diplomacy in State and the resources in DOD – being one obvious proof of this'.[9] To rectify this mismatch in authority and resources, proposals were launched for the revision of the Information and Educational Exchange Act of 1948 (the Smith-Mundt Act), the original legislation authorising the State Department to conduct information and cultural activities abroad. According to Pentagon officials, Smith-Mundt, which precluded the dissemination of information within the USA, was based on 'an outdated model of global communication'.[10] Significantly, in September 2008 the White House nominated Doran for the position of Assistant Secretary of State for International Information Programs in the State Department. As an independent report stated in October 2008:

> The 'militarization of diplomacy' is noticeably expanding as DOD personnel assume public diplomacy and assistance responsibilities that the civilian agencies do not have the trained staff to fill. In the area of security assistance ... a number of new DOD authorities have been created, reducing the role of the Secretary of State even more in this vital area of US foreign policy.
>
> (American Academy 2008: 6)

How the credit crisis will impact on the gigantic military budget remains to be seen, and current opinion remains divided on this point (Yglesias 2008; Youssef 2008). But a necessary cut-back in the military budget, accompanied by a regeneration of the State Department and a large-scale improvement in diplomatic resources, could be the best possible outcome from this year's financial turmoil.[11]

Building a new consensus?

At present, the public diplomacy outlook of the USA is marked by a recognition of the changing global environment but a desire to do nothing but control it. The challenge for the coming decade is to accommodate the rising powers of the twenty-first century within a credible institutional framework of rules and norms before the existing post-World War II structures are undermined further, for example through 'axis of oil' alternatives creating a 'world without the West' (Weber 2007). There are precedents, such as the gradual incorporation of Japan into the structures of global governance via the OECD, the Trilateral Commission and the original G6, and analysts such as John Ikenberry (2008) have argued that 'Chinese economic interests are quite congruent with the current global economic system – a system that is open and loosely institutionalized and that China has enthusiastically embraced and thrived in'. The appointment of Justin Lin Yifu as the World Bank's chief economist was a clear step in this direction, and large-scale Chinese investments to shore up Citibank, Morgan Stanley and Merrill Lynch in 2007 and 2008 demonstrated the interest of Beijing in maintaining a stable financial environment.[12] By the end of January 2008 there were at least US$60 billion of East Asian investments in American, British and Swiss banks, and this trend has continued through the year as the credit crisis battered major banks across the USA and Europe. In the energy sectors, some have floated the idea of a 'consumer cartel' of oil-using nations, led by the USA and China, to bear down on the increasing resource-led power of the axis of oil (Kurlantzick 2008).

The conditions do exist for the building of transnational networks to manage an international system based on multipolarity and power-sharing, not on implicit or explicit US hegemony. Indeed, the situation can be compared to that of the early 1970s, when the USA faced damaged prestige, a weakening economic position and the need to engage with others to solve common problems such as environmental decline. Building a public diplomacy approach for these challenges, the State Department's Bureau of Educational and Cultural Exchange in 1973 advocated the direction of exchange programmes 'to stimulate institutional development in directions which favourably affect mutual comprehension'. The study of interdependence (Keohane and Nye 1974) led to a growing focus on 'transnational as well as transgovernmental coalition-building' and the role of knowledge-based or issue-based communities in achieving consensus and establishing norms for the management of common problems (Risse-Kappen 1995a: 30, 1995b: 38).

The implications of this period for the conception of the national interest and a resulting multilateral public diplomacy still need to be fully taken into account. Recently Anne-Marie Slaughter has offered an overview of the value of transnational networks as a necessary extension of the function of the state. This framework of global governance, with the building of networks between government officials and non-governmental organizations (horizontal) and government officials and supranational organizations (vertical), leads to a greater level of policy convergence, regulatory reach, normative compliance, and cross-border cooperation. For Slaughter, accountability will remain in place through both the national level and 'a hypothetical global polity' (although one assumes that this polity will remain largely bound by national frames of reference) (Slaughter 2004: 29).

What is not clear in analyses such as Slaughter's, however, is how far this network-centric approach affects understandings of the national interest. For Nye (2004a: 7, 10–11), soft power offers 'the ability to manipulate the agenda of political choices in a manner that makes others fail to express some preferences because they seem to be too unrealistic. ... If a country can shape international rules that are consistent with its interests and values, its actions will more likely appear legitimate in the eyes of others.' The assumption remains in the scenario sketched by Slaughter that the USA, because of its unparalleled governmental and non-governmental outreach, will still be in the driving seat when it comes to asserting the rules of relationships. The state may be in a transition phase from 'unitary' to 'disaggregated', but there appears to be little recognition of how this will affect the state's understanding of its interests, role and main constituencies. Risse-Kappen has rightly referred to 'transgovernmental coalitions' and 'informal networks of officials' that 'involve behaviour of bureaucratic actors which could be regarded as *disloyal* by their home governments'. The establishment of shared norms and values across state boundaries must lead to a *reconfiguration* of national interest within a broader context (Risse-Kappen 1995b: 34). This will have to be constantly renegotiated as the boundaries to sovereignty and autonomy are assessed and altered with every case.

However, Slaughter has contributed to other important studies on the future of US foreign relations which indicate that these demands could become accepted and tolerated within the higher reaches of the policy-advice establishment. The final report of the Princeton Project on National Security, of which Slaughter was co-director (alongside Ikenberry), did point towards a reconfiguring of US power in a changing world. Recognizing that 'America can no longer rely on the legacy institutions of the Cold War', the report admitted that managing the global economy 'will become increasingly difficult' in an era when the multipolar world is no longer made up predominantly of 'close allies of the United States' (Princeton 2006: 7, 15). The clues to where the report seeks solace in this environment are soon made clear:

> [T]he objective of creating and maintaining a benign international environment remains crucial to our long-term security, today more than ever due to increasing global interdependence. In practice, it means safeguarding our alliances and promoting security cooperation among liberal democracies … avoiding the emergence of hostile great powers or balancing coalitions against the United States, and encouraging liberal democracy and responsible government worldwide.
>
> (Princeton 2006: 16)

This statement is followed by a clear realization that a reiteration of national security as purely national is not going to work.

> A successful strategy must begin by identifying and pursuing common interests with other states rather than insisting that they accept our prioritization of common threats. … The most enduring source of American national security is to do everything possible to ensure that citizens of other countries see US power the same way … so that they are willing to join their power with ours in the service of larger common goals.
>
> (Princeton 2006: 17–18)

The US can still take the lead by promoting governments worldwide that are popular, accountable and rights-regarding (PAR), utilizing global networks to open up and interlink societies through an array of 'formal and informal multilateral tools'(much as Slaughter described in *A New World Order*). To solidify this democratic community, the reform of existing institutions is important but not enough. For a strong enough liberal order to be maintained, a 'concert of democracies' is required that could effectively operate as a 'security community' and 'a framework in which [liberal democracies] can work together to effectively tackle common challenges'. Should existing institutions fail – presumably through the ill-advised or malign behaviour of non-democracies – then the concert will be available as an alternative forum for action.

The moral logic of this position is powerful, but its relation with the changing realities of global power are worrying. The motive is not just to create a more effective world order, but to reshuffle existing institutions and create new ones in order to sustain US global leadership into the twenty-first century. Recognition of the challenges to come concerning the rise of other powers is short-circuited by a desire to maintain the hegemonic position of the USA as the prime 'global public goods provider'. By establishing the concert of democracies at the centre of a revamped US-led order, the legitimate use of US military power can be reorientated around a repositioning of international law away from existing bodies such as the UN. But the geo-economic and geo-political shifts that have occurred since the report was completed in 2006 put all of this in a very different light. While the financial world of the 1990s was dominated by footloose hedge funds, the rise of huge sovereign wealth funds (total wealth estimated at US$3300 billion by the end of 2007)[13] under the control of OPEC and Far Eastern governments may well have an impact on the future room for manoeuvre of the world's largest debtor nation, the USA.

The test case? Iran

Since 2005 there have been moves by the US to formulate a strategy towards Tehran, but the bottom line has always been the de facto refusal to grant the Islamic regime legitimacy and reinstate full diplomatic relations. As a result, instead of being used to normalize relations, all contacts have been used, either overtly or covertly, to promote regime change. The first fruits of this approach in relation to Iran came to light in March 2006, with an unclassified State Department cable entitled 'Recruiting the Next Generation of Iran Experts: New Opportunities in Washington, Dubai and Europe'.[14] This was part of Secretary of State Condoleeza Rice's (2006) new strategy, transformational diplomacy, the stated aim of which was 'to build and sustain democratic, well-governed states that will respond to the needs of their people and conduct themselves responsibly in the international system'. The cable announced the formation of an Office of Iranian Affairs to coordinate a network of 'outreach posts' for political/economic reporting, the most significant being the Regional Presence Office in Dubai, UAE, designed to connect with the Iranian people and 'promote freedom and democracy in Iran'. Around the same time, US$85 million in emergency funding was earmarked for the promotion of democracy in Iran, including support for dissidents and exiles groups,

24-hour radio and television broadcasting, increasing internet gateways and study opportunities for Iranians to go to the USA. There are plenty of pro-democracy, anti-Islamic fundamentalist groups inside Iran, and the political situation there is unstable enough for there still to be some hope that they can shift the political pendulum in a more Western-orientated direction. However, telegraphing the fact that they are tools in a policy aimed at regime change placed potential allies of the USA in an impossible situation. It turned those demanding human rights and free speech into no more than acolytes and agents of the enemy power. In the words of the Iranian Nobel Peace Prize-winner and human rights activist Shirin Ebadi, 'whoever speaks about democracy in Iran will be accused of having been paid by the United States' (Fisher 2006). As with Iraq, the influence of hard-line exile groups was affecting Washington's thinking, to the detriment of their countrymen still inside Iran. What is more, the efforts to engage with Iranians and bring them to the USA via cultural diplomacy initiatives and exchange programmes have stumbled up against the US security state. Visa requirements and the implicit branding of all Iranians as suspects by the Department of Homeland Security's staff has led to delays, humiliations, frustrations, and above all a disastrous negative image of the USA. 'It is fair to say', writes a recent commentator, 'that security procedures make it much more difficult and expensive for sponsored exchange programs to keep up with the demands made on them to promote better connections and understanding with the Islamic world' (Ballow 2004: 120). These kinds of programmes only work successfully if they are run according to a sense of openness, not paranoia. But the general policy environment has to allow this.

Successful diplomacy relies on mutual recognition of the status of all parties involved, a recognition tinged with respect for the others' interests and capabilities. As Ivo Daalder stated soon after the announcement that negotiations on Iran's nuclear programme would begin, 'we must be clear that we are willing to settle all our differences through negotiations – including, ultimately, re-establishing economic and diplomatic relations and providing security guarantees as part of a regional framework'.[15] Such an approach has never materialized because it has never been the intention.[16] Rice's transformational diplomacy was, in the case of Iran, little more than the strategy of pre-emption applied to the field of diplomacy and public diplomacy. Accepting the efforts of the EU-3 to broker a deal, there has been little sign that a US-led 'concert of democracy' could either enforce its will on Iran or garner enough legitimacy to act with force. Neither is there any reason to assume that this will change. Meanwhile, instead of direct diplomatic engagement, rumours of pre-emptive military action persisted (Hersh 2008; Owen 2008).

Leading a global community of fate?

The Princeton report (2006: 28) made clear that 'when the rest of the world develops confidence that the United States is genuinely seeking an economic system that responds to the needs of, and promises benefits for, all countries, U.S. credibility and goodwill are likely to be enhanced'. In relation to the importance of this statement for the public diplomacy strategy of the Obama administration, it is worth contrasting it here with the work of Ulrich Beck, the developer of the 'risk society' thesis (Beck 1992). In *Power in the Global Age* Beck talks of the need to forge a transnational cooperative public sphere that coordinates itself with the realities of globalization. The resultant 'strategic power' stems not from its cover for the extension of national power and the right of imperial-style intervention (the national writ universal, as appears to be the case in Nye and Slaughter) but from its creation of new forms of governance that transform the defensive hierarchical nation-state into the progressive 'network state' (Beck 2005: 18, 219, 231). Beck's call for a reconfiguration of global politics may conveniently bypass the realities of the shifting distribution of global power, but it is still necessary.

The assumption of Nye, Arquilla and Ronfeldt, and others is that the Soft Powers of the twenty-first century will be those who abide by a normative set of ideas that are close to prevailing global norms such as liberalism, pluralism and autonomy and that have access to multiple channels of communication, enabling a greater influence over how issues are framed (Nye 2002; Ronfeldt and Arquilla 2007). However, the critical factor enabling a state to take on a leading role that others will follow – the factor of credibility – is at present a limitation. As Habermas appositely puts it, 'the normative authority of the United States was completely undermined during the Bush years' (see Habermas 2006).

Nevertheless, there are possibilities. American ideals continue to resonate around the globe, and no other system offers such powerful symbols and motivating narratives. In the Middle East, for instance, many still hope to 'replace the Arab nightmare with the American dream'.[17] However, the USA needs to increasingly become one nation among many, recognizing its ideals appeal widely but equally accepting that their appropriateness for universal application is not taken for granted.[18] The issue is towards which goals these ideals should be directed. Beck argues for a necessary shift away from realpolitik and mercantilist national interest towards an appreciation of the 'global community of fate' in the context of global risk, which currently presents itself in the dimensions of environmental decline, financial instability and terrorism. During the Bush years only the cause of anti-terrorism led to an American demand for increased transnational cooperation, and even then this was in the context of constructing a US-centred global 'surveillance state' that transverses – both openly and surreptitiously – all other jurisdictions (Beck 2002, 2005: 12). The result was a 'false cosmopolitanism' that continues to pursue the confluence of American (national) and global (universal) interests. The insistence on maintaining sovereignty and autonomy in an era of increasingly fluid boundaries can only lead to a downward spiral of negative regulation.

There is a desperate need, above all, to move away from an insistence on developing strategic communication in support of a narrowly defined national interest. The emphasis on managing the news cycle, the central drive in US public diplomacy in recent years, can be dated back to the Clinton administration and the inability to explain the US position or deal with misinformation during the Kosovo and Haiti crises.[19] Under George W. Bush this emphasis has only escalated across the whole spectrum of government, from the Pentagon to the White House (Office of Global Communications 2002–5) and the State Department (Under-Secretary of State for Public Diplomacy and Public Affairs). Secretary of State Condoleeza Rice's implementation of transformational diplomacy did not veer from this trend. Democracy promotion is all very well, but the provision of basic needs should come first. Funding for the US Agency for International Development was cut, while at the same time the White House-run Millennium Account, operating outside of established government channels, was created and extended (Scott-Smith and Mos 2009).

The American approach can be contrasted with the so-called new public diplomacy, an outlook that recognizes the need for governments, in an era of increasing information awareness, to connect with their publics to carry out foreign policy. The merits of this are twofold. First, it will foster and maintain a greater democratic legitimacy for policies. Second, it will open up opportunities to make use of the extra reach, both in terms of issues and access, of private citizens, businesses and non-governmental organizations (NGOs) abroad (Melissen 2005).

This is a fundamental shift away from much of the debate surrounding US public diplomacy, which tends to focus on the 'narrow, mechanistic terms of delivery rather than content' and the assessment of information as no more than 'an area of increasing strategic competition'.[20] The issue of global warming could be one important catalyst that both causes a gradual shift in perception on national interest and lays the basis for a new public diplomacy strategy. In the face of resistance to climate change legislation by the federal government, by June 2006 nine US states had passed greenhouse gas emission reduction targets, and more than half of all states now use public funds for energy efficiency and renewable energy programmes (Selin and VanDeever 2007). This widespread constituency could be tapped in combination with a reconfiguration of US national interest and an increasing interaction with other nation-state, business and NGO partners.

However, these transitions are going to be difficult to negotiate, particularly in a world where competition and resource nationalism are becoming ever more pronounced. Writing in the midst of a financial crisis on a scale beyond that of 1929, it is worth reflecting on how the American twentieth century was closely associated with a grand narrative of abundance. If the twenty-first century is going to have a grand narrative of anything, it is going to be based on dealing with scarcity. The shifts in interest-recognition and self-perception that will be required to deal with this are way beyond anything that has so far emerged from the petty debates over the US image and how to repair it.

Notes

1 Between September 2001 and September 2004, for instance, at least 17 reports were issued on the need to reform US public diplomacy efforts in a rapidly changing global environment. See the list at http://pdi.gwu.edu/merlin-cgi/p/downloadFile/d/8758/n/off/other/1/name/PDBooks,Articles,Websites (accessed 24 October 2008).

2 Nye himself refers to his own source as Peter Bachrach and Morton Baratz, 'Decisions and Non-Decisions: An Analytical Framework,' *American Political Science Review*, 57 (1963), pp. 632–42.

3 'Russian proposal for European security would sideline NATO', *International Herald Tribune*, 27 July 2008. Online. Available at: http://www.iht.com/articles/2008/07/27/europe/nato.php (accessed 17 September 2008). 'Russia's security proposal doesn't threaten NATO, official said', *International Herald Tribune*, 28 July 2008. Online. Available at: http://www.iht.com/articles/2008/07/28/europe/nato.php (accessed 17 September 2008).

4 On the World Bank see the unprecedented criticism by its former chief economist Joseph Stiglitz in *Globalization and its Discontents* (Penguin: Harmondsworth, 2003).

5 Speech online. Available at http://www.defenselink.mil/speeches/speech.aspx?speechid+1199 (accessed 2 June 2008).

6 Report is available online at http://www.publicdiplomacy.org/37.htm (accessed 18 September 2008).

7 Ibid.

8 Gregory was a member of the Defense Science Board Task Force.

9 Dr Michael Doran, Statement to the House Armed Services Committee, 15 November 2007. Available at: armedservices.house.gov/pdfs/TUTC111507/Doran_Testimony111507.pdf (accessed 18 September 2008).

10 'Bill would amend Smith-Mundt Act', *Inside the Pentagon*, 17 July 2008.

11 See Kristin Lord, 'The State Department, not the Pentagon, should lead America's public diplomacy efforts', *Christian Science Monitor*, 29 October 2008. Lord makes the pertinent point that Gates' call for an increased use of US soft power to further US national interest is exactly not what should be happening. 'In most circumstances, the Department of Defense should not serve as the most visible face of the United States overseas.' Neither should soft power be seen in military-like terms as a strategic asset to be deployed at will by the Secretary of Defence (never mind the military itself).

12 'The citadels of the global economy are yielding to China's battering ram', *Guardian*, 23 April 2008; 'Foreign investments in US banks draw attention', *npr*, 6 February 2008. Available at: http://www.npr.org/templates/story/story.php?storyId= 18754222 (accessed 18 September 2008)

13 'Sovereign wealth funds grow to $3,300bn', *Financial Times*, 30 March 2008.

14 Cable available at: http://thinkprogress.org/2006/03/01/iran-doc/ (accessed 30 October 2008).

15 'The Iran Talks,' 31 May 2006, America Abroad Weblog, Brookings Institution. Available at: http://www.brookings.edu/opinions/2006/0531iran_daalder.aspx?p=1 (accessed 30 October 2008).

16 In late 2008, the Bush administration announced its aim to open an 'interests section' diplomatic post in Tehran (should the Iranians agree). This was not to be an official embassy-type outlet but another effort 'to reach out to the Iranian people' by facilitating cultural exchanges, visa applications and public diplomacy activities. Bilateral government-to-government diplomacy continues to remain taboo.

17 A comment of an Al Jazeera television producer in the documentary *Control Room* (Jehaine Noujaim 2004).

18 See Anne-Marie Slaughter, 'Reviving American Ideals', *International Herald Tribune*, 18 May 2007, and the subsequent response from those who objected to its continuing unipolarity and one-sidedness, such as David Rieff: 'Slaughter's entire argument, for all its talk of the need for humility, is a reiteration of this 'exceptionalist'

conception'. Available at: http://www.iht.com/articles/2007/05/23/opinion/edlet.php (accessed 24 September 2008).

19 See the information on the FAS website concerning 'International Public Information', Presidential Decision Directive (PDD) 68, 30 April 1999. Available at: http://www.fas. org/irp/offdocs/pdd/pdd-68.htm (accessed 24 September 2008).

20 See Scott Lucas, 'The Past, Present, and Futures of Public Diplomacy and Political Warfare', *Libertas*. Available at: http://www.libertas.bham.ac.uk/publications/articles/ index.htm (accessed 24 September 2008); Rhiannon Vickers, 'A New Public Diplomacy for the Information Age', Paper presented at the International Studies Association annual conference, New Orleans, March 2002.

Bibliography

Advisory Group on Public Diplomacy for the Arab and Muslim World (2003) 'Changing Minds, Winning Peace', Washington, DC. Available at: www.state.gov/documents/ organization/24882.pdf (accessed 5 January 2010).

American Academy of Diplomacy (2008) 'A Foreign Affairs Budget for the Future'. Available at: www.academyofdiplomacy.org/publications/FAB_report_2008.pdf (accessed 5 January 2010).

Ballow, B. (2004) 'Academic and Professional Exchanges with the Islamic World: An Undervalued Tool', in W. Rugh (ed.) *Engaging the Arab and Muslim Worlds through Public Diplomacy,* Washington, DC: Public Diplomacy Council.

Bamford, J. (2005a) *A Pretext for War: 9/11, Iraq, and the Abuse of America's Intelligence Agencies,* New York: Doubleday.

—— (2005b) 'The Rendon Group', *Rolling Stone*, 988. Available at: http:// www.rollingstone.com/politics/story/8798997/the_man_who_sold_the_war (accessed 5 January 2010).

BBC (2008) 'Brown Urges New US-Europe Links', *BBC News*, 18 April 2008. Available at: http://news.bbc.co.uk/1/hi/uk_politics/7353824.stm. (accessed 5 January 2010).

Beck, U. (1992) *Risk Society: Towards a New Modernity*, London: SAGE Publications.

—— (2002) 'The Terrorist Threat: World Risk Society Revisited', *Theory Culture and Society*, 19: 39–55.

—— (2005) *Power in the Global Age: A New Global Political Economy,* Cambridge: Polity.

Center for Strategic International Studies (CSIS) (2007) 'A Smarter, More Secure America', Commission on Smart Power. Available at: http://www.csis.org/component/ option,com_csis_pubs/task,view/id,4156/type,1/ (accessed 5 January 2010).

De Haas, M. and van der Putten, F.-P. (2007) *The Shanghai Cooperation Organisation: Towards a Full-Grown Security Alliance?*, Amsterdam: Netherlands Institute of International Relations.

Fisher, W. (2006) 'Buying Democracy in Iran', 16 June. Available at: http://www.tompaine. com/buying_democracy_in_iran.php (accessed 30 October 2008).

Gough, S (2003) 'The Evolution of Strategic Influence', USAWC Strategy Research Project. Available at: http:www.fas.org/irp/eprint/gough.pdf (accessed 5 January 2010).

Gregory, B. (2005) 'Public Diplomacy and Strategic Communication: Cultures, Firewalls, and Imported Norms', APSA conference on International Communication and Conflict, George Washington University, Washington, DC, August.. Available at: www8. georgetown.edu/cct/apsa/papers/gregory.pdf (accessed 5 January 2010).

Habermas, J. (2006) *The Divided West,* Cambridge: Polity.

Hersh, S. (2008) 'Preparing the Battlefield', *New Yorker.* Available at http://www. newyorker.com/reporting/2008/07/07/080707fa_fact_hersh (accessed 5 January 2010).

Huq, A. (2008) 'How to Manage Imperial Decline', *Asia Times,* 18 October. Available at: http://www.atimes.com/atimes/Middle_East/JJ18Ak03.html (accessed 30 October 2008).

Ikenberry, G.J. (2008) 'The Rise of China and the Future of the West', *Foreign Affairs,* January–February. Available at: http://www.ituassu.com.br/china_ikenberry_fa.pdf (accessed 30 October 2008).

Jacques, M. (2006) 'America Faces a Future of Managing Imperial Decline', *Guardian,* 16 November. Available at: http://www.guardian.co.uk/commentisfree/2006/nov/16/comment.usa (accessed 30 October 2008).

Keohane, R. and Nye, J., Jr (1974) 'Transgovernmental Relations and International Organizations', *World Politics* 27: 39–62.

Khalaf, R. (2008) 'With Friends Like These, Who Needs Enemies', *Financial Times,* 15 September. Available at: http://www.ft.com/cms/s/0/9bfea064–833a-11dd-907e-000077b07658.html?nclick_check=1 (accessed 30 October 2008).

Kurlantzick, J. (2008) 'Can Public Diplomacy counter Resource Nationalism', USC Public Diplomacy Blog. Available at: http://uscpublicdiplomacy.com/index. php/newsroom/pdblog_detail/060928_can_public_diplomacy_counter_resource_nationalism/ (accessed 30 October 2008).

Leverett, F. (2008) 'Black Is the New Green', *The National Interest,* January–February.

Mahbubani, K. (2008) *The New Asian Hemisphere: The Irresistible Shift of Global Power to the East,* New York: PublicAffairs.

Melissen, J. (2005) 'The New Public Diplomacy: Between Theory and Practice', in J. Melissen (ed.) *The New Public Diplomacy: Soft Power in International Relations,* London: Macmillan.

National Defense Strategy of the United States (2005) Available at: http:// www.globalsecurity.org/military/library/policy/dod/nds-usa_mar2005.htm (accessed 5 January 2010).

Nye, J.S., Jr (2002) 'The Information Revolution and American Soft Power', *Asia-Pacific Review,* 9: 60–76.

—— (2004a) *Soft Power,* New York: PublicAffairs.

—— (2004b) 'The Decline of America's Soft Power', *Foreign Affairs,* May–June: 83. Available at: http://ics.leeds.ac.uk/papers/vp01.cfm?outfit=pmt&folder=7&paper=1944 (accessed 5 January 2010).

—— (2008a) *The Powers to Lead,* New York: Oxford University Press.

—— (2008b) 'Public Diplomacy and Soft Power', *Annals of the American Academy of Political and Social Science,* 616.

—— (2008c) 'Recovering American Leadership', *Survival,* 50.

Owen, D. (2008) 'Warning Signs of an Israeli Attack on Iran', *Times Online.* Available at: http://www.timesonline.co.uk/tol/comment/columnists/guest_contributors/article 4926251.ece (accessed 30 October 2008).

Princeton Project on National Security (2006) 'Forging a World of Liberty under Law: US National Security in the 21st Century', September. Available at: http://www.princeton. edu/~ppns/report/FinalReport.pdf (accessed 5 January 2010).

Rice, C. (2006) 'Transformational Diplomacy'. Available at: http://www.state.gov/ secretary/rm/2006/59306.htm (accessed 30 October 2008).

Risse-Kappen, T. (1995a) *Bringing Transnational Relations Back In,* Cambridge: Cambridge University Press.

—— (1995b) *Cooperation Among Democracies: The European Influence on US Foreign Policy,* Princeton NJ: Princeton University Press.

Ronfeldt, D. and Arquilla, J. (2007) 'The Promise of Noöpolitik', *First Monday.* Available at: http://firstmonday.org/htbin/cgiwrap/bin/ojs/index.php/fm/article/view/1971/1846 (accessed 5 January, 2010).

Scott-Smith, G. and Mos, M. (2009) 'Democracy Promotion and the New Public Diplomacy', in I. Parmar, L. Miller and M. Ledwidge (eds), *New Directions in U.S. Foreign Policy,* London: Routledge.

Selin, H. and VanDeever, S. (2007) 'Political Science and Prediction: What's Next for US Climate Change Policy?', *Review of Policy Research*, 24: 1–27.

Slaughter, A.-M, (2004) *A New World Order,* Princeton, NJ: Princeton University Press.

Weber, S. (2007) 'A World without the West', *The National Interest,* January.

Yglesias, M. (2008) 'The Coming Military Spending Surge', *American Prospect*, 16 October. Available at: http://www.prospect.org/cs/articles?article=the_coming_military_spending_surge (accessed 30 October 2008).

Youssef, N. (2008) 'Both McCain and McCain would Rebuild US Forces', *McClatchy Newspapers*, 22 October. Available at: http://news.yahoo.com/s/mcclatchy/20081022/pl_mcclatchy/3079604 (accessed 30 October 2008).

11 Cheques and balances

The European Union's soft power strategy

Christopher Hill

Introduction

Soft power is associated more with the European Union (EU) than with any other actor, as the EU has a track record of using the relevant instruments and an ideology that celebrates the values inherent in the concept. This chapter examines the EU's record, first in terms of the historical context, and then in terms of the dilemmas that have occurred over the last decade as the EU has finally entered the realm of military collaboration. In that respect it focuses particularly on the dimensions of transatlantic relations, and of the institutional ramifications. The chapter concludes by examining the role of soft power in relation to some of the main foreign policy issues confronting the EU, and its implications for its longer-term role in the world, particularly in the context of the European Security Strategy (ESS).

The EU was associated with soft power long before its recent arrival in popular parlance. The European Economic Community (EEC) had its origins in the problem of war and peace but had no collective political capacity in world affairs built in to its founding treaties. Its external relations revolved around first commercial diplomacy and second the dilemma of how to manage the rapidly expanding number of ex-colonies associated with member states. These activities were inherently political but the power at stake was barely fungible. As a result the European Community (EC), as it gradually and revealingly became known, began to suffer from an influence deficit. It was frustrating, especially for French politicians wanting to see Europe develop as a 'third force' in international relations, not to be able to mobilize collective action during crises such as the 1967 Middle East war and the deepening conflict in south east Asia. Conversely, only the smaller member states could have envisaged up giving up sovereignty in foreign policy in the way that had been done for trade policy. Indeed, one of the inhibitions to developing a political dimension to EC external relations was Paris's insistence on keeping it intergovernmental, and effectively subject to French leadership. Thus when an embryo European foreign policy finally emerged in 1970, it was limited to pure diplomacy, and a cautious and intermittent version at that.

The attempts at foreign policy coordination that developed during the 1970s soon began to be understood as both unique and limited, by comparison to the foreign policies of states. François Duchêne's label of 'civilian power' caught on (Duchêne 1972), not least because it had the quality of making a virtue out of the necessity of avoiding any talk of defence policy, which would have upset NATO, on the one hand, and Italo-German pacifism, on the other. It also caught the spirit of the times, which were those of détente in Europe, and a strong reaction against the bloody denouement of the Vietnam war. For enthusiasts for the European project it also led to the conclusion that foreign policy might, after all, turn out to be a motor force for integration, rather than having to wait for the prior completion of a federal structure. A civilian power might be able to promote harmony in international politics at the same time as appearing a progressive project within the Community, in so doing attracting popular support.

This hope ran almost immediately into the obstruction represented by British, Danish and Irish accession in 1973. The Danes and the British were ultra-protective of their national freedom of manoeuvre, while the Irish were nervous of any kind of alliance, even a non-military one, which might call their neutrality into question. All three, however, gradually came to see that foreign policy cooperation had the potential to enhance national interests more than subvert them, and thus cautiously to support the process known as European Political Cooperation (EPC). In the case of the UK, which as a large state and permanent member of the UN Security Council had the potential to make or break EPC, the realization dawned, as it had in France beforehand, that it could shape the direction of the emerging European foreign policy, and use it as a multiplier of British national influence. This was particularly evident given that the UK was effectively 'present at the creation' of EPC, having being allowed to participate as a pre-accession state since 1971 – in sharp contrast to its position with respect to the Common Agricultural Policy (CAP) and other policies deriving from the Rome Treaties.

What is more, the UK, rather more than France, was content to have European foreign policy coordination restricted to pure diplomacy, so that the defence aspects could lie undisturbed in NATO. Indeed, British membership acted as a guarantee of the status quo in this respect, since London always vetoed any French attempts to augment the EC's capabilities. Thus a working distinction grew up between 'defence', which the EC did not do, and 'security', which it increasingly did, but via 'civilian' means, such as promoting the Conference on Security and Cooperation in Europe (CSCE). This distinction eventually encouraged the much wider interpretation of 'security' which has become the orthodoxy in both academic and policy circles over the last 20 years (Buzan 1989, 1991).

Part of the civilian power approach was the hope that European influence might be felt in the world through a process of emulation, whereby other groupings of states would also pursue the goals of integration and a zone of peace. Even if that were not to prove possible, there was still the possibility that individual states would be influenced. Subsequently the argument was extended through the notion of 'normative power', in other words the EU's capacity to shape the norms of international politics through the impact of its example on other actors (Manners 2002). 'Civilian power' was self-explanatory in that it made a virtue of the EC's lack of a military dimension; 'normative power' has not been so directly part of practitioners' discourse, but it has pointed up the influence of the EU at the level of values, in part through what it is rather than what it does. The two taken together come close to Nye's conception of soft power as the ability to get others to want what you want, although the issues of agency and intentionality remain open for interpretation.

The above picture disguised the fact that the EC/EU did in fact have some hard power capacity right from the beginning, if hard power using means to pressure others into doing what they do not (necessarily) want to do. Coercion – sticks rather than carrots – was present in the use of economic sanctions of various kinds, and even the denial or delaying of a potential accession to the Community. Thus arguably General de Gaulle used hard power when twice denying Britain's requests to enter the EEC. So far as foreign policy was concerned the explicit use of economic weapons for political ends – as opposed to pressures within the parameters of the Lomé system for development policy, or of the General Agreement on Trade and Tariffs (GATT) rounds of trade negotiations – began only in the early 1980s, with protests against the Iranian seizure of US hostages and the imposition of martial law in Poland (Nuttall 1992). The EC's reputation for economic power grew steadily through its leverage over impoverished ex-colonies, and in particular through its ability to engage the USA in trade 'wars', such as that over poultry in the early 1960s. But its wider foreign policy was bound to be hamstrung unless it could deploy these same economic weapons for other unrelated purposes, through what Henry Kissinger had called 'linkage' policies, which the Europeans at this time were far too cautious to claim for themselves.

Sanctions became an increasingly common instrument during the 1980s, for the EC and other players, as a substitute for the dangerous use (or threat) of military force. However, there were limits to the extent to which the European could resort to them without calling into question their own good faith over adherence to existing agreements and to international law. They also had solid interests in not disturbing profitable economic relationships (as when refusing to back-date sanctions against Iran over the hostage crisis) or calling into question a general preference for constructive engagement – even with Apartheid South Africa, against which serious sanctions were never imposed (Treverton 1988: 12; Hill and Smith 2000: 400–1). This ambivalence about coercive strategies meant that such hard power as the EC wielded during the Cold War amounted to little more than a rubber fist inside a velvet glove. The concealment, both of what was done and what might be done, was aided by the prominence of positive sanctions, or inducements, in external relations. Although conditionality was as yet beyond the horizon, the accession of Greece, Spain and Portugal in the 1980s was pushed through because of the perceived need to stabilize countries just emerged from dictatorship, while the agreements of various kinds signed with Turkey – and eventually most other Mediterranean countries – were designed as much to achieve a zone of regional civility as to hustle market opportunities. The Euro-Arab Dialogue begun in 1974 was transparently a way to catch Arab oil-exporters in a web of cooperation and mutual understanding, with the distant carrot left dangling of possible support for the Palestinians. A whole raft of political dialogues seemed to promise most regions in the world the possibility of privileged relations with the rich and evolving project of European integration.

This use of inducements, and in particular what was to be termed by Gabriel Munuera 'the power of attraction', meant that the EC was speaking the language of soft power, rather like Molière's '*bourgeois gentilhomme*', all unawares (Munuera 1994: 52–3). But the lack of the soft/hard distinction at the time, and the apparent remoteness of access to the military instrument, meant at least that there was no theological dispute over the appropriate means of foreign policy. The USA, coming off the painful experience of failed force in Vietnam, had to think about how a superpower could make plausible threats without always having to implement them, and thus was preoccupied with 'coercive diplomacy' (George *et al.* 1971). The EC, at best, had the option of diplomatic coercion, assuming this notion went beyond an oxymoron. Since this sat well with Europeans' self-image, or what would now be called their collective identity, that is, of a peaceful group of states in retreat from colonialism, there appeared to be few major choices confronting them. Even the foreign policy principals, such as the UK and France, took a defensive view of world affairs in the 1970s and 1980s, being short of resources and themselves scarred by such memories as Dien Bien Phu, Suez and Cyprus.

It was this mentality that led to the cautious approach in the early years of the Yugoslav crisis after 1991, when the Europeans clung to the idea that the status quo might be restored and were deeply reluctant to risk becoming embroiled in the conflicts breaking out all over the Balkans. For this they were sharply criticized, and eventually self-critical, as the growing concern for human rights within European civil societies led to outrage at the inactivity governments and their representatives showed in the face of atrocities such as those at Srebrenica in 1995. The mood against interventionism in Europe thus began to change, albeit too slowly for many Bosnians, as the grip of the Cold War faded and the sense of the triumph of Western values mounted. This was, within a few years, to break the taboo against giving the EU (as it had by now become) the ability to use military force. The use of hard power seemed at once more desirable and less risky. This was symbolized by the judgement of the German Constitutional Court in 1994 that the use of the armed services beyond the national frontier might in certain circumstances be once again legitimate.

Ambivalence in Washington

The USA for the most part had watched the emergence of European diplomacy with occasional irritation but a sense of security that NATO would not be endangered by a new European third force. A certain ambivalence derived from a wish to see the Europeans take a greater share of the security and defence burden within the alliance, and from an historic approval of the compliment paid to the USA by the integration project. Since the Gaullist era, and the French withdrawal from the military command structure of NATO (combined with criticisms over Vietnam), there had also been a sensitivity over any signs of France trying to turn the EC into a rival to NATO, or even a mere caucus within it. Thus in 1983, when Paris looked to revive the dormant Western European Union as a way of boosting integration and giving the Europeans extra leverage with the USA, Washington made a deliberately heavy-handed démarche to stop the process in its tracks – by playing the British card, which was not so difficult given that after 10 years of membership London was now a key factor in EPC.

Such watchfulness did not prevent a continuing scorn in Washington throughout the 1980s about European attempts to act politically in international relations. The usual refrain was 'where's the beef?', echoing Walter Mondale's famous (if notably unsuccessful) election slogan of 1984. The USA knew that in the event of diverging views their European allies were limited by their dependence on US armed strength, by their own reluctance to use force, and by the difficulties they had in reaching agreement – the Six having become Nine in 1973, Ten in 1981 and Twelve in 1986. These issues were interconnected, in that because some member states genuinely thought that NATO was the most efficient producer of security, and some were constrained by domestic pacifism, they were always unlikely to agree with those who wanted to push ahead with a European defence project, whether for integrationist or interventionist reasons. In some, like Italy, or Belgium, these conflicting feelings beat within the same breast, creating a degree of cognitive dissonance over support for the Alliance and enthusiasm for Europe's role in the world. As the external environment changed so the balance altered between the two tendencies: NATO seemed less necessary, and perhaps in decline, while the hopes for an effective common European foreign policy grew. The Treaty of Maastricht, ratified in 1993, was a high point of these hopes. Not only did it put the attempt to create a Common Foreign and Security (sic) Policy (CFSP) on a legal footing for the first time, but it said that the Policy would cover 'all questions related to the security of the Union, including the eventual framing of a common defence policy, which might in time lead to a common defence' (Treaty of European Union, Article J4.1, 1993, reproduced in Hill and Smith 2000: 155). In contrast, this wording was permissive rather than prescriptive, and few imagined that it could soon be built upon by actual institutions and capabilities.

For its part the USA was not too perturbed in principle. In practice it soon, under the incoming Clinton administration, began to feel frustrated that grandiose claims for Europe's new international role could not even be matched in its immediate neighbourhood. As Yugoslavia disintegrated and descended into savagery, the Europeans at first could not agree on a diagnosis and then refused to do more than contribute to monitors and barrier forces (in the form of British and French troops) which in practice did little more than stand on the sidelines. The USA at this point started to call urgently for military action, if not from the Europeans alone then via a consensus on lifting the arms embargo to the Bosnians and striking hard at the (Serb and Croatian) aggressors. In this the USA was to be frustrated, to the point where it ultimately resorted to the use of its own air power to bring Belgrade to the negotiating table, at Dayton in 1995 (Simms 2002).

European actions after Dayton spoke loudly of an acceptance that the critics – of incoherence, indecision and excessive rhetoric – might have a point. On the one hand, the EU as a whole accepted a responsibility for securing the peace in Bosnia through the administration of what became a virtual protectorate. On the other, the UK and France concluded that the difficulties which their troops had on the ground before 1995, in trying to make the peace without being able ever to threaten war, meant that they needed more support from their European partners, specifically in the form of a rapid reaction force which would not depend on Washington. This led to the St Malo meeting of December 1998, which in turn proved to be the genesis of the European Security and Defence Policy (ESDP) agreed a year later at the Helsinki EU Council. Thus, seven years on from Maastricht, catalysed by the tragedy in the Balkans, the Europeans had indeed 'framed' a common defence policy and brought themselves to the very edge of acquiring the instrument of military force.

Was this, then, at last the dawn of an era of hard power for the EU? Even a decade later the answer is not wholly clear. An academic dispute has arisen, for example, over whether the very existence of the ESDP nullifies the EU's status as a 'civilian power'. On one side are those such as Karen E. Smith in London, and Nicole Gnesotto in Paris (not by chance, perhaps, located in the two most 'realist' member states) who believe that the very possession of military power, whether used or not, changes the character of European foreign policy, leading it away from a reliance on dialogue, discussion and Arnold Wolfers' 'milieu goals' towards solipsism, self-interest and coercive diplomacy (Smith 2001; Gnesotto 2004). Against this view is the position argued by Stelios Stavridis and Hanns Maull (Stavridis 2001; Maull 2005) to the effect that because the EU retains a distinctive set of aims in world politics, which might be labelled 'democratic' or 'civilized', they would only be prepared to use force in defence of these ends, probably legitimized by a United Nations mandate (Stavridis 2001; Maull 2005). From this viewpoint the EU will remain a civilian power until it starts to behave like a traditional great power, regardless of the capabilities it possesses. Nor does the military dimension *necessitate* a change in attitudes or behaviour.

Regardless, however, of what label we choose to reserve for Europe as an international actor, it is evident that there is something unique about its conformation, as a congeries of relatively rich states which have agreed to forego a degree of national independence in the interest of achieving a 'politics of scale' (Ginsberg 1989). At the same time the project is a difficult and cautious one, much complicated by the regular addition to the mix of extra states with their own foreign policy traditions. Regardless, therefore, of whether the EU claims in principle to dispose of the full range of instruments and capabilities, it is still limited to what it can agree on, and sustain over a period of time. In the nature of things, with 27 democracies, this means that the use of military force, but also of the lesser forms of coercion, is always going to be difficult and the exception far more than the rule. The failure to meet the first headline goal, of a rapid reaction force of 60,000 men by 2003, and the lack of use of the 13 battlegroups that succeeded it (on paper, at least) bears out the point. The EU does not fight battles, and would still find it virtually impossible to face down the kind of challenge posed by Slobodan Milosevic or the genocidal Hutus in the first half of the 1990s.

The European security strategy of 2003: a step change?

Twenty-two ESDP missions between 2003–9 might seem to contradict this view, but none have involved imposing solutions on recalcitrant parties. They have been valuable, and often courageous in their own terms, but essentially they amount to small-scale barrier forces or policing missions, usually on the frontier of civil-military activity. In short, they still mostly represent soft power, and are likely to do so for the foreseeable future. It remains true that this burst of activity has occurred since the attack of 11 September 2001 (9/11) on the USA, which had a profound impact on European thinking about international relations in general and the EU's own role in particular. It was no longer possible to feel comfortable with the assumptions of the first post-Cold War decade, in which the EU's distinctive approach had seemed validated, with force apparently anachronistic and therefore conventional defence policy much less of a priority. The activities of al-Qaeda were not those of an aggressive nation-state engaged in border-crossing, but their power had been facilitated by the hospitality of the Taliban in Afghanistan and the availability of training camps in the Pakistani badlands. This meant that the Europeans had at the least to confront the issue of whether to support their American ally in counter-measures against 'rogue states', and at most to admit the possibility that they too might suffer attacks from terrorists receiving succour from distant regimes. Moreover these regimes were unlikely to prove susceptible to the language of 'appeasement', in the original meaning of the word, which describes well the normative direction of EU foreign policy, although avoided in European capitals for its pejorative associations.[1]

The war on terror convinced many European policymakers, however, that they had to go beyond election-monitoring and barrier forces to enter the world of preventive actions, even war-fighting. This would be necessary for substantive reasons, but also to convince the USA that it was not alone in facing the new threats – and that it might therefore be persuaded to consult more with its allies before engaging in precipitate action. Thus the member states came to the view that they needed 'to do hard power', and to make a reality of the ESDP. This led to the rash of missions described above, but more significantly also to the drafting of an 'ESS', in direct imitation of the United States' National Security Strategy, albeit in much shorter and pithier form. The ESS first appeared as a draft in the summer of 2003 when it included a willingness to envisage 'preventive defence'. This move was backed away from in the version finalized six months later, which nonetheless still referred to the possible need for 'early and robust interventions' (European Security Strategy, December 2003).

The ESS was intended as a diplomatic signal – certainly to the USA, but also to possible adversaries of the West as a whole, that the EU was not the soft underbelly of the alliance. Rather, it would be increasingly capable of responding powerfully to attacks without having to be dependent on Washington, and it could not be counted on to act merely as a persistent brake on the latter's more combative instincts. But it also represented a step-change in the Union's own thinking, whereby it acknowledged that Europe might indeed have enemies, and was not just a post-modern observer of other people's conflicts, to be prevented or resolved. From now on, at least in principle, the EU was willing to get involved in counter-terrorist operations, and perhaps also peace-*making*. This would be in contrast in the first case to the coordination over national anti-terrorist measures, which had been taking place under the auspices of the Trevi group since 1975, and in the second to peace-*keeping*, which the EU had always been keen to support, even if member states had undertaken most of the action, via the UN.

The ESS was not quite the definitive strategy document, or 'one of the best EU documents ever written', described by some (Missiroli 2008). Nor is it the 'soft power strategy' of my title. It is actually more a survey of possible threats and roles for the EU than a clear attempt to settle priorities and provide direction for tactical decisions (Hill 2008). Where it does become specific the ESS tends to become merely arbitrary, as with the recommendations for strategic partnerships to be created with Russia, Japan, China, Canada and India, in that order (but not Brazil or South Africa). This did not inspire confidence in any follow-through, and so it proved with the quiet abandonment of these priorities, and a second edition of the Strategy in December 2008 which was surprisingly low-profile and banal (European Council Conclusions, December 2008).

What the ESS does do is deliberately to interweave hard and soft power elements, in fact making an attempt to leave the very dichotomy between the two behind, since it only draws attention to the EU's international deficiencies. To the dispassionate observer it can be seen as either a fudge, or an honest attempt to move into a half-way house, accepting that significant joint military strength will take many years, but opening up for the first time the possibility of real combat operations, anathema for so long to many member states, including the crucial player of Germany.

The ESS employs a reasonable tone, but in the context of the EU's diplomatic tradition it represents talking tough. The reference to the importance of 'effective (sic) multilateralism' was a clear concession to the US view that burdens had to be genuinely shared if there were to be two pillars in NATO. Moreover, the ESS explicitly provided a framework for thinking coherently about the many diverse dimensions of EU external relations, thus leaving behind the historical obsession with mere 'consistency', while implying the redundancy of the Pillars system. It also moved beyond regional concerns to assert Europe's global responsibilities. It saw security, especially in relation to Weapons of Mass Destruction (WMD) and terrorism, as indivisible, and legitimized European interventions in third countries, by military means if necessary. All this goes well beyond soft power, even if an observer used to the EU talking itself up, might be justified in a degree of cynicism over the extent to which paper commitments will translate into concrete change in both capabilities and actions.

There are plenty of observers with this last cast of mind in the USA. The US Ambassador to NATO, Victoria Nuland, recently called for 'a stronger, more capable European defence capacity. An ESDP with only soft power is not enough' (quoted in Keohane 2008: 6). This judgement is rather hard on the ESDP, which has certainly gone beyond soft power, but it demonstrates how expectations continue to rise relentlessly. This is paradoxical given the past scepticism of observers such as Richard Holbrooke and Robert Kagan that the EU could ever make the qualitative leap to the hard power level (Holbrooke 1998; Kagan 2003). What is more, there are good reasons for doubting that the USA would be quite so keen on a fully-fledged EU as military actor were one to be achieved – it would almost certainly be much more independent of Washington in foreign policy terms. But this is the way the debate is inevitably conducted: a grand rhetoric with long-term implications, generated largely by short-term preoccupations.

The ESDP thus tends to be seen in the USA more as an extension of soft power than as a qualitative shift in European will or capacity. This is not surprising given the fact that its missions have not yet taken on the high end of the Petersberg tasks (themselves to be expanded by the Treaty of Lisbon), that is, tasks where there is a risk of serious involvement in violent conflict. Such missions as those in the Congo, or Chad, are potentially dangerous, while the EU is committed to a major role in the unstable statelet of Kosovo. European troops are also exposed in the Lebanon (albeit not in any formal ESDP mission). As a result the ESDP missions are beginning to attract serious military analysis (Siebert, 2007), just as the range and extent of European member states' troop deployments taken together are becoming more widely known (Giegerich and Wallace 2004; International Institute of Strategic Studies 2008). Two million EU citizens are in uniform, even if it is probable that less than 15 per cent are deployable to trouble-spots and then only by permission of the national capitals. The EU undoubtedly has the potential – that is, the size, wealth, technology and political weight – to be a superpower, and thus to leave the world of soft power far behind, but it is still, after nearly four decades of foreign policy activity, more than one step-change away from being so.

The era of the Treaty of Lisbon

The Lisbon Treaty, if ratified, will allow for further developments in hard power, by its provision for Permanent Structured Cooperation (Biscop 2008). This mechanism enables a variable geometry approach to defence cooperation, which is the only feasible way of making progress given the enormous disparities in the armed services, resources and strategic cultures of the 27 member states. The development of a defence dimension in this way should also be facilitated by the fact that the USA, from the latter years of the Bush administration on, has become more relaxed than ever before about the idea of a European pillar within NATO, and indeed is to some extent encouraging its development, having moved beyond the strictures of the 'Berlin Plus' arrangements of 2003, which sought to ensure that NATO (and thus the USA) had a virtual veto on what could practicably be done with the ESDP. The USA now recognizes that it needs the Europeans to operate in the grey area between shooting wars and pure diplomacy, where Gulliver is not always well-equipped to act (a weakness Stanley Hoffmann alerted us to three decades ago; Hoffmann, 1968, 2005).

Operating in this grey area, however, means that the newly arriving elements of military force in the EU's portfolio are not yet being used for *compellance*, which is the essence of hard power. Rather their function is to attempt to bring stability and structure to fragile states and to turbulent regions. When challenged, as could have been the case in the Congo, or as would undoubtedly be the case in Darfur, the EU would still be likely to retreat – or, more probably, *qua* EU, not to turn up in the first place (as since 2006 in the Lebanon, where the presence of French, Spanish and Italian troops does not signify EU-wide agreement on an ESDP mission). Indeed, the EU as such has never taken a stand militarily. This is not necessarily a condemnation; getting involved in civil wars (which is what these conflicts mostly are) is a high-risk enterprise, while 'standing firm' over time, as in Iraq and Afghanistan is usually both costly and controversial. In such circumstances even superpowers make prudential judgements about tactical retreats (as the USA did in Lebanon in the 1980s and Somalia in the 1990s, and the Soviet Union did in Afghanistan in the mid-1980s).

However, there are places where the EU does want to move things decisively in its preferred direction, on the basis of clear interests. One such is North Africa, from where the tide of illegal immigration seems unstoppable, and where Islamic fundamentalism has been making steady gains. The EU foresaw some of this in the 1990s. Its Barcelona process was a classic use of soft power to tackle the problems through prevention rather than cure. Most judgements, a decade or more on, are that the process has failed, with much money unspent, migration flows continuing, often connived at by Maghrebian governments, and some terrorist cells implanted inside western European societies. French President Sarkozy's initiative for a new Mediterranean Union, soon after taking office, was a tacit recognition of the fact. The counter-factual, however, must always be born in mind; it is possible that things would have been even worse without the EU's determined efforts to engage with the problems of unemployment and cultural misunderstandings. Moreover the alternative strategy, pursued in parallel (and contradiction) by France in Algeria, is that of backing repressive governments willing to crack down hard on any sign of Islamic fundamentalism, with the resulting human rights abuses predictably fostering further opposition. Yet it has to be accepted that, as with similar US tactics in Latin America during the 1960s, this brutal form of realpolitik has kept the unwanted political change at bay. Similarly tough measures – which can only so far be pursued at the national level – were reputedly taken by the USA and the UK to deter Colonel Gaddafi from continuing his plans to acquire a nuclear weapon. Soft power can affect the broad context, but once militant and determined antagonisms arise, it is out of its depth.

On Iran, where the EU sees itself as sharing a vital interest with the whole international community, of which it sometimes presumes to be the agent, diplomacy has again been in the forefront. The concern here relates to the general stability of the Middle East and the possibility that Tehran might sponsor nuclear terrorism inside Europe. Accordingly the Europeans, led by the EU-3 of the UK, France and Germany (to the initial annoyance of Italy and Spain), have managed to lead a united European diplomatic effort over six years, attempting to keep Iran in play through negotiations and to prevent the conflict with the USA and Israel from erupting into violence. This soft power strategy had some success in its first two years, until Iran backed away from its initial agreement not to engage in the enrichment and reprocessing of nuclear fuel. The EU clearly accepts that it cannot coerce Iran into anything, and that persuasion is its only hope. Sanctions are of merely symbolic value here, to keep the USA onside. Indeed, the unstated major aim of European diplomacy from 2004–8 was to play for time in the hope of forestalling a military attack on Iran, which would be less likely with a Democrat in the White House. There may also have been some element of a deliberate division of labour, along the lines of good cop/bad cop, between Washington and the EU-3, which (if true) would qualify the picture of unbridled antagonism between the Bush administration and its European critics. For their part the Europeans may not even be so alarmed at the prospect of an Iranian bomb. As Christoph Bertram (2008) has recently pointed out, whatever is said in public, the West's deterrent capability is such that it could in practice live with a modest Iranian nuclear capability, as it does with Pakistan's. The real problem, even greater in the latter case, is the prospect of technology and fissile material getting into the wrong hands through either malicious intent or the collapse of the states concerned.

Thus on big issues where there is no need for, or possibility of, the kind of benign occupation the EU practises in the Balkans, the Europeans still fall back, for perfectly good reasons, on various forms of soft power. Others, indeed, seem to value the kind of 'structural' resources that the EU has at its disposal (Keukeleire 2004). Although it routinely calls for more European contributions to hard power, the USA has come to rely on the EU's main instruments, notably enlargement, post-war reconstruction and election monitoring, and attempts to harness them to its own ends. China and Russia have also woken up to their importance, although they are more than content for the EU to remain a civilian superpower, without the capacity to heighten their own sense of threat.

The Treaty of Lisbon itself contains a number of important elements for the foreign policy agency of the EU (Whitman and Juncos 2009). Apart from Permanent Structured Cooperation, discussed briefly above, there are three developments to note. First, external policymaking comes under the overall control of someone who was to be called a foreign minister, until the crisis over the planned Constitution induced more caution. The first appointment, Catherine Ashton, has the title of the High Representative (HR), as has been the case since the Treaty of Amsterdam in 1997. The innovation lies in the fact that the HR will also be a vice-president of the Commission and thus bring together what have previously been two separate and at times competing strands of foreign policy. There is no guarantee that in practice this will resolve the problems of coherence which afflict the EU's exercise of any kind of power in the world, but it has some potential to do so. The second development is a true innovation, viz. the replacement of the rotating Presidency by an appointed individual who will serve for 30 months, renewable once and who will (jointly with the HR, which will create its own problems) be the human face, and principal agent, of the EU in international relations. In itself this should be a neutral development so far as soft or hard power is concerned, since while the president will be primarily occupied with representation at high-level meetings, there is no reason in principle why this kind of diplomacy might not also involve pressure and the threat of coercion – indeed, access to the resources of the Community via the Commission might make it easier to threaten negative sanctions, through the withdrawal of financial or commercial benefits. Of course, the high profile of the new President might also encourage an exaggerated sense of what the EU can and should do to shape events. Failure would then rebound sharply on its reputation and influence.

The third foreign policy innovation of the Treaty of Lisbon is for the longer term, namely the development of an External Action Service, which would be a major step towards a common diplomatic service for the EU. By its nature this would merely extend the repertoire for the exercise of soft power, but insofar as its successful development would betoken a greater commitment to common actions it might also foster more assertiveness in external relations. Already military staff from the ESDP side of the Brussels institutions are starting to liaise with EU Delegations when serving on missions in the field. If not yet formal military attachés they are at least a visible sign of the EU's having begun to acquire some interesting new capabilities.

A strategy for soft power?

For the future, at least in the EU context, it may make no particular sense to distinguish between hard and soft power given that the EU has over the last three decades increasingly gained confidence over the use of the coercive instruments it has always possessed – threats of economic sanctions – while also acquiring aspects of the traditional underpinning of statecraft, that is, military power. At the same time it retains strict self-denying ordinances on what use may be made of coercion, for reasons of both necessity and values. Thus while the default setting for the EU in foreign policy is soft power, it is stretching that category by increasingly flexing its economic muscles and by deploying armed services, which however peaceful their intentions always have the potential to change someone else's reality against their will. Its activity is increasingly in the grey middle part of the hard/soft continuum.

This means that there is a built-in (and possibly creative) ambiguity over the power the EU wields in specific situations. How are counter-terror measures, for example, to be thought of? They may involve preemptive strikes, or measures such as conniving in rendition, where the law is a marginal consideration. We should not forget that even pacifistic Germany was capable 30 years ago of an effective commando raid to rescue hostages from a plane at Mogadishu, while British and French forces have been engaged in various rescue missions in Sierra Leone and the Lebanon which always had the potential to become a firefight. This kind of operation is right on the cusp of the hard/soft divide. Conversely, as events since the US invasion of Iraq have shown, the barrel of a gun always needs to be accompanied by wider social and political measures if military gains are to be consolidated.

The various ESDP missions are similarly neither clearly hard nor soft in the 'power' they represent. While primarily irenic in purpose, they embody an EU presence which cannot be ignored, and a reminder that political settlements are not simply about the exchange of diplomatic memoranda. For persuasion takes many forms, some distinctly asymmetrical in terms of the capacity of the parties to influence outcomes. The EU often has the advantage in such situations, but an effective use of the tools at its disposal, while keeping within the limits ordained by cautious intergovernmentalism, must involve Joseph Nye's (2008) category of 'smart power', with a premium placed on perceptive leaders capable of distinguishing between different contexts, and between the instruments most appropriate for use on any given occasion. This, which in other times would have been referred to as 'statesmanship', was picked up by EC's Enlargement Commissioner Olli Rehn in a lecture in which he stressed the need for coherence in 'using the whole spectrum of policy instruments and economic resources' (Rehn 2008). But we should remember that the EU, as with any other actor, is not capable, however smart its leadership might be, of just pulling out of the toolbox any kind of instrument, or identifying the precise spanner with which to crack a particular nut. In practice, and especially post-St Malo, the EU will always dispose of what might be termed 'halfway power', where the possible element of coercion is ambiguous, being mixed with, or even hidden by, the softer, more acceptable face of persuasion and example.

To take things a step further, the '[r]ationalism in supporting multilateralism', which is what Lord Patten (2007) has said is the purpose of soft power, is necessary but not sufficient. However much it would prefer to retain its faith in policy planning, and in conflict prevention, the EU will also need to make use, for a range of unforeseeable circumstances, of diverse combinations of instruments, and possibly newly confected ones, rather than rely on precise strategies and the advance calibration of resources. Moreover, while the demands will keep coming, all forms of the exercise of power are expensive, in terms not only of budgetary expenditure but also political costs – as we have discovered with the popular reaction against enlargement, which had been pushed forward largely for foreign policy reasons. Those who demand more EU military capacity make no bones about the fact that it will require an overall increase in defence spending – and risks. But all the EU's international power is expensive at some level, as we have always known when thinking about opening up agricultural trade to developing countries. The real issue, therefore, is less that of soft versus hard power, than that of the balance of responsibilities – international versus internal, vital interests versus desirable outcomes. The EU, no less than Germany and Japan which have also practised cheque-book diplomacy, cannot count either on it being effective or on continuing to have the resources to underpin it. Not only will it be difficult to find more resources for foreign and defence policy, but its existing balance-sheet, particularly now that the very bases of Western wealth are in question, cannot be taken for granted, especially given the competition. It is striking how China, long seen as either weak or reliant on the military strength inherent in its huge size, is now a practised exponent of soft power on a global scale, which has led to alarm-bells ringing in both Europe and the USA (Alden 2007; Suzuki 2009). The EU and its member states will need to think carefully about both the inherent limits to their global role, and the comparative advantages they possess by virtue of an unusual range and variety of available means. For if the EU is unlikely to become a player in a traditional great power balance it does at least have the means to exert some checks on the behaviour of a surprising range of other actors. 'Structural power', however, probably overstates the case, given the limits on the EU's ability to convert size, wealth and trading position into political leverage.

Given the increasingly blurred line between hard and soft power in the case of the EU it is not plausible to argue that the EU needs to formulate a 'soft power strategy'. There can, indeed, be no strategy for the use of the *means* of foreign policy, whether particular or general, in isolation from the *ends* being pursued. To be sure, if the overriding aim is – as perhaps it was during the civilian power era – to limit oneself to the use of soft power, with no coercive element, then it would be sensible to think how that can and should be done over the long term. Because in that event the means would, to a large extent, determine the ends of foreign policy. Until economic sanctions started to be used in the 1980s the EC limited itself to a mixture of exhortation, mediation and milieu goals such as détente. In the contemporary environment, where a much wider range of foreign policy instruments is available to the EU, a soft power strategy is conceivable for a specified purpose, but not as a template for European foreign policy as a whole. For example, in relations with Turkey, which is a NATO ally for many member states, it almost goes without saying that the only appropriate means come under the heading of soft power – diplomacy, economic cooperation, shared regulatory structures. This is true whatever end is sought, and in truth the member states cannot agree on whether that end should be Turkish accession, or rather some form of privileged partnership. In other words the nature of the issue generally determines the range of available instruments. However, even with a friendly state like Turkey, pressure is as much a part of the diplomatic spectrum as is discussion, as illustrated by the history of relations over the 46 years since the Association agreement was signed. It may be imputing too much collective rationality to the Community/Union over this period to say that it has been 'smart' in its deployment of the various means open to it, but broadly speaking the Europeans have been successful in maintaining good relations with Turkey without actually having to admit it to their group. Only in 1974, when Ankara decided to invade Cyprus did the strategy (to the extent it deserves the name) break down. Since then the carrot of membership has had to be brought almost within Turkey's grasp, but it has not yet been handed over, much to the understandable frustration of many Turks.

Thus in this important case, as in others, the EU's soft power resources have proved effective in delivering most of what is wanted – including, as so often, the avoidance of real change given that the member states cannot agree on what form it should take. The category of soft power is irrelevant in such cases, as both the nature of the issue and the relationship with the particular third country rule out some of the theoretically available instruments *ab initio*. Where soft power as a concept can add value for the practitioner in European foreign policy is in drawing attention away from the now outmoded distinction between 'civilian' and military power, where the EU is always at a disadvantage, and towards the need for all actors in the international system, including the USA and other powerful nation-states, to engage more in the arts of negotiation and linkage politics, which means understanding the interplay which takes place continually between domestic populations, and between them and governments, whether their own or others'. In this complex phase of international politics, requiring more sophistication than displayed in the relatively crude versions of realism or crusading which have too often passed for foreign policy expertise in the past, the EU is a leader. Given the power of language, and of branding, it is best to avoid being damned by association with 'soft power', which in any case understates the capacity for coercive behaviour present even in the EU's economic instruments. However, the Europeans have certainly shown what can be done with this kind of approach – and, sadly, what cannot.

Note

1 'Appeasement' originally referred to the process of making peace. Only after Munich in 1938 did it take on the connotations of cowardice and weakness. (Gilbert, 1966)

Bibliography

Alden, C. (2007) *China in Africa*, London: Zed.

Bertram, C. (2008) 'For a New Iran Policy', *Centre for European Reform Bulletin*, Issue 59, April/May.

Biscop, S. (2008) 'Permanent Structured Cooperation and the Future of the ESDP', Egmont Paper 20, Brussels: Royal Institute of International Relations.

Buzan, B. (1991) *People, States and Fear: An Agenda for International Security Studies in the Post-Cold War Era*, 2nd edn, Brighton: Harvester Wheatsheaf. [1st edn, Wheatsheaf 1983].

Duchêne, F. (1972) 'Europe's Role in World Peace', in R. Mayne (ed.) *Europe Tomorrow: Sixteen Europeans Look Ahead*, London: Fontana.

Edwards, G. and Rijks, D. (2008) 'Boundary Problems in EU External Representation', in L. Aggestam, F. Anesi, G. Edwards, C. Hill and D. Rijks, *Institutional Competences in the EU External Action: Actors and Boundaries in CFSP and ESDP*, Report No. 6–7, Stockholm: SIEPS.

European Union (2008) *Presidency Conclusions*, 11–12 December, Brussels .

European Security Strategy (2003) 'A Secure Europe in a Better World', 12 December 2003, Brussels: European Union. Available at: http://www.consilium.europa.eu/uedocs/cmsUpload/78367.pdf

George, A.L., Hall, D.K. and Simons, W.E. (1971) *The Limits of Coercive Diplomacy: Laos, Cuba, Vietnam*, Boston, MA: Little, Brown.

Giegerich, B. and Wallace, W. (2004) 'Not Such a Soft Power: The External Deployment of European Forces', *Survival: Global Politics and Strategy*, 46(2): 163–82.

Gilbert, M. (1966) *The Roots of Appeasement*, London: Weidenfeld & Nicolson.

Ginsberg, R.H. (1989) *Foreign Policy Actions of the European Community: the Politics of Scale*, Boulder, CO: Lynne Reinner.

Gnesotto, N. (2004) 'European Strategy as a Model', Editorial, *Newsletter*, No. 9., January 2004, Paris: European Union for Security Studies.

Hill, C. (2008) 'The European Security Strategy Reconsidered', in C. Franck and G. Duchenne (eds) *L'action extérieure de l'Union européenne: Rôle global, dimensions matérielles, aspects juridiques, valeurs*, Louvain-la-Neuve: Academia Bruylant.

Hill, C. and Smith, K.E. (eds) (2000) *European Foreign Policy: Key Documents*, London: Routledge, in association with the Secretariat of the European Parliament.

Hoffmann, S. (1968) *Gulliver's Troubles; or, the Setting of American Foreign Policy*, New York: McGraw-Hill.

—— (2005) *Gulliver Unbound: the Imperial Temptation and the War in Iraq*, Lanham, MD: Rowman & Littlefield.

Holbrooke, R. (1998) *To End a War*, New York: Random House.

International Institute for Strategic Studies (2008) *European Military Capabilities: Building Armed Forces for Modern Operations*, London: IISS Strategic Dossier.

Kagan, R. (2003) *Of Paradise and Power: America and Europe in the New World Order*, New York: Alfred A. Knopf.

Keohane, D. (2008) 'The Strategic Rise of Defence Policy', *Issues*, 25, March 2008, Paris: EU Institute for Security Studies.

Keukeleire, S. (2004) 'EU Structural Foreign Policy and Structural Conflict Prevention', in V. Kronenberger and J. Wouters (eds) *The European Union and Conflict Prevention. Legal and Policy Aspects*, The Hague: T.M.C. Asser Press.

Manners, I. (2002) 'Normative Power Europe: A Contradiction in terms?', *Journal of Common Market Studies*, 40(2), pp. 235–258.

Maull, H. (2005) 'Europe and the New Balance of Global Order', *International Affairs*, 81(4): 775–99.

Missiroli, A. (2008) 'Revisiting the European Security Strategy – beyond 2008', *EPC Policy Brief*, April 2008, Brussels: the European Policy Centre.

Munuera, G. (1994), *Preventing Armed Conflict in Europe: Lessons from Recent Experience*, Chaillot Paper 15/16, Paris: Western European Union Institute for Security Studies.

Nuttall, S.J. (1992) *European Political Cooperation*, Oxford: Oxford University Press.

Nye, J. (1990) 'Soft Power', *Foreign Policy*, Number 80: 153–71.

—— (2008) *Powers that Lead*, New York: Oxford University Press.

Patten, Lord (2007) 'Peace-making in the Middle East and the Role of Europe', ELIAMEP Annual Lecture, Athens, 20 September 2007, transcript of lecture and discussion period, availale at: http://www.eliamep.gr/en/european-integration/events-european-integration/annual-lecture-2007/ (accessed 12 January 2010).

Rehn, O. (2008), 'Europe's Smart Power in its Region and the World', Speech at St Antony's College, Oxford, 1 May 2008, http://www.sant.ox.ac.uk/seesox/pdf/rehn_speech2008.pdf. (accessed 12 January, 2010).

Siebert, B.H. (2007), *African Adventure: Assessing the European Union's Military Intervention in Chad and the Central African Republic*, Cambridge, MA: MIT Security Studies Program Working Paper.

Simms, B. (2001) *Britain's Unfinest Hour: Britain and the Destruction of Bosnia*, London: Penguin.

Smith, K.E. (2000) 'The End of Civilian Power Europe: A Welcome Demise of Cause for Concern?', *The International Spectator*, 35(2): 11–28.

—— (2005) 'Beyond the Civilian Power EU Debate', *Politique européenne*, 17 (Autumn): 63–82.

Stavridis, S. (2001) ' "Militarising" the EU: the Concept of Civilian Power Europe Revisited', *The International Spectator*, 36(4): 43–50.

Suzuki, S. (2009) 'Chinese Soft Power, Insecurity Studies, Myopia and Fantasy', *Third World Quarterly*, 30(4): 779–93.

Treverton, G.F. (ed.) (1988) *Europe, America and South Africa*, New York: Council of Foreign Relations.

Whitman, R. and Juncos, A. (2009) 'The Lisbon Treaty and the Foreign, Security and Defence Policy: Reforms, Implementation and the Consequences of (non-) Ratification', *European Foreign Affairs Review*, 14(1): 25–46.

12 The myth and reality of China's 'soft power'

Shogo Suzuki

Introduction

As a rising power, the People's Republic of China's (PRC) use of soft power is of considerable importance to the international order, and has been garnering much interest in recent years. Chinese cultural influence appears to be on the rise, as evidenced by the mushrooming of Chinese government-sponsored cultural centres, the 'Confucius Institutes' across the world, as well as the growing number of people learning the Chinese language. The spectacular opening ceremony of the 2008 Beijing Olympic games also sought to remind viewers of the world of China's charm through pageantries drawing on Chinese historical heritage and culture. It was a strong reminder of the rich sources of soft power that the PRC could draw on.

Soft power has been conceptualized by Joseph S. Nye, Jr (2004: 5) as the ability to get 'others to want the outcomes that you want' through the power of attraction. Chinese analysts' definitions of soft power do not differ radically from this definition (Zhang 2004: 10, 2007: 576; Li 2008: 291), even though some have departed from Nye's broadly state-centric perspective by arguing that 'soft power applies not only to nations, but also regions, organizations and even individuals' (Wang and Lu 2008: 427). Yet, there is much that is unknown about China's soft power. This is partly related to the fact that Chinese policy elites themselves did not pay much attention to this concept until the beginning of the twenty-first century (Cho and Jeong 2008: 456–8; Wang and Lu 2008: 426), and also because the rise of China's soft power was not seen as a potential challenge to the West and was not taken seriously. Any concerns with China's growing power was related to its military, or 'hard' power. Furthermore, in the post-Cold War mood of 'liberal triumphalism', scholars' attention was focused mainly on how the USA had maintained its preponderance for so long, and how its soft power had contributed to this.

Things have changed greatly since then. China's growing confidence in the international political arena, coupled perhaps with a sense of diminishing American power resulting from the prolonged wars in Iraq and Afghanistan, has made the Beijing leadership less shy about announcing China's rise and its intention to reclaim its 'rightful' place alongside the great powers of international society. Not surprisingly, debates on the PRC's soft power have been profoundly influenced by this development, often leading to misunderstandings about the nature of Chinese soft power by both Chinese and Western observers.

What, then, is Chinese soft power and its content? The aim of this chapter is to give an overview of Chinese and Western debates on the PRC's soft power, as well as to explore the content of Chinese soft power. It argues that debates on China's rise to power have led to erroneous interpretations of this (admittedly sometimes vague) concept. While Chinese scholars tend to exaggerate the extent of the PRC's soft power, Western pundits have been equally guilty of overestimating Chinese soft power's influence in the international order.

Chinese debates on soft power

China's debates on its soft power are inextricably linked with its rise in the international community. China's threat to the military balance of power was a hot topic in the 'China Threat' debate of the late 1990s, but this was of course more to do with 'hard', military/material power. For its part, Beijing, stung by international fears and criticisms of its growing material might and negative international image, kept a low profile. However, China's impressive growth in its economic and political clout continued, and Beijing's claims that it was a 'developing country' with limited capacity for power soon began to lose their credibility. Furthermore (as will be explored below), Beijing's attempts to allay its neighbours' fears through its 'good neighbour' diplomacy paid dividends. In the context of growing international criticism of US unilateralism and interventionist foreign policies, many of the PRC's neighbours became increasingly accommodating of China's growing power. There thus resulted a lively domestic debate about 'China's peaceful rise' (*heping jueqi*) and how to enhance Chinese power, which 'was in effect an intention to declare China's expansion of national power and its presumed forthcoming rise to global power status, and to gain acceptance of this declaration from neighbouring Asian countries (Cho and Jeong 2008: 467).

Soft power – known in Chinese as *ruan shili, ruan liliang* or *ruan quanli* – was, and is increasingly, seen to play a crucial role in this process, and there is very little doubt that the Chinese elite take soft power very seriously. Leaders make frequent references to the need to project China's soft power (Li 2008: 288–91). The Chinese Communist Party (CCP) Central Committee report adopted at the Seventeenth Party Congress in 2007 stated that China needed to 'enhance culture as part of the soft power of our country' (China.org.cn 2007). A Chinese scholar has also noted that soft power is just as important to China's rise as is hard power: 'if one of them is zero, no matter how large the value of the other is, the total value of the comprehensive power [of the PRC] will be zero' (Yan 2006: 12; Men 2007: 6–7).

The reasons for the PRC's interest in soft power are threefold. First, as can be seen from above, the rise of China means that 'Chinese policy makers and analysts are naturally interested in the question of what makes for great powers'

(Wang and Lu 2008: 435), and they see soft power as 'an important indicator of a state's international status and influence' (Li 2008: 299; Yan 2006). Second, with wars between great powers becoming an increasing rarity, the Chinese are now of the belief that competition between these states will take the form of soft power competition (Wang and Lu 2008: 435). As Zhao Changmo (2004: 1) states, 'as a developing state [China] has still not been able to claim leadership. In the process of constructing soft power and using it to play an international role, it is inevitable that we will encounter Western ideological obstruction, particularly the interference from American cultural hegemonism'. It is thus imperative for the PRC to develop its soft power if it is going to fulfil its long-cherished dream of attaining equality with the great powers of the international community. Finally, the development of soft power is seen as an important means by which to allay fears that China is a rising power with intentions of upsetting the international material and normative status quo (Li 2008: 300–1; Wang and Lu 2008: 435–6).

The sources of China's soft power

Chinese debates on the sources of soft power tend to adhere to Nye's (2004: 11) conceptualization, namely that soft power derives from a state's culture, 'political values (when it lives up to them at home and abroad)' and 'foreign policies (when they are seen as legitimate and having moral authority)'. Of these three, Chinese culture has been one of the most promoted 'sources' of Chinese soft power in recent years. While Nye's original work had examined the role of contemporary popular American culture and its role in enhancing US soft power, Chinese scholars tend to look to history (Wang and Lu 2008: 431). The most obvious is traditional Chinese arts and crafts, ranging from Peking Opera, calligraphy, Chinese medicine, Chinese language to classical literature. As mentioned above, the opening ceremony of the Beijing Olympics drew heavily on these themes, and this suggests that the Chinese believe these facets of Chinese culture to be the most readily identifiable for a non-Chinese audience. The opening of Confucius Institutes is also believed by some to be based on the notion that 'language-culture is the core of soft power, and in the process of national construction and exporting soft power, as well as participating in the competition [between soft powers], it plays a pioneering, foundational role' (Duan 2008: 48).

As regards political values, a perhaps less obvious aspect which gets heavily promoted as part of the PRC's soft power is traditional Chinese political philosophy, particularly Confucianism. Chinese Scholars note that traditional Chinese political philosophy promotes the 'kingly way' (Zhang 2007: 576) of 'harmony without suppressing differences' through the pursuit of 'equality, cooperation based on trust and benefit' (Men 2007: 15–16) which brought about peace development in the ancient East Asian international system and its institutional expression, the tribute system (cf. Fairbank 1968; Zhang 2001). This, of course, appears to be an implicit criticism of recent US foreign policy and its proponents, who have been particularly forthright in their demands for international homogeneity based on democratic governance and even explored the idea of a hierarchical international society with liberal democracies at the apex of this order (Buchanan and Keohane 2004; cf. Reus-Smit 2005). Chinese analysts argue that at a time when there is serious disillusionment with Western culture, which can allegedly lead to 'extreme egoism, material fetishism, confused values, utilitarianism, and unethical tendencies' (Men 2007: 19; also see Zhang and Li 2003: 47), traditional Chinese political values of 'harmony' are drawing the increased attention of the world.

China's soft power draws on contemporary political developments as well. Chinese intellectuals assert that the 'vitality' of the PRC's 'socialism with Chinese characteristics (*Zhongguo tese shehui zhuyi*)' is an important source of China's soft power. Men Honghua (2007: 29), for instance, claims that 'institutions support soft power'. China, he states, has continuously striven to improve its domestic governance. 'In recent years, alongside economic development, the construction of the rule of law has been promoted on a large scale ... in a certain way, institutional renewal can ensure a state's leading role in international relations.' This point overlaps with recent debates on the rise of great powers (*daguo jueqi*), where domestic institutional development was frequently mentioned as a key variable in facilitating a state's rise to power (Tang 2007), and is indicative of Chinese elite thinking that enhancing the PRC's soft power will also facilitate its entry into the club of great powers.

Perhaps the greatest contemporary source of Chinese soft power in the area of political values is the PRC's model of development, which has more recently been dubbed the 'Beijing Consensus' by Joshua Cooper Ramo. According to Ramo (2004: 4) the 'Beijing Consensus' is characterised by a 'desire to have equitable, peaceful high-quality growth' but 'does not believe in uniform solutions' – such as economic and political liberalization often propagated by the West – but a 'ruthless willingness to innovate and experiment' and a 'lively defense of national borders and interests'. As Cho and Jeong (2008: 463) note, '[t]he fact that the major force initially disseminating the Beijing Consensus is neither the Chinese government nor Chinese scholars but rather foreign scholars and foreign media is a very encouraging sign' of international status and recognition, and Chinese analysts have been eager to jump on the bandwagon of the 'Beijing Consensus'. Yu Keping (2006: 11–12; also see Gill and Huang 2006: 20), for instance, claims that the PRC's model of development is garnering the increasing interest of developing states because of the perceived failures of neoliberal financial restructuring programmes undertaken in Latin America, Asia and Russia. In contrast, 'China has upheld its own modernization strategy and reform and opening up policies, creating a miracle of fast economic growth' (Yu 2006: 12), and this has helped it to become a great power. Evidence of the increased profile of the Beijing model of development and subsequent growth of the PRC's soft power is given by citing various international voices of praise for China's trajectory of development. Chinese commentators proudly note that in the 2004 Shanghai Conference for Scaling Up Poverty Reduction and Global Learning Process, the chief of the World Bank 'called for the world to share China's experience in poverty reduction' (Zhang *et al.* 2005: 21). The PRC's developmental model has allegedly provided inspiration for countries such as Russia or India (Men 2007: 36). Zhang and Li (2003: 46) provide further evidence by noting that:

> ... political parties, organizations and figures from 110 counties sent more than 200 messages of congratulations on the eve of the Chinese Communist Party's sixteenth Party Congress, expressing their praise of China's socialist system, affirmation of the fruits of China's reform and opening policy, and admiration for the Party's governing abilities.

Finally, in the realm of foreign policy, Beijing's recent 'good neighbour policy' is frequently cited as a source of Chinese soft power. It is noted that 'China's independent (meaning resistant to outside pressure, free from alignment, non-ideological and non-confrontational) foreign policy and its orientation toward 'peaceful rise' have made China appealing' (Wang and Lu 2008: 429). While less timid about flaunting its aspirations and expectations towards attaining the status of a great power, the PRC has been at pains to avoid being seen as a 'revisionist power' and has sought to construct an image of a 'responsible great power (*fu zeren daguo*)' which plays an active part in maintaining international order. To this end, the PRC has settled a number of its territorial disputes with its neighbours. It has joined a growing number of multilateral institutions, and has played an increasingly proactive role within them (Gill and Huang 2006: 21–3).

Chinese commentators are keen to contrast this new, cooperative foreign policy with that of the USA. Zhang and Li (2003: 48) claim that this approach 'resolutely upholds the use of peaceful means to solve international disputes, and does not engage in power politics'. Furthermore, it 'opposes any pretexts to interfere in the internal affairs of other states, as well as the strong threatening, invading, bullying or overturning weaker states. China ... has never allowed others to force their social institutions and ideology upon us' (Zhang and Li 2003: 48). At a time when US foreign policy based on the Bush Doctrine often seen as characterized by 'contempt for international law and institutions' and 'little concern for either legitimacy or the moral dimensions of the exercise of power' (Van Ness 2004/5: 39; also see Nye 2004), Beijing's 'good neighbour' approach has indeed at times looked less 'revisionist' than Washington's unilateralism. Moreover, it earns the support and praise from the so-called 'Third World', which is a support base the Chinese have often relied on.

Western views of Chinese soft power

While the Chinese elites have been busy analysing China's soft power, Western commentators have also been paying increasing attention to this new facet of China's growing power. Many of their debates so far, however, have reflected increased anxieties that a 'decline in American soft power' is 'relative – largely a comparative decline based on the rise of other powers – in particular the rapid emergence of China as a US 'peer competitor' and a growing source of international influence, investment, and political and economic power'

(Congressional Research Service 2008: 3; also see Pang 2007: 4). While noting that the unpopular US foreign policies under the Bush administration have partly contributed to this, Ramo (2004: 3) seems to sum up this sentiment nicely when he claims that 'China is assembling the resources to eclipse the US in many essential areas of international affairs and constructing an environment that will make US hegemonic action more difficult.' There are some similarities to Chinese thinking that different types of 'soft powers' are in an inherently competitive relationship with one another. However, this statement is perhaps explicit in its thinking that competition between US and PRC soft power is a zero-sum game.

It is thus not surprising that Chinese soft power has been frequently seen as something of a threat. The 'Chinese model of development' or 'Beijing Consensus' has garnered the most attention in this context. International attraction to this model could, according to some, lead to environmental degradation. In his influential book, *Charm Offensive*, Joshua Kurlantzick (2007: 163–4) claims that 'China's growing soft power also could lead it to export its environmental problems', and that this 'environmental recklessness' will '[spread] across borders as China's global influence grows'. Worst of all, perhaps, is the threat that Chinese soft power poses to cherished liberal values of democracy and goals to achieve 'good governance' across the globe. Kurlantzick (2007: 56–7) has claimed that China's model of development 'stands in direct contrast to democratic liberalism, the economic and political model emphasizing individual rights and civil liberties that has underpinned the societies of the West', and it appears that his sentiments are shared among policymakers as well. Washington is also reported to have despatched a senior official to investigate China's growing influence, and 'determine how much can be put down to simply business and how much China plans to export its own political system and power' (BBC News 2006).

Western analysts often cite Beijing's alleged undermining of political and economic reform programmes that aim for some form of democratization and transparency in governance – often administered by institutions such as the International Monetary Fund (IMF). An important, overarching factor in this development is China's 'positive image'. With reference to Africa, Kurlantzick (2006: 1–2) states that Beijing 'offers African nations an alternate consumer for resources, *a model of successful development*, and trade policies that can be more benign than Western initiatives' and could undermine Western efforts to promote democratic governance 'and strengthen some of the continent's worst regimes'.

Chinese soft power: myth or reality?

The discussions above would seem to indicate the 'arrival' of Chinese soft power on the world stage, with significant implications for the international community. It is important, however, to exercise caution in taking these debates at face value. While very few would dismiss Nye's intuitively plausible arguments about the importance of and necessity to cultivate soft power out of hand, it is extremely difficult (methodological difficulties notwithstanding) to determine *how* and to *what extent* soft power would enable a state to achieve its political goals (Wang and

Lu 2008: 446). As the images of anti-American protestors wearing Nike shoes and jeans demonstrates, it is never very clear as to how American popular culture would result in enhanced soft power for the USA. This point is particularly relevant in the case of China, as various studies and commentaries on the degree of the PRC's power and influence have often been vulnerable to hyperbole. Gerald Segal (1999) starkly reminded us of this during the height of the 'China Threat' debates of the late 1990s by pointing out to the greatly exaggerated reports of China's economic and military power and concomitant international influence. Our examinations below suggest, however, that the steady stream of commentaries by both Chinese and Western analysts on the PRC's soft power have been unable to escape this all too familiar trap.

The primary reasons for this can be traced back to the relative closeness these individuals often enjoy with political decision makers and their agendas. Robert Cox (1996: 87) has famously noted that '[t]heory is always *for* someone and *for* some purpose', and this observation is certainly of great relevance with regard to recent debates on Chinese soft power. Within the PRC, public intellectuals and academics are increasingly being called upon by the Beijing leadership to provide policy advice. The former often require the maintenance of personal connections to the political elite in order to maintain their influence (Glaser and Saunders 2002). In this social environment – coupled with continued restrictions on free speech – it is perhaps not surprising that many pundits may tend to emphasize the positive achievements of the CCP and link these with assertions of China's growing soft power. Western analysts, of course, do not operate under the same political restrictions that their Chinese counterparts have to. However, it is worth noting that many recent studies on Chinese soft power have been produced by American or American-based scholars. This is partly a reflection of the greater strategic importance Asia holds for the USA, but the strong emphasis on exploring Chinese soft power and the potential *threat* it poses to US primacy does suggest that Washington's political interests in maintaining American hegemony in the face of a rising China inform many of these works (Suzuki 2009). These factors, in turn, result in tendencies by Western analysts to exaggerate the degree of influence Chinese soft power enjoys, as well as ignore any complexities which may exist within debates of the PRC's soft power.

Exaggerating the influence of Chinese soft power

In the case of Chinese studies of the PRC's soft power, 'exaggeration' tends to manifest itself in the form of glossing over any negative aspects of Chinese culture, political values, and foreign policy, while trumpeting the 'attraction' that China has enjoyed in recent years. In the field of foreign policy, PRC commentators make much of Beijing's 'good neighbour' and 'independent' foreign policy. There is a certain ring of truth to this claim: many scholars do not regard the PRC as a 'revisionist power' and note that China has taken huge strides in attempting to conform to various international norms (Johnston 2003). The high level of anti-American sentiment during the Bush administration may have improved the

PRC's *relative* international image to a certain degree as well. Yet, Beijing's foreign policy continues to have serious 'problems of legitimacy' because of its 'few qualms about cutting political and economic deals with corrupt and even brutal, dictators' (Gill and Huang 2006: 28).

Similar problems bedevil debates on Chinese political values as well. Men (2007: 17), for instance, confidently claims that China's rise to power 'has made people reexamine the tremendous power of Chinese traditional culture based on Confucianism', but the causal relations between traditional (political) culture and China's growth today is never clear. More serious, perhaps, are the dubious Chinese claims to soft power on the basis of traditional political philosophy (and the international order which was based on it). While many Chinese scholars have been keen to point out that China was traditionally a benevolent hegemon, such arguments were formulated in the wake of the 'China Threat' debates, and were designed to serve a very specific *political* purpose of 'proving' that historically China was never a threat. The historical record, however, shows that imperial China was far from the 'benevolent' Confucian ideal (Johnston 1995). Furthermore, it is important to note that Confucian political philosophy was inherently *hierarchical*, with a strong paternalistic notion that the morally cultivated should lead those more fallible to happiness and attain cosmic harmony. Such 'hierarchical cultural relations where the goal is to transform enemies into friends follows the logic of the other technique of imperial violence ... conversion' (Callahan 2008: 755). This notion of Chinese superiority is reinforced when we consider that Beijing's 'principles such as 'live peacefully with neighbors, bring prosperity to them, and provide safety to them' and a 'harmonious world' are all taken from Confucianism' (Cho and Jeong 2008: 471). These reflect 'a thirst in China for 'Chinese solutions' to world problems, and a hunger for nationalist solutions to global issues, especially when they promote a patriotic form of cosmopolitanism' (Callahan 2008: 759), as well as a 'sentiment that the Chinese people must tomorrow take over the mission that has been carried by Americans since World War II ... , the mission of civilising the world' (Nyíri 2006: 106). Such sentiments will hardly do much to add to China's attraction, particularly in the developing world where the search for independence included a struggle to overcome notions of cultural and racial hierarchy (Suzuki 2009).

The links between the achievements of contemporary Chinese political values – 'socialism with Chinese characteristics' – and Chinese soft power are questionable as well. With regard to the domestic political system of China, any claims that these contribute to the PRC's soft power often simply amount to assertions, and there is evidence that the same views are not shared by others outside of China. While Zhang and Li (2003: 46) claim that the PRC's political institutions have created a 'free, democratic, rich and strong China which has produced huge influence throughout the world, particularly among the developing states', it is obvious that this is far from the case. First, Beijing still has far to go with regard to making China a truly 'free' and 'democratic' state. As a report prepared for the United Nations (UN) Office of the High Commissioner for Human Rights (UN Document 2008) notes, the PRC still suffers from wide-spread human rights abuses and general restrictions on political rights. The angry anti-China protests that took place during the Beijing Olympic torch relay in the UK, France and the USA amply demonstrated widespread antipathy towards Beijing's repressive policies and served as a sharp reminder of how fragile China's soft power actually was.

Overstating the 'threat' of Chinese soft power

If Chinese scholars make the mistake of overstating the positive influence of Chinese soft power, many Western pundits have been equally guilty of exaggerating the influence that Beijing and its 'charm' enjoys for the sake of 'looking' for threats to Western interests. For instance, it is claimed that 'China has so quickly created a positive image of itself in Africa that it now rivals the United States, France and international financial institutions for influence' (Kurlantzick 2006: 1), undermining liberal goals of propagating democracy and respect for human rights. The IMF's failure to get Angola to accept its restructuring programmes is thus linked to China's soft power, namely China's offer of unconditional aid (Kurlantzick 2006: 1, 2007: 97–103). This perspective, however, overstates the efficacy of Chinese soft power. Downs (2007: 56–7) highlights the one-sided nature of these arguments when she states:

> The near-myopic focus on China's role in changing Luanda's position on pursuing a formal financial arrangement with the IMF has obscured the … dominant role played by soaring oil revenues in reducing the Angolan government's interests in IMF and other lending facilities provided by Western donors …

Furthermore, Chinese foreign policy is not as attractive as is often assumed by Western pundits, even in the so-called 'Third World', where China allegedly enjoys huge respect. The PRC and its enterprises' ruthless quest for natural resources, coupled with exploitation of local workers, has resulted in a considerable rise in anti-Chinese sentiment (Alden 2005; *Le Monde* 2008). Furthermore, it is worth noting that the peoples of the developing world are not mindless, empty vassals waiting to be filled with 'Chinese soft power'. Assuming that peoples of the developing world are oblivious to these potential pitfalls robs them of their own agency (Suzuki 2009).

China is also blamed for propagating 'autocratic development' epitomized by the 'Beijing Consensus'. In a typical statement of this genre, Kurlantzick (2007: 56) states that 'China clearly promotes its socioeconomic model through speeches overseas, a model of top-down control of development and poverty reduction in which political reform is sidelined for economic reform.' However, he ignores the fact that it is *other states* that have shown interest in the 'Beijing Consensus' of their own accord, as the various statements by non-Chinese statesmen seem to indicate. Furthermore, while it is true that China's policies since the 1980s have been successful in bringing about spectacular economic growth for China, they have also resulted in blatant inequalities, combined with 'widespread corruption'. This of course 'call[s] into question the sustainability and long-term appeal of China's development and the so-called 'Beijing Consensus'' (Gill and Huang 2006: 28). It is difficult to imagine that other states are ignorant of this aspect of the Chinese developmental model, and this view is shared even by Chinese scholars who generally hold positive views about China's attraction (Yu and Zhuang 2005: 203; Cai 2006: 324; Men 2007: 53; Zhang 2007: 577).

Other potential threats are also linked to Chinese soft power, often with weak causal links. Gill and Huang (2006: 18), for instance, state that the opening of Confucius Institutes and the teaching of Mainland Chinese language which utilizes 'readings from a Beijing perspective, rather than the traditional Chinese characters used in Taiwan or Taiwan-based points of view … serve to advance China's foreign-policy goal of marginalizing Taiwan's international influence'. Strangely, they miss the fact that the learning of Chinese can also open doors to understanding *Taiwanese* perspectives, given that both the PRC and Taiwan use Mandarin Chinese as their official languages. Kurlantzick's aforementioned claim that China's increased soft power would lead to growing 'environmental recklessness' is another case in point. His 'linking global environmental damage to Chinese soft power implies that pollution will spread because other states somehow feel a strong sense of attraction to the environmentally unfriendly Beijing model of economic development, and that its devastating effects on the environment mean very little to them' (Suzuki 2009). In fact, Beijing has faced frequent complaints from its neighbours about the devastating impact China's pollution has on their environment. Such behaviour hardly suggests that other states are impressed and attracted to the 'Beijing Consensus' of development. In fact, one could argue that China's scant regard for environmental degradation causes the *reduction* of China's attractiveness, and similar concerns have been raised by Chinese commentators as well (Zhang 2004: 13).

Ignoring complexities

The wish to stress the importance of Chinese soft power – whether as a positive or negative force – has also led to the ignoring of any complexities within China's 'charm offensive' or Chinese debates that surround them. This seems to be particularly prominent in some Western analyses. First, because of their implicit concerns over the 'threat' posed by Chinese soft power, many commentators seem to ignore the fact that many Chinese analysts remain highly sceptical about the strength and efficacy of the PRC's soft power. Indeed, Li (2008: 296) states that the 'dominant view among Chinese interlocutors on the current state of China's soft power is that China has made much headway and has great potential, but its soft power lags behind both its own hard power growth and that of the soft power of other major powers'. One Chinese scholar has bluntly argued that 'those who say that Chinese culture has universal appeal or China is an agenda-setter in international institutions today are fooling themselves' (Zhan 2006: 5), and many agree. Some have, as mentioned above, noted the darker sides of China's recent development (such as high levels of pollution) that may diminish the appeal of the PRC's model of development. Zhang (2007: 577) has also noted that 'the attraction of Chinese culture cannot be discussed at the same level of that of America's', as evidenced from the ubiquitous presence of Mickey Mouse or MTV. Others have focused on the difficulty in proving how interest in Chinese language or culture is evidence of growing soft power on the part of the PRC. Zhan Yijia (2006: 5) notes perceptively:

> ... one could say, 'If you look at the world, Confucius Institutes are growing in numbers abroad, there are more people studying China and researching China, and there is more reporting and attention paid to China by the foreign media ... if China isn't a great power in soft power terms, how could it have such attraction? While it's true that this explains the tremendous attraction China has, but this attraction is just an expression of interest in the trading opportunities China gives to multinational companies, the Chinese consumers market and cheap labour. Overseas attention paid to China and the recent enthusiasm towards Chinese culture is based on a desire to make more money from China by understanding it better.

Second, there is a problematic assumption that there exists a monolithic Chinese political elite bent on subverting Western interests, particularly by selling the 'Beijing Consensus' abroad. However, there does not necessarily appear to be any sort of 'consensus' among the Chinese elite. For a start, even though the 'Beijing Consensus' is discussed quite extensively within the PRC, it is important to note that the term only appeared in the lexicon of the Chinese policymaking circles *after* Ramo's influential work appeared. As Wu Shuqing (2007, emphasis added) notes, the '"Beijing Consensus" was brought forward spontaneously by *international opinions* against the background of China's fast economic development.' It was not as if there existed a 'consensus' from the start, and even today some analysts argue that 'if there is a consensus in Beijing, then it is a consensus that the reforms in China are still incomplete' (Zhang 2004: 11; Wu 2007). Without a clear and complete understanding of what exactly its developmental model consists of, it is difficult for Beijing to 'sell' its so-called 'Beijing Consensus'. It is thus not surprising that Wang and Lu (2008: 429; also see Cho and Jeong 2008: 465) come to the conclusion that 'the Chinese government has not sought to use the Beijing consensus to compete against the Washington Consensus'.

Finally, there is a tendency among some analysts to lay too much emphasis on the potential revisionism behind Beijing's intentions and see Chinese soft power as directed primarily *against* the West, neglecting the fact that the PRC's 'charm offensive' targets multiple audiences. The multifaceted nature of China's 'charm offensive' is most visible in Beijing's recent foreign policies which aim to cultivate the image of a status quo power that upholds the material and normative status quo of the international community. The post-Cold War international order has so far been characterized by American unipolarity. In such an environment, the PRC has no choice but to ensure it fulfils certain normative expectations espoused by the

West. China's economic growth, which is increasingly tied to CCP legitimacy, depends on stable political and economic relations with the developed states. Furthermore, this is the only way to prevent the reemergence of 'China Threat' theses, and ensure that the international community does not develop hostility towards the PRC. Given that the cultivation of soft power is seen as a means by which to allay fears of a rising China (as mentioned above), it is not surprising that Chinese foreign policy behaviour aimed at bolstering its soft power are hardly what we would characterize as 'revisionist'. Indeed, contrary to allegations that China's growing influence in Africa results in the strengthening of undemocratic rulers and increases in human rights abuses, Gill *et al.* (2007: 13–14) point out that '[p]rogressives in the Chinese policy-making elite … have suggested scaling back relations with Khartoum in an attempt to burnish China's image and international reputation', and in 2007 the PRC government removed Sudan's 'preferred trade status' and refused to 'provide financial incentives to Chinese companies to invest in Sudan'.

Consequently, even analysts who tend to view Chinese soft power through a more threatening lens are forced to acknowledge that Beijing has not necessarily posed a threat to the international order, and claim that the PRC has used its soft power in positive ways, as can be seen from its participation in United Nations Peacekeeping Operations (UNPKO), or the brokering of multilateral talks for the North Korean nuclear crisis (Kurlantzick 2007: 155–60). Both of these activities contradict China's oft-cited image as a 'defender' of sovereignty and autocrats: in the case of UNPKO, post-Cold War operations have increasingly taken on intrusive forms, with the goal of transforming war-torn societies into market-capitalist, liberal democracies (Paris 2004). Such social engineering mandates often suspend the host state's sovereignty and effectively treat the peoples of the host state as children (Bain 2003). Participating in such operations certainly does gain China kudos among the Western powers as a 'responsible great power' and Beijing indeed intends to do just this (Suzuki 2008). However, these activities do go against China and many post-colonial states' opposition to hierarchy and paternalism which characterized imperial rule, and such seeming contradictions cannot be explained by pundits who see 'isolated autocrats' as the target audience for the PRC's 'charm offensive' to promote its soft power (Kurlantzick 2007: 54).

Conclusion

Chinese soft power is a relatively new concept in Chinese foreign policy, and has been subject to much debate and misunderstanding, as has been demonstrated in this chapter. Given how recently Beijing has begun promoting its soft power, it is perhaps fair to say that despite their highly strategic motivations, the Chinese elite have to date been unable to articulate a concrete, unified soft power policy. There is still no consensus about what the so-called 'Beijing Consensus' actually constitutes, and the fact that the PRC's 'charm offensive' is directed to multiple audiences means that Beijing's various policies are often shot with contradictions.

Furthermore – the hyperbolic analyses by Chinese and Western commentators notwithstanding – it is still too early to say whether or not the PRC has succeeded in 'getting others to want the outcomes' that it would like, and if the policymaking circles in Beijing are not sure about China's soft power, neither is their 'target audience'. The results of surveys concerning the PRC's appeal show quite a large variation. A BBC World Service Survey reported that 'China's influence on the world is viewed as positive by a majority or plurality of citizens in 14 of the 22 surveyed countries', and 48 percent saw 'China's influence as positive, 10% higher than those who say the same for the United States' (Gill and Huang 2006: 23–4). Similarly, a poll conducted among Australians by the Lowy Institute for International Policy in 2005 found that 69 per cent had 'positive' feelings for China, compared for 58 per cent for the USA (Cook 2005: 1). Conversely, a 2008 multinational public opinion survey conducted by the Chicago Council on Global Affairs (2008: 5) found that while the majority of respondents in the USA, Japan, South Korea, Indonesia and Vietnam believed that China would soon be the leader of Asia, a surprising number were 'either "somewhat" or "very" uncomfortable with the idea of China one day becoming the leader of Asia'. Of South Koreans 77 per cent gave negative responses, and while the developing states such as Indonesia or Vietnam tended to be more positive, the percentages were '45 and 39, respectively'. In terms of 'diplomatic soft power' and 'political soft power', the PRC lagged behind both the USA and Japan, and lost out to Japan in terms of 'cultural soft power' among respondents in South Korea and the USA (Chicago Council on Global Affairs 2008: 14).

All of this means that as far as becoming a 'great power' in terms of soft power – something which the Chinese call *ruan shili daguo* – the PRC has a long way to go. In addition, the Beijing leadership may also have to deal with a resurgence of American soft power. At the time of writing, the Bush administration is in its final days, and the inauguration of president-elect Barak Obama may bring in a very different foreign policy and international image and improve American soft power, which has taken quite a battering in recent years. However, this does not imply that there will inevitably be an intensified, zero-sum competition between Chinese and American soft power. Our experiences with multiculturalism have demonstrated that multiple cultures and traditions can coexist with one another, and it is quite plausible to suggest that the world can feel a mutual attraction to Chinese and American 'charm'. Recent analyses of Chinese soft power appear to have fallen into a strange realist trap of seeing Chinese and Western bids for the world's hearts and minds in zero-sum terms. This not only clouds our understanding of this latest facet of Chinese foreign policy, but also could result in unhelpful images of one another and can prevent a rising China and the West from coexisting with one another. The rise of China is on the horizon, and both the Chinese and the rest of the world understands this well. The challenge, then, is to work out a way of accommodating this rising power without disrupting the fragile international order. A nuanced understanding of Chinese soft power which moves beyond the myopia and fantasy of 'threats' should be one step that needs to be taken towards this end.

212 *Shogo Suzuki*

Bibliography

Alden, C. (2005) 'China in Africa', *Survival*, 47(3): 147–64.

Bain, W. (2003) *Between Anarchy and Society: Trusteeship and the Obligations of Power*, Oxford: Oxford University Press.

BBC News (2006) 'Chinese Influence in Brazil Worries US', 3 April. Available at: http://news.bbc.co.uk/1/hi/world/americas/4872522.stm (accessed 9 April 2008).

Buchanan, A. and Keohane, R.O. (2004) 'The Preventive Use of Force: A Cosmopolitan Institutional Proposal', *Ethics and International Affairs*, 18(1): 1–22.

Cai, T. (2006) 'Tansuo Zhong de "Zhongguo Moshi" ', in K. Yu, P. Huang, S. Xie and J. Gao (eds) *Zhongguo Moshi Yu 'Beijing Gongshi': Chaoyue 'Huashengdun Gongshi'*, Beijing: Shehui kexue wenxian chubanshe.

Callahan, W.A. (2008) 'Chinese Visions of World Order: Post-hegemonic or a New Hegemony?', *International Studies Review*, 10: 749–61.

Chicago Council on Global Affairs (2008) 'Soft Power in Asia: Results of a 2008 Multinational Survey of Public Opinion'. Available at http://www.thechicagocouncil.org/UserFiles/File/POS_Topline%20Reports/Asia%20Soft%20Power%202008/Chicago%20Council%20Soft%20Power%20Report-%20Final%206-11-08.pdf (accessed 11 January 2009).

China.org.cn (2007) 'Full Text of the Eesolution on CPC Central Committee Report'. Available at: http://www.china.org.cn/english/congress/229158.htm (accessed 20 May 2008).

Cho, Y.N. and Jeong, J.H. (2008) 'China's Soft Power: Discussions, Resources, and Prospects', *Asian Survey*, 48(3): 453–72.

Cook, I. (2005) 'Australian Speak 2005: Public Opinion and Foreign Policy', Lowy Institute for International Policy. Available at: http://www.lowyinstitute.org/Publication.asp?pid=236 (accessed 11 January 2009).

Cox, R.W. (with Sinclair, T.J.) (1996) *Approaches to World Order*, Cambridge: Cambridge University Press.

Downs, E.S. (2007) 'The Fact and Fiction of Sino-African Energy Relations', *China Security*, 3(3): 42–68.

Duan, Y. (2008) 'Ying shili-ruan shili lilun kuangjia xia de yuan-wenhua guoji tuiguang yu kongzi xueyuan', *Fudan jiaoyu luntan*, 6(2): 48–51.

Fairbank, J.K. (ed.) (1968) *The Chinese World Order: Traditional China's Foreign Relations*, Cambridge, MA: Harvard University Press.

Gill, B. and Huang, Y. (2006) 'Sources and Limits of Chinese 'Soft Power'', *Survival*, 48(2): 17–36.

Gill, B., Huang, C. and Morrison, J.S. (2007) 'Assessing China's Growing Influence in Africa', *China Security*, 3(3): 3–21.

Glaser, B.S. and Saunders, P.C. (2002) 'Chinese Civilian Foreign Policy Research Institutes: Evolving Roles and Increasing Influence', *China Quarterly*, 171: 597–616.

Interview (2007) China Foundation for International Strategic Studies, Beijing, 23 April.

Johnston, A.I. (1998) *Cultural Realism: Strategic Culture and Grand Strategy in Chinese History*, Princeton, NJ: Princeton University Press.

—— (2003) 'Is China a Status Quo Power?', *International Security*, 27(4): 5–56.

Kurlantzick, J. (2006) 'Beijing's Safari: China's Move into Africa and Its Implications for Aid, Development and Governance', *Policy Outlook*, November, Carnegie Endowment for International Peace.

—— (2007) *Charm Offensive: How China's Soft Power Is Transforming the World*, New Haven, CT: Yale University Press.

Le Monde (2008) 'Chinois en Zambie: l'amitié entre les peuples, sauce aigre-douce'. Availalble at: http://www.lemonde.fr/web/imprimer_element/0,40_0@2–1004868, 50–1110879,0.html (accessed 25 October 2008).

Li, M. (2008) 'China Debates Soft Power', *Chinese Journal of International Politics*, 2(2): 287–308.

Men, H. (2007) 'Zhongguo ruan shili pinggu yu zengjin fanglüe', in H. Men (ed.) *Zhongguo: ruan shili fanglüe*, Hangzhou: Zhejiang renmin chubanshe.

Nye, J.S., Jr (2004a) *Soft Power: The Means to Success in World Politics*, New York: PublicAffairs. pp. 199.

—— (2004b) 'The Decline of America's Soft Power: Why Washington Should Worry' (Nye 2004a: 5), *Foreign Affairs*, 83(3): 16–20.

Nyíri, Pál (2006) 'The Yellow Man's Burden: Chinese Migrants on a Civilizing Mission' (Nye 2004a: 11), *The China Journal*, 56: 83–106.

Pang, Z. (2007) 'China's Soft Power', presentation at The Brookings Institution, Washington DC, 24 October. Available at: http://www.brookings.edu/~/media/Files/events/2007/1024_china/1024_china.pdf (accessed 9 January 2009).

Paris, R. (2004) *At War's End: Building Peace After Civil Conflict*, Cambridge: Cambridge University Press.

Ramo, J.C. (2004) *The Beijing Consensus*, London: The Foreign Policy Centre.

Reus-Smit, C. (2005) 'Liberal Hierarchy and the Licence to Use Force', *Review of International Studies*, 31(5): 71–92.

Segal, G. (1999) 'Does China Matter?', *Foreign Affairs*, 78(5): 24–36.

Suzuki, S. (2008) 'Seeking "Legitimate" Great Power Status in Post-Cold War International Society: China and Japan's Participation in UNPKO', *International Relations*, 22(1): 45–63.

—— (2009) 'Chinese Soft Power, Insecurity Studies, Myopia and Fantasy', *Third World Quarterly*, 30(4): (Nye 2004b) pp. 779–793.

Tang, J. (2007) *Daguo jueqi*, Beijing: Renmin chubanshe.

UN Document (2008) 'Compilation Prepared by the Office of the High Commissioner for Human Rights, in Accordance with Paragraph 15(B) of the Annex to Human Rights Council Resolution 5/1: People's Republic of China (including Hong Kong and Macao Special Administrative Regions (HKSAR) and (MSAR)), 16 December, UN Document A/HRC/WG.6/4/CHN/2.

Van Ness, P. (2004) 'China's Response to the Bush Doctrine', *World Policy Journal*, 21(4): 38–47.

Wang, H. and Lu, Y.-C. (2008) 'The Conception of Soft Power and its Policy Implications: a Comparative Study of China and Taiwan', *Journal of Contemporary China*, 17(56): 425–47.

Wu, S. (2007) 'The "Washington Consensus" and "Beijing Consensus"', *People's Daily Online*. Available at: http://english.peopledaily.com.cn/200506/18/print20050618_190947.html (accessed 5 September 2007).

Yan, X. (2006) 'The Rise of China and its Power Status', *Chinese Journal of International Politics*, 1(1): 5–33.

Yu, K. (2006) ' "Zhongguo moshi": jingyan yu jianjie', in K. Yu, P. Huang, S. Xie and J. Gao (eds) *Zhongguo moshi yu 'beijing gongshi': chaoyue 'huashengdun gongshi'*, Beijing: Shehui kexue wenxian chubanshe.

—— and Zhuang, J. (2005) 'Re huati yu ling sikao (dai houji): guanyu 'bejing gongshi' yu zhongguo fazhan moshi de duihua', in P. Huang and Z. Cui (eds) *Zhongguo yu zuanqiuhua: huashengdun gongshi haishi beijing gongshi*, Beijing: Shehui kexue wenxian chubanshe.

Zhan, Y. (2006) 'Zhongguo shi ruan shili daguo ma?', *Shijie zhishi*, 20: 5.

Zhang, J. (2004) ' "Beijing gongshi" yu zhongguo ruan shili de tisheng', *Dangdai shijie yu shehui zhuyi*, 5: 10–14.

—— (2007) 'Lun ruan shili yu zhongguo fazhan', *Fazhi yu shehui*, 12: 576–7.

Zhang, Y. (2001) 'System, Empire and State in Chinese International Relations', *Review of International Studies*, 27(5): 43–63.

Zhang, Y. and Huang, R., et al. (2005) *Zhongguo guoji diwei baogao*, Beijing: Renmin chubanshe.

Zhang, Z. and Li, H. (2003) 'Guoji zhengzhi zhong de zhongguo ruan shili san yaosu', *Zhongguo tese shehui zhuyi yanjiu*, 4: 45–9.

Zhao, C. (2004) 'Zhongguo xuyao ruan shili', *Liaowang xinwen zhoukan*, 23, 7 June, p.1.

13 Responding to my critics and concluding thoughts

Joseph S. Nye, Jr

When I wrote *Bound to Lead* two decades ago, I observed that power is like the weather. Everyone talks about it, but few understand it. I also observed that power is like love, easier to experience than to define or measure. Those observations reinforce the conclusion of Edward Lock's thoughtful chapter in this volume: 'humility is essential in our analysis of power not because such a posture is somehow ethically superior to hubris, but instead because it presents a practical necessity when we understand power correctly.'

Although I have defined power in behavioural terms as the ability to affect others to produce the outcomes one wants, there are many definitions of power. As Steven Lukes (2007) and others have noted, power is a primitive and contested term, and the definitions and perspectives that analysts choose reflect their interests and values. There is no one answer, though there is something to be said for using definitions that are consistent with the dictionary if we wish to communicate with practical people as well as other theorists. While I appreciate the comparison that Lock (and Lukes before him) have made between my humble work and that of Foucault, I would submit that my simpler definition and focus is closer to the dictionary usage and more accessible to policymakers. The fact that I wanted to address both theorists and policymakers may account for some of the limitations of my work as well as its impact (TRIP 2008).

The word 'power' is somewhat like the word 'cause', which the dictionary defines as 'anything producing an effect or result'. In the enormous complexity of relationships and long causal chains, it is sometimes arbitrary which we single out as a 'cause', and our choice is affected by our interests in analyzing and affecting the world. Lock correctly points out that power can be conceived in structural as well as relational terms. A teenager chooses a fashion to attract another teenager, but the sub-culture of what is fashionable is set by someone other than the teenager. He cites Thomas Schelling's definition of strategy as the conditioning of one's behaviour on the behaviour of others. From that point view, power is a theory of interdependent decisions.

Lock is correct that my early formulations focused more on the agent than the subject of power, in part because I was looking at the question of American power in international relations, and I was dissatisfied by the way it was theorized by those who were writing about American decline. Similarly, Geraldo Zahran and

Leonardo Ramos correctly point out that my first two books that introduced the term 'soft power' were focused on larger questions of American foreign policy and it was not until 2004 that I focused a book on soft power as such. More recently in *The Powers to Lead*, I applied the concept of soft power to leadership, where as Locke notes, I broaden the focus and stress three dimensions: leaders, followers, and how the relationships between them vary with contexts. While I have made efforts to keep my definitions consistent among the books, the treatment of power is clearly affected by my changing interest and focus.

Power behaviour and resources

In their well reasoned chapter, Zahran and Ramos criticize me for saying that 'the distinction between hard and soft power is one of degree, both in the nature of the behaviour and in the tangibility of the resources', without providing any definition of tangibility. I was simply relying on the common dictionary usage of tangible as something that can be touched, but they are correct in pointing out that I should have made it more clear that intangibility is not a *necessary* condition for soft power. I define soft power in behavioural terms as the ability to affect others to obtain preferred outcomes by co-option and attraction rather than coercion or payment, and I was careful to use language that suggested an imperfect relationship ('tend to be associated, are usually associated') between soft power behaviour and the intangibility of the resources that can produce it.

I agree with their statement that command power can create resources that can create soft power at a later phase, and co-optive power can create hard resources. As they say, command power can be used to build institutions that will provide soft power resources in the future, and co-optive behaviour can be used to generate hard power resources in the form of military alliance or economic aid. Similarly, a tangible hard power resource like a military unit can produce both command behaviour (by winning a battle) and co-optive behaviour (attraction) depending on how it is used – witness the effect of American naval units in improving the attractiveness of the USA in Indonesia after the Tsunami relief operations in 2005. And intangibility can be a characteristic of hard power instruments and resources. The words used to threaten are as intangible as the words used to attract, and in the virtual domain of cyber power, intangible bits can be used to attract others or to destroy infrastructure systems that have enormous physical consequences.

I argued that 'the general association is strong enough to allow the useful shorthand reference to hard and soft power'. This had the unfortunate effect of blurring the important distinction between behaviour and resources even though I explicitly used a behavioural and relational definition of power. I overstressed intangibility of resources because the then fashionable neorealist international relations literature was dominated not merely by a tendency to define power in terms of resources, but primarily tangible resources. One might call this 'the concrete fallacy'. Something is a power resource only if you can touch it, or drop it on a city or on your foot. I wanted to persuade analysts and policy makers to broaden their perspectives and see that power – the ability to affect others to obtain preferred outcomes – does not require tangibility. That usage of the term soft power seems to have succeeded in the sense that many analysts now pay more attention to intangible power resources, but strictly speaking, Zahran and Ramos are correct. In behavioural terms, soft power includes both the agenda setting and preference setting that Lukes (2007) calls the second and third faces of power and it can be created by *both* tangible and intangible resources.

Tangibility receives less emphasis in my more recent work on leadership where the concrete fallacy is less of a problem. I say in *The Powers to Lead* (2008) that soft power means getting the outcomes one wants by attracting others rather than manipulating their material incentives. It co-opts people rather than coerces them, but I also point out that sometimes people are attracted to others by myths of invincibility. In some extreme cases, known as 'the Stockholm syndrome', fearful hostages become attracted to their captors. Even if Zahran and Ramos are correct that under hegemony, coercion and consent are complementary, that is not the same as saying that soft power is always rooted in hard power. Sometimes it is and sometimes it is not. I still believe there is a distinction between coercive and attractive behaviour in many instances. As Lukes (2007) argues, there are rational and non-rational modes by which the third face of power operates, and empowering and disempowering ways by which agents influence subjects' formulation of their preferences and self-interest. Within the rubric of soft power, one can still distinguish indoctrination from free choice.

Janice Bially Mattern (2007) describes 'verbal fighting' as coercive communicative exchange that leaves little room for subjects' refusal. While some American soft power is rooted in verbal fighting and fits a Gramscian description of a hegemony of controlled discourse, not all is. Values do not have to be universal in an absolute sense for some to be more widely shared than others in some periods and contexts. American values are not universal in some absolute sense, but many are similar to the values of others in an information age where more people want participation and freedom of expression. When democratic values are widely shared, they can provide a basis for soft power in multiple directions, both to and from the USA. Americans may benefit but simultaneously find themselves constrained to live up to values shared by others if the USA wishes to remain attractive. Given the political diversity and institutional fragmentation of international relations a full Gramscian hegemony over discourse is difficult to maintain. Many countries and groups have different values. Contrary to some of my critics' charges, I believe that liberal values are far from universal. Otherwise, there would be more uniformity of views than now exists (Nye 2007). Perhaps that is why I have regarded neo-Gramscian analysis and the idea of a globalist historic bloc emerging in the 1970s and dominating discourse as interesting but too procrustean.

In any event, the failure to distinguish power behaviour from the resources that can produce it has been a problem for all power analyses, not just soft power. Many an article has compared countries' power in terms of their military resources, but sometimes the less well endowed party prevails. An actor has access to the power resources that may be available to it, but whether it can translate those resources into desired outcomes depends upon the context and its skills in power conversion. For example, France and the UK had more tanks than Germany in 1940, but Germany had a better strategy for power conversion and thus obtained the outcomes it wanted.

Commentaries on soft power frequently confuse behaviour with the resources that produce it. For example, Niall Ferguson (2003) described soft power as 'non-traditional forces such as cultural and commercial goods,' and then dismissed it on the grounds that 'it's, well, soft'. Of course drinking coke or wearing a Manchester United shirt does not necessarily convey power. But this view confuses the resources that may (or may not) produce behaviour with the behaviour itself. Whether the possession of power resources actually produces favourable outcomes depends upon the context of a relationship between agent and subject of power. A similar frequent mistake is to refer to economic sanctions as a form of soft power. But there is nothing soft about sanctions if you are on the receiving end. They are clearly intended to coerce rather than attract, and thus a form of hard power. The confusion arises because economic *resources* can produce both hard and soft power behaviour. The soft power of a country rests primarily (though not entirely) on three resources: its culture (in places where it is attractive to others); its political values (when they are shared and effectively applied); and its foreign policies (when they are seen as legitimate and having moral authority.) But whether these resources can be converted into behavioural power or not depends upon relationships in different contexts.

Public opinion polls can measure the existence and trends in potential soft power resources, but they are only a first approximation for behavioural change in terms of outcomes. Where opinion is strong and consistent over time, it can have an effect, but its impact in comparison to other variables can only be determined by careful process tracing of the sort that historians do. Christopher Layne argues that 'the fact that the state controls public opinion rather than being controlled by it in the realm of foreign policy is a fact that undermines the logic of soft power'. Layne is correct to point out that many governments in many contexts are only weakly constrained by public opinion, but his statement is too simple. It ignores direct effects, matters of degree, types of goals and interactions with other causes.

Regarding specific goals, soft power often works along the lines of Layne's two-step model where there are political and bureaucratic filters between the masses and the elites, but sometimes there is a one step model with direct effects on policymakers that does not go through public opinion. Gorbachev's embrace of perestroika and glastnost was influenced by ideas learned in the USA by Alexander Yakovlev. And while the end of the Cold War involved multiple causes, there is ample testimony by former Soviet elites about how the ideational component interacted with their economic decline. As Georgi Shaknazarov put it, 'Gorbachev, me, all of us were double thinkers' (Nye 2004: ch. 2) Even with the two step model, public opinion often affects elites. Public opinion in other countries can create an enabling or disabling environment for specific policy initiatives. For example, in regard to Iraq in 2003, Turkish officials were constrained by public and parliamentary opinion and unable to allow the American 4th Infantry Division to cross their country. The Bush administration's lack of soft power hurt its hard power. Similarly, Mexican President Vicente Fox wished to accommodate George W. Bush by supporting a second UN resolution authorizing invasion, but was constrained by public opinion. When being pro-American is a political kiss of death, public opinion has an effect on policy that Layne's simple proposition does not capture.

Moreover, in addition to specific goals, countries often have general goals (or as Arnold Wolfers termed it, 'milieu goals') such as democracy, human rights, and open economic systems. Here the target of soft power *is* broad public opinion and cultural attitudes. Most historians who have studied the period agree that in addition to troops and money, American power to promote such goals in post war Europe was strongly affected by culture and ideas. As Gier Lundestad (1998) argued, 'federalism, democracy, and open markets represented core American values. This is what America exported.' That made it much easier to maintain what he called an 'empire by invitation.'

Layne's analysis is also marred by his confusion of power resources and power behaviour. Following Leslie Gelb (2009), he says the definition of soft power has become fuzzy through expansion. 'Nye has expanded the definition beyond "pure" attraction (without coercion or inducements) to include both economic statecraft – used as both a carrot and as a stick – and even military power. ... Soft power now seems to mean everything.' But this is simply wrong. Gelb (and Layne) confuse the actions of a state seeking to achieve desired outcomes with the resources used to produce those outcomes. As explained above, this means that many different types of resources can contribute to soft power, not that the term 'soft power' can mean any type of behaviour.

Theory and the changing context of international relations

Soft power is an analytical concept, not a theory. At one point, Layne acknowledges that 'soft power touches on multiple literatures about IR theory', but then he goes on to treat it as a theory, or as an adjunct to liberal or institutional theory. His paper contains a long list of pet peeves (some of which I share) about liberal theory from democratic peace theory, to democracy promotion, to multilateralism, to Woodrow Wilson, but this is not really a critique of soft power. He is simply inaccurate when he states that 'soft power is nothing more than a catchy term for the bundle of liberal international policies that have driven US foreign policy since World War II and which are rooted in the Wilsonian tradition'. The concept fits with realist, liberal or constructivist perspectives. Since it is a form of power, only a truncated and impoverished version of realism would ignore soft power. Traditional realists did not.

The practice and discipline of international politics has been heavily influenced by realist theory. Although Robert O. Keohane and I complained about the narrow focus of the dominant realist paradigm in *Transnational Relations and World Politics* in the 1970s, Baldwin and others criticized us for too much deference to the realist model which portrays states as the main actors, security as their major goal, and military force their ultimate instrument. In the context of many anarchically organized state systems, this model was a reasonable approximation of reality (Keohane and Nye 1972, 1977). Classical realists from Thucydides to Machiavelli to Hans Morgenthau had a broad conception of power. E.H. Carr (1993) referred to the power over opinion alongside military and economic power.

By the 1980s, however, Kenneth Waltz' (1979) *Theory of International Politics* developed a parsimonious theory that tried to explain the stability of a bipolar world. This neo-realism stripped away the richness of classical realism and treated power largely as a set of concrete measurable resources. While Waltz occasionally paid lip service to the limitations of material power, Baldwin (2002) points out that such statements were inconsistent with his theory. When I set out to write *Bound to Lead* at the end of the 1980s, I first compared the traditional military and economic power resources of different countries, but found that something was still missing – the ability of states to set the agenda and affect the preferences of others mostly through intangible resources. That led me to conceptualize the idea of soft power along the lines accurately described by Zahran and Ramos.

Power is a relational concept, and it makes little sense to describe a relationship without specifying both parties and the context of the relationship. Following Jack Nagel, David Baldwin (2002) points out, one cannot make a meaningful statement that 'x causes' without specifying 'y' and conditions. Similarly we cannot say that someone has power without specifying the domain of targets of influence and the scope of issues within which they have influence. Statements about power always depend upon a specified or implied context. Your boss may have great power over you in the workplace, but none in your home. Athletic skills may make a student powerful on the playground but not in the classroom. And athletic ability in pole vaulting does not mean athletic power in the shot put. Superiority in tanks may make a nation powerful (in terms of producing desired outcomes) if a battle is fought in a desert, but not if the battle is fought in a swamp.

In international relations, the implied context has been the anarchical structure in a system of states that is described in the realist paradigm. That has led both analysts and statesmen to the shorthand of treating power as resources that can be possessed. Lock is correct that 'the more we treat power as a possession of actors, the more we are likely to then seek to identify what attributes or resources an actor has that make it powerful'. That perpetuates the 'vehicle fallacy that scholars (including Nye) have repeatedly warned against', and 'implies that we can successfully evaluate the exercise of power by the USA simply by examining what it is the USA does and without even considering those over whom American power is exercised'. This commits the classic strategic error of neglect of the enemy. Quoting Sun Tzu, Philip Taylor points out in his chapter, that if you do not know the other, you are likely to lose the battle.

Nonetheless, the widespread practice in international relations is to use the shorthand of treating power as resources that can be possessed rather than a hypothetical relationship. Statesmen, journalists, and many analysts have little patience with the psychological niceties of first, second and third faces of power in behavioural terms. They want something concrete and measurable. Most net assessments of power compare resources that are likely to produce successful outcomes in many contexts, and ultimately war, and then discount them depending on their view of the characteristics of the society that may lead to imperfect power conversion from resources into outcomes. Particularly when making judgements about power transitions among states and how that affects expectations and military investments, statesmen and analysts seek the comfort of measurable resources. Although this may give some comfort (even if false) about the relative ranking of states and power transitions, it does not provide much help in judging the diffusion of power to non-state actors.

Analysis of power transition among states has a history that goes all the way back to Thucydides, but power diffusion is less well understood. As the nature of international politics changes, the implied context of the realist model makes less sense and that calls into questions some of the projections based on power resources of states. I have used the metaphor of a three dimensional chess game to describe how it is becoming impossible to imply a single context in terms of the distribution of power resources. On the top chessboard, the distribution of military power resources is largely unipolar and likely to remain so for some time. But on the middle chessboard, the distribution of economic power resources among states has been multipolar for more than a decade, with the USA, Europe, Japan and China as the major players, and others gaining in importance.

The bottom chessboard is the realm of transnational relations that cross borders outside of government control, and it includes actors as diverse as bankers electronically transferring sums larger than most national budgets at one extreme, and terrorists transferring weapons or hackers threatening cyber-security at the other. It also includes new challenges like pandemics and climate change. On this bottom board, power resources are widely dispersed, and it makes no sense to speak of unipolarity, multipolarity or hegemony of states. Success in dealing with these issues requires cooperation among states and that often requires the use of soft power and institutions. Failure to understand this distribution of power resources was one of the main problems of the neo-conservatives and assertive nationalists who guided the Bush Administration. By focusing so single mindedly on the traditional top board of military resources, they failed to obtain their preferred outcomes. They forgot that in three dimensional games, the player who focuses only on one board is likely to lose.

The future of American soft power

Declinism is making a comeback, and there are many comments today about the sinking power of the USA, particularly after the recent financial crisis. However, there is always a danger of the golden glow of the past. American soft power has always had its limits. John Krige's chapter serves as a useful reminder that even in the 1960s, France was able to set limits on the American capacity to create institutions to unify Europe and constrain national options. As the old joke goes, the American government's soft power ain't what it used to be, but maybe it never was. At the same time Inderjeet Parmar's interesting chapter about the role of American foundations in fostering transnational contacts among private citizens in the Kissinger and Salzburg seminars reminds us that much of the soft power of a country is generated by its civil society. That was impressive in the past, and still is.

Giles Scott-Smith sees the current American problem as one of declining power, including soft power, but as Fareed Zakaria (2008) has argued, the situation may be less one of American decline than the 'rise of the rest'. If power were always a zero sum relationship, this might be a distinction without a difference. Whether power relations are zero sum or positive sum depends upon the intentions of the actors. For example, in a classic balance of military power, if all countries seek stability, the strength of one need not be at the cost of another. Or to take a soft power example, China's President Hu Jintao has spoken about the importance of increasing China's soft power. If that is for the purposes of limiting American soft power in Asia, it would be zero sum. But to the extent that an increase of China's attractiveness in the USA and American attractiveness in China helps leaders in both countries preserve a stable and beneficial economic relationship, the increase of China's soft power is not a zero sum situation.

One of the points that I develop in my book on leadership is that it is a mistake to think of power – the ability to affect others to obtain preferred outcomes – simply as 'power over' rather than 'power with' others. By empowering one's followers, an attractive leader can increase the prospects of being able to achieve his or her preferred outcomes. Sometimes traditional realists say this possibility has little relevance in the context of international relations where relative gains outweigh absolute gains, but that is not always the case. Take the case of climate change where greenhouse gases emitted anywhere on the planet can lead to damages all over the planet. China has now overtaken the USA as the 'superpower of CO_2', and is adding nearly two new coal fired plants per week. Their emissions can damage the USA, but it is farfetched to think in nineteenth-century terms of bombing the plants, or applying trade sanctions that could have counter productive effects. Conversely, by helping China develop and implement technologies for carbon capture and storage, the USA can empower China and also help achieve its own preferred outcomes. The rise to prominence of such transnational global commons issues creates a different type of international politics that often requires a positive sum approach to power.

At the same time, it is not clear that American soft power is in permanent decline. Not only did a recent poll show that the USA ranks highest in attraction among countries polled in Asia (Chicago Council on Global Affairs 2008) but the election of Barack Obama in 2008 helped to restore faith in American values in many parts of the world. As a high-ranking British political leader remarked to me in November 2008, 'in one stroke, the election of Obama has changed the American image in the eyes of billions of people, showing the extraordinary capacity of the United States to renew itself'. Of course, symbols must be followed by policy, but it is worth remembering that in the Vietnam War period, the USA suffered a great loss of soft power but was subsequently able to recover when it changed its policies.

Scott-Smith is correct, of course, that American soft power and public diplomacy depend upon credibility which has been sorely missing over the past eight years. The new administration has yet to be fully tested, but to the extent to which it emphasizes provision of global public goods, it will be able to pursue a positive sum approach to its national interest that can make it more attractive in the eyes of others. The importance of American leadership on these issues rests on the simple proposition of collective goods theory that if the largest member of the group does not take the lead, it is very difficult for the smaller members to organize collective action.

In addition, style will matter in the restoration of American soft power. Scott-Smith is correct that for American public diplomacy to be credible, it will have to avoid the dangers of an over-militarized and state-centric approach. Power becomes less hierarchical in an information age, and networks become more important. To succeed in a networked world requires leaders to think in terms of attraction and co-option rather than command. Leaders need to think of themselves as being in a circle rather than atop a mountain. That means that two-way communications are more effective than commands. Parmar's chapter gives fascinating examples such as Kissinger's remark about the importance of 'the crucible of informal conversation,' and a young Czech participant at the Salzberg Seminar observing that 'this is the best propaganda because it's not propaganda'. Perhaps this is merely an effective way to establish a neo-Gramscian hegemony as Zahran and Ramos would put it, but it involves an interactive discourse that fits with Lukes' rational and empowering choices. Moreover, in terms in Lock's strategic view of power, it involves recognition that the sharing of values can be interactive and binding on the USA as well as others. As he points out, the neoconservatives were right to warn about 'Gulliverization' and America being tied down by countless norms and rules. But to a large extent, the future of American soft power will depend upon accepting rather than rejecting such multilateral approaches.

American soft power is generated only in part by what the government does through its policies and public diplomacy. The generation of soft power is also affected in positive (and negative) ways by a host of non-state actors within and outside the USA. Those actors affect both the general public and governing elites in other countries, and create an enabling or disabling environment for government policies. As mentioned earlier, in some cases, soft power will enhance the probability of other elites adopting policies that allow us to achieve our preferred outcomes. In other cases, where being seen as friendly to the US administration is seen as a local political kiss of death, the decline or absence of soft power will prevent us from obtaining particular goals. Even in such instances, the interactions of civil societies and non-state actors may help to further general milieu goals such as democracy, liberty and development. And this sharing of general values will be a two-way street.

Interestingly, military analysts trying to understand counter-insurgency have rediscovered the importance of soft power. Sophisticated military men have long understood that battles are not won by kinetics alone. Angus Taverner opens his valuable chapter with a quotation that 'a battle is not lost until the losing side believes that it has lost', and reminds us of Clausewitz' dictum that 'all military action is intertwined psychological forces and effects'. In the documentary film 'Control Room,' an Al Jazeera reporter observes that if a commander does not have an information strategy, he does not have a strategy. But Taverner warns against the danger of thinking of information campaigns in terms that misunderstand the essence of soft power. 'The military has to understand that soft power is more challenging to wield in terms of the application of military force – particularly if what that force is doing is not seen as 'attractive.' If the other levers of soft power are not pulling in the same direction, then the military cannot create favourable conditions on its own. Except at the tactical level, the military options for the use of soft power have to been seen in a larger policy context.

This is particularly true of the struggle against Islamist extremist terrorism. As Philip Taylor correctly points out, terror is about audiences and is more akin to theatre than war. It is essential to 'know the other' and to understand that cyberspace is a critical battlefield. There is very little likelihood that we can ever attract people like Mohammed Atta or Osama bin Laden. We need hard power to deal with such hard cases. But the current terrorist threat is not Samuel Huntington's clash of civilizations. It is a clash within Islam between a diverse mainstream and a small minority who want to coerce others into their simplified and ideologized version of their religion. We cannot win unless the mainstream wins. We cannot win unless the number of people the extremists are recruiting is lower than the number we are killing and deterring. That equation is hard to balance without soft power. One cannot win hearts and minds without it. In the information age, it is not whose army wins, but whose story wins. Early in 2006, then Secretary of Defense Donald Rumsfeld said of the administration's global war on terror, 'In this war, some of the most critical battles may not be in the mountains of Afghanistan or the streets of Iraq but in newsrooms in New York, London, Cairo and elsewhere.' As *The Economist* commented about Rumsfeld's speech, 'until recently he plainly regarded such a focus on 'soft power' as, well, soft – part of "Old Europe's" appeasement of terrorism'. Now he realizes the importance of winning hearts and minds, but 'a good part of his speech was focused on how with slicker PR America could win the propaganda war' (*The Economist* 2006). Unfortunately, Rumsfeld forgot the first rule of advertising: if you have a poor product, not even the best advertising will sell it.

Smart power

I developed the term 'smart power' in 2003 to counter the misperception that soft power alone can produce effective foreign policy. I defined it as the ability to combine hard and soft power resources into effective strategies (Nye 2004). Unlike soft power, it is an evaluative concept as well as a descriptive concept.

Soft power can be good or bad from a normative perspective, depending on how it is used. Smart power has the evaluation built into the definition. That is why Layne is confused when he says 'smart power – which can be dubbed Soft Power 2.0 – has superseded Soft Power 1.0 in the US foreign policy lexicon'. He is more correct when he says the concept (unlike soft power) lends itself to slogans.

In 2007, Richard Armitage and I co-chaired a bipartisan commission at the Center for Strategic and International Studies that helped to popularize the concept of smart power in an effort to affect the direction of American foreign policy. We concluded that America's image and influence had declined in recent years, and that the USA had to move from exporting fear to inspiring optimism and hope. The Commission pointed out that the Pentagon is the best trained and best resourced arm of the government, but there are limits to what hard power can achieve on its own. Promoting democracy, human rights and development of civil society are not best handled with the barrel of a gun. It is true that the American military has an impressive operational capacity, but the practice of turning to the Pentagon because it can get things done leads to an image of an over-militarized foreign policy.

We argued that the USA can become a smart power by once again investing in global public goods – providing things people and governments in all quarters of the world want but cannot attain in the absence of leadership by the largest country. Development, public health, coping with climate change and maintaining an open stable international economic system are good examples. We argued that by complementing American military and economic might with greater investments in soft power resources, and focusing on global public goods, the USA can rebuild the framework that it needs to tackle tough global challenges.

Layne may disagree with Armitage and my particular policy conclusions, but he is not correct that 'reduced to its fundamentals, smart power is about promoting democracy and good governance, and economic development in the expectation that by doing so the USA can remove the grievances that fuel terrorism and the kind of instability that causes states to fail'. As an evaluative term, smart power can be applied to many different policies in different contexts, and its descriptive content can also fit different situations. Christopher Hill's fascinating history of the benefits and costs of Europe's use of soft power provides an interesting example of how the term can be used to criticize Europe's reluctance to invest in hard power resources and instruments. Hill critiques the European Security Strategy of December 2003 for 'failing to interweave hard and soft power elements'. As he says, 'an effective use of the tools at its disposal, while keeping within the limits ordained by cautious intergovernmentalism, must involve Joseph Nye's category of "smart power", with a premium place on perceptive leaders capable of distinguishing between different contexts and between the instruments most appropriate for use on any given occasion'. While the evaluative aspect of 'smart power' can lend itself to slogans, Hill's European example shows that the descriptive content of balancing hard and soft resources to create effective strategies in varying contexts makes the concept more than just a slogan. And it is certainly not simply 'soft power 2.0'.

Conclusion

Soft power is more relevant than ever, but we need to have a more sophisticated appreciation of where it fits in the international relations of a global information age. We need more studies like the chapters in this book that explore both the nature of the concept, as well as empirical studies of policy examples and limitations. Some academic theorists object to the combination of theory and policy. As Zahran and Ramos say, through a neo-Gramscian lense, my work 'provides us with a brilliant case of the role organic intellectuals play in the creation of ideas and mental images that give support and conscience to the historic bloc'. Perhaps it would have been better if I had thought up the concept of soft power in the abstract rather than as a product of trying to think about the sequential problems of declinism and triumphalism in American foreign policy. But I find the interaction of theory and practical policy to be a fruitful dialogue so long as one remembers Lock's opening injunction about the importance of humility. There are no final answers about power. Each analyst and each age brings interests and values that colour their treatment of the subject, but it is incumbent upon each analyst to strive for objectivity, realize their biases, listen to criticism and adjust their thinking to accommodate new facts rather than merely serve their preferences. That is what I have tried to do in this response to the helpful criticisms presented in these chapters.

Bibliography

Baldwin, D. (2002) 'Power and International Relations', in W. Carlsnaes, T. Risse and B. Simmons (eds) *Handbook of International Relations*, London: SAGE Publications.

Bially Mattern, J. (2007) 'Why "Soft Power" Isn't So Soft: Representational Force and Attraction in World Politics', in F. Berenskoetter and M.J. Williams (eds) *Power in World Politics*, London: Routledge.

Carr, E.H. (1940) *The Twenty Years' Crisis, 1919–1939: An Introduction to the Study of International Relations*, London: MacMillan.

Center for Strategic and International Studies (2007) *CSIS Commission on Smart Power: A Smarter, More Secure America*, Washington, DC: CSIS.

Chicago Council on Global Affairs (2009) *Soft Power In Asia: Results of a 2008 Multinational Survey of Public Opinion*, Chicago, IL: Chicago Council.

Ferguson, N. (2003) 'Think Again: Power', *Foreign Policy*, March/April.

Gelb, L. (2009) *Power Rules: How Common Sense Can Rescue American Foreign Policy*, New York: Harper Collins.

Institute for the Theory and Practice of International Relations (2009) *One Dimension or Many? TRIP Survey of International Relations Faculty in Ten Countries*, Williamsburg, VA: College of William and Mary.

Keohane, R.O. and Nye, J.S, Jr (1972) *Transnational Relations and World Politics*, Cambridge, MA: Harvard University Press.

—— (1977) *Power and Interdependence*, Boston, MA: Little Brown.

Lukes, S. (2005) *Power: A Radical View*, 2nd edn, London: Palgrave MacMillan.

Lundestad, G. (1998) *Empire by Invitation: The United States and European Integration, 1945–1997*, New York: Oxford University Press.

Nye, J.S., Jr (1990) *Bound to Lead: The Changing Nature of American Power*, New York: Basic Books.

—— (2004) *Soft Power: The Means of Success in World Politics*, New York: PublicAffairs.

—— (2007) 'Notes for A Soft Power Research Agenda', in F. Berenskoetter and M.J. Williams (eds) *Power in World Politics*, London: Routledge.

—— (2008) *The Powers to Lead*, New York: Oxford University Press.

The Economist (2006)

Waltz, K. (1979) *Theory of World Politics*, Reading MA: Addison-Wesley.

Zakaria, F. (2008) *The Post American World*, New York: Norton.

Index